P9-DEX-324

irreverent

guide to

Vancouver

other titles in the

irreverent guide

series

Frommer's®

irreverent
guide to
Vancouver

3rd Edition

by
Paul Karr

WILEY

a disclaimer

Please note that prices fluctuate in the course of time, and travel information changes under the impact of the many factors that influence the travel industry. We therefore suggest that you write or call ahead for confirmation when making your travel plans. Every effort has been made to ensure the accuracy of information throughout this book and the contents of this publication are believed correct at the time of printing. Nevertheless, the publishers cannot accept responsibility for errors or omissions or for changes in details given in this guide or for the consequences of any reliance on the information provided by the same. Assessments of attractions and so forth are based upon the author's own experience and therefore, descriptions given in this guide necessarily contain an element of subjective opinion, which may not reflect the publisher's opinion or dictate a reader's own experience on another occasion. Readers are invited to write to the publisher with ideas, comments, and suggestions for future editions.

Your safety is important to us, however, so we encourage you to stay alert and be aware of your surroundings. Keep a close eye on cameras, purses, and wallets, all favorite targets of thieves and pickpockets.

about the author

Paul Karr is an award-winning writer and editor based in the U.S. and Canada. To update this edition of Irreverent Vancouver, he quaffed microbrews from mainland to island and back, test-drove fig leafs at Wreck Beach, and learned to spell "colour" and "neighbourhood" the Canadian way. He loves British Columbia, and he'll definitely be back soon.

Published by JOHN WILEY & SONS, INC.

111 River Street
Hoboken, NJ 07030

ISBN 0-7645-3926-4
ISSN 1524-4342

Interior design contributed to by Tsang Seymour Design Studio

For information on our other products and services or to obtain technical support, please contact our Customer Care Department within the U.S. at (800) 762-2974, outside the U.S. at (317) 572-3993 or fax (317) 572-4002.
John Wiley & Sons, Inc. also publishes its books in a variety of electronic formats. Some content that appears in print may not be available in electronic formats.

Manufactured in the United States of America
5   4   3   2   1

what's so irreverent?

It's up to you.

You can buy a traditional guidebook with its fluff, its promotional hype, its let's-find-something-nice-to-say-about-everything point of view. Or you can buy an Irreverent guide.

What the Irreverents give you is the lowdown, the inside story. They have nothing to sell but the truth, which includes a balance of good and bad. They praise, they trash, they weigh, and leave the final decisions up to you. No tourist board, no chamber of commerce will ever recommend them.

Our writers are insiders who feel passionate about the cities they live in and have strong opinions they want to share with you. They take a special pleasure leading you where other guides fear to tread.

How irreverent are they? One of our authors insisted on writing under a pseudonym. "I couldn't show my face in town again if I used my own name," she told me. "My friends would never speak to me." Such is the price of honesty. She, like you, should know she'll always have a friend at Frommer's.

Warm regards,

Michael Spring

Michael Spring
Publisher

contents

introduction

You know pretty much what to expect when you come to Vancouver, right? A picture-postcard setting so idyllic it's turned the city into Hollywood North. An ethnic melting pot that has made for one of the most diverse restaurant and shopping scenes around. A lifestyle so altogether seductive that people come for the weekend and stay forever. You think it sounds like public relations puffery, and you want the real scoop. Sorry to disappoint you, but most of it's true.

Like Rio, Sydney, or Hong Kong (to which it's often compared), Vancouver has a setting that is genuinely jaw-dropping. Nature's a major Mother in these parts—the interplay of jagged mountain peaks, sandy beaches, and clear blue waters embracing the downtown core is a hard one to beat. Even the most jaded travel writers tend to pile on the pretty adjectives, so feel free to gasp and gawk. On a gray day, when the clouds hide the mountains and there's a light drizzle falling, the scenery's still attractive, in a moody sort of way. Granted, the rain can drive you crazy. Don't come in January, or you may be in for days of chilly, unrelenting drizzle. Then again, if the gods are smiling, you can play tennis outdoors in mid-December. Snow is mostly a day here or there, a week at most. If you want it under your skis, the slopes of Grouse Mountain are no more than a half-hour from downtown. Summers can be a long parade of golden days that stretch way into October, with nights cooled by sea breezes. All of this helps explain why the rest of Canada, a little snarkily, calls Vancouver "Lotus Land."

Nobody works here, easterners figure—everyone's too drugged by the scenery. In fact, Vancouverites, by and large, bust their butts as much as everyone else does these days. Here, as in any major city, a crammed calendar equals success. And don't forget, you've got to be in the office at six, if you want to run on eastern time. It's just that locals can—and do—wrap the kind of lifestyle most people would kill for around their 12-hour workdays. Slaving away in a cubicle somehow doesn't seem so bad when you can take your lunch break on the beach.

What other city has a vast downtown acreage that's more wilderness forest than park? Where else can you—and this example gets trotted out all the time—ski in the morning and sail in the afternoon? And how about those miles and miles of public beach, all clean, almost all sandy? No doubt about it, if you're an outdoorsy type, it's a nice place to live.

For years, this outer beauty almost worked against Vancouver. It was seen as the stereotypical blonde: great to have on your arm, but not too much between the ears. Now that's all starting to change. The arts scene is thriving. And not just the big mainstream organizations, but scads of small groups performing edgy, exciting stuff. And festivals? Film, theater, written word—there's invariably something happening. But not, repeat, *not* on the professional sports scene. Ironically, in a city in which every second person appears to be surgically attached to his in-line skates or squash racket, to say that the city's pro sports teams lack *oomph* is an understatement.

What can't be understated is how vibrantly multicultural the city is. Less a melting pot (which suggests homogenization), it's more of a mosaic. Ethnic groups tend to keep their identities, which only adds to the city's texture. Even on the predominantly white-bread West Side, you can pick up foreign language newspapers—*Ming Pao*, *Sing Tao*, *Kanada Kurier*—that are all published locally. A few doors down, a produce store stocks frozen Chinese dumplings beside the cabbages, a deli makes its own hummus and *tzatsiki*, and a baker creates delicate Portuguese pastries. Go to the Punjabi market on Main Street, and you could be in Bombay or Calcutta. Drive to Richmond, all of 20 minutes away, and you feel like you're in Taipei or Hong Kong.

The figures bandied around vary, but one source maintains that in the city itself (not including the surburbs), more than 40 percent of the faces are recognizably *not* WASP. Anywhere else a population this mixed could be a formula for trouble, but Vancouver muddles along very amicably for the most part. Violence between Asian street gangs erupts occasionally, but otherwise, what racism exists is mostly kept under wraps. It's a tolerant city in general. You can be gay, you can be straight, you can be just about anything you want, and nobody's going to hassle you.

A famous Canadian columnist once called Vancouver "the village at the edge of the rain forest." Walking around downtown flanked by urban "cliffs" of concrete and steel, it's hard to imagine that just 200 years ago this was all West Coast jungle, inhabited only by the Coast Salish native peoples. Then, in 1792, along came Captain Vancouver. Soon the fur trade got underway, and in 1886, what had become a small frontier town was named Vancouver. Today, sprawling east into the Fraser Valley, north as far as the mountains will let it, and south across the Fraser delta, the region houses close to two million.

Not bad for a little more than a century.

What jump-started the tourism business—and the city's major growth spurt—was the coming of the World's Fair in 1986. Money flooded in (much of it from Asia), property values rocketed overnight, and shiny office towers shot up like tulips after a warm spring rain. Too fast, too soon, said many, as the wrecker's ball swung at heritage buildings, leaving scant evidence that Vancouver ever had a past. The population has mushroomed, but roads and public transit haven't kept pace. Rush hour starts early and ends increasingly later, and gridlock is common. In its urban design, this city is, in many ways, still a small town.

That goes for its humanity, too. You won't run into the attitude you do in New York City or Chicago. For the most part, people here are out to help you, not fleece you. Carry a map and look lost, and, dollars to donuts, someone will offer to show you the way. On the downside, you can sit at a bar for hours before anyone strikes up a conversation. And oddly, although well-mannered everywhere else, far too many Vancouverites become pigs on the road. An amber light means speed up. A red means go like hell. Pedestrians waiting patiently for a crosswalk aren't especially law-abiding either. It's all about self-preservation on the roadways here.

Preservation in general is a big issue in Vancouver. Citizens don't generally get too excited about politics (can you say "apathy"?), but let development threaten what little is left of the city's history, or any of the natural wonders, and the adrenaline starts pumping. Stanley Park, like all parks, is sacrosanct. Any other city would have blasted a six-lane highway through it years ago. Instead commuters here cheerfully put up with snail-slow traffic. Even axing a tree in your own backyard can require a city permit. This is, after all, the city that gave birth to Greenpeace.

It's those unspoiled green spaces and that scenic variety—and let's not forget the pool of local production talent—that attracts movie crews by the score. But is Vancouver really Hollywood North? Well, on any given day, your chances of seeing a production crew are better than even. Lights, camera, and action are part of everyday life. Even when they're forced to wait at the crosswalk so a "police car" can rocket past for the camera, locals stay cool. Seeing Sharon Stone or Tom Cruise on the street doesn't faze them. It's unhip to gawk.

One feature that does open the eyes of crews from L.A. and elsewhere is the cleanliness of the city. You want Vancouver to stand in for some other burg? You'd better be ready to truck in some garbage. Dropping your gum wrapper on the street is a no-no here. Vancouver is also safe—with the usual caveat that it's foolish to cruise dark alleys at night.

On a sunny afternoon, at English Bay Beach, with a steady parade of tanned, muscled bods of all sexes jogging past, and white-sailed boats scudding across the water, you feel like you're in your own small slice of heaven—or at least in the final take of a beer commercial. But that apparently laissez-faire attitude is on a tight rein. One out-of-towner was right on the money when he assessed the timbre of the city as "a mix of hedonism and Calvinism." Though recently loosened, the archaic liquor laws here still have Europeans rocking with laughter. Smoking is verboten just about everywhere. On the other hand, puffing squiffily on a joint in public isn't likely to land you in the slammer.

Ah yes, drugs. The city does have its seamy side. Venture

off the tourist beat, and you can find yourself shoulder to shoulder with addicts, dealers, deadbeats, and drunks. The HIV rate is horrifying on the downtown's east side, as are the numbers of those who end up in the morgue with a tag on their toe. When Vancouver is cruel, it's cruel, and not just on the streets. Wander away from the beaten tracks of the North Shore mountains, and you'll find Mother Nature has claws in the form of ravines, sudden fogs, and turbulent rivers. But let's not think about that. It's much more pleasant to sit at a sidewalk cafe, kick back with a latte, and watch the world go by.

Cafes, tea shops, noodle houses—folks here eat out in astonishing numbers in an astonishing number of restaurants. Two thousand? Three thousand? Nobody knows precisely how many places there are where you can pick up a fork or a pair of chopsticks, but sufficient to say that huge competition plus access to the most varied larder in Canada adds up to lively cuisine. And you can't beat the price; it's the best deal in North America.

For a quintessential Vancouver moment, get some of that great food to go, and take it and a blanket down to Jericho Beach around sunset. As you dine on wood-smoked salmon or authentic dim sum, the day fades, the clouds are rose-colored, the sea is a limpid aquamarine, and the low sun turns the downtown towers into a flashing, gleaming city of gold. You don't want to leave, do you? Didn't think so.

Need a vacation from your vacation? Vancouver can even provide that. Nearby Vancouver Island makes either a great day trip from Vancouver *or* a great couple-of-days trip in and of itself. Lying just off the British Columbian coast, it's only an hour and a half ferry ride away (and almost as close to Washington state); once there, you'll find the island to be huge and beautiful, with loads of beaches, mountains, tour outfitters, and the like. Fish restaurants abound, and some of Canada's best parks hunker down along the wet western coast. Without a car, though, you'll probably want to spend most of your time in Victoria—a snuggly, quite British little city on the island's southern tip. This is the kind of town where you can get tea and scones almost anytime, where the beer is much better than usual, and where a healthy mixture of locals, immigrants, hippies, students, and tourists makes for a decently good time. Our call? Definitely worth a sidetrip.

Vancouver Neighborhoods

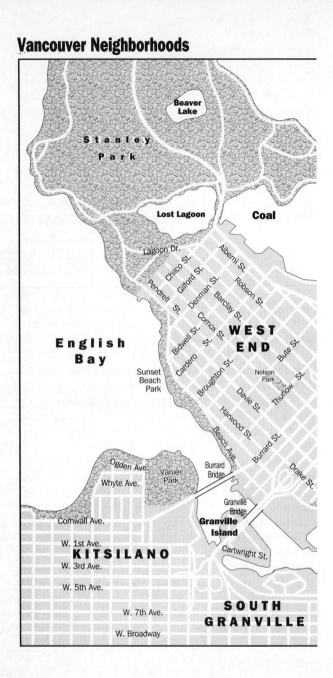

Beaver Lake

Stanley Park

Lost Lagoon

Coal

Lagoon Dr.

Chilco St.

Pendrell St.

Gilford St.

Denman St.

Alberni St.

Robson St.

Barclay St.

Comox St.

English Bay

Bidwell St.

WEST END

Cardero

Bute St.

Sunset Beach Park

Broughton St.

Nelson Park

Davie St.

Thurlow St.

Harwood St.

Beach Ave.

Burrard St.

Drake St.

Ogden Ave.

Vanier Park

Burrard Bridge

Whyte Ave.

Granville Bridge

Cornwall Ave.

Granville Island

W. 1st Ave.

KITSILANO

W. 3rd Ave.

Cartwright St.

W. 5th Ave.

W. 7th Ave.

SOUTH GRANVILLE

W. Broadway

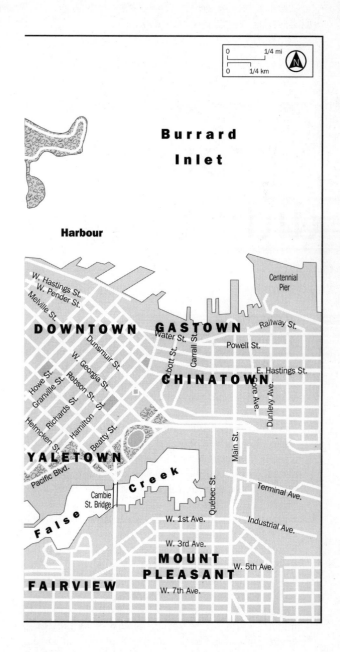

you probably didn't know

What's that squishy sound?... Yes, we've heard all the jokes—"Old Vancouverites don't die, they rust"—and fair enough, the city does get its share of the wet stuff. But so does Seattle, for Pete's sake. In fact, Vancouver has no more precipitation than most other cities in Canada—it's just that elsewhere, a lot of it falls as snow. All in all, Vancouver has a distinctly un-Canadian climate. It's warm when the rest of the country is in deep freeze. And it's never hot and sticky in summer, which is not only a relief to inhabitants, but also helps keep the sky haze-free for movie and television lighting crews. But don't think you can predict the weather in Vancouver. Whether you need to pack an umbrella, for example, depends on where you're headed. The jagged coastal mountains can cause rain clouds to unleash their load, so the closer you get to them, the better your chances of getting wet. You can leave a sunny downtown and be pummeled by a deluge as soon as you cross the Lions Gate Bridge. Conversely, you can often escape a gloomy day in the city by driving 40 minutes south to the seaside suburb of White Rock, where crowds can be seen sunning themselves in languid fashion on the boardwalk. Yes, those *are* palm trees in the West End; it does get that warm on Canada's west coast. Moreover, the seasons evolve gently rather than with the sudden shock of a Montreal spring. While the rest of the country may be flattened by heat waves in June, Vancouverites are wondering whether to turn the furnace on again. Winters are long and dreary—lotsa rain, a bit of snow occasionally, but, on the bright side, with daytime temperatures that average 2° Celsius (35° Fahrenheit). When the summer does eventually deign to start, it's worth waiting for: hot days, zero humidity, and cool nights.

Why is the West Side west of the West End?... Don't get them mixed up. The West End refers to the residential section of downtown. The West Side, the address south of downtown every wannabe wants, is generally considered to be west of Cambie Street (although the definition keeps changing). And then there's West Vancouver, which is across the Lions Gate Bridge, west of the Capilano River—and north of downtown! Go figure.

How should I drive onto the Lions Gate Bridge?... Anywhere else, four lanes of traffic attempting to converge into one (as they do at the North Shore end of the Lions Gate Bridge) would be an invitation to chaos, fender-benders, elevated fingers, and blaring horns. Not here. Instead, everyone takes turns. You go first, then I go, then the car behind you, and so on. Nobody will abuse you if you inadvertently jump in out of turn. They'll just think you're from out of town and don't know any better.

When will the Big One hit?... At a subconscious level, everyone in the region knows that humongous tectonic plates are continually shifting beneath the sea. But the image of major earthquakes followed by the mother of all tsunamis didn't keep people awake nights, even though experts have long predicted that Vancouver will be hit by a major earthquake sometime in the next 200 years. New buildings are designed to withstand quakes and aftershocks, bridges have been brought up to par, and most folks add a clause to their home insurance. Beyond that? Only when the news reported a minor tremor once in a rare while did Vancouverites think that maybe they *should* keep empty jugs filled with water, and drop some cash on a battery-run radio. Just in case. Well, that all changed in March 2001, when— sure enough—a decent-sized tremor *did* hit the city. No, it wasn't the Big One, and sure, the epicenter was actually down near Olympia, Washington (yet another reason for locals to look down their noses at those heathen imperialists to the south). Still, it was enough to give people pause.

Why is David Duchovny not Vancouver's favorite son?... For four seasons, Vancouver basked in the reflected limelight created by *The X-Files*, the celebrated TV series filmed just down the street. Imagine! Vancouver prided itself on being studiously cool in the presence of Duchovny downing a morning cappuccino in a local coffee bar. It was understood that one kept mum—especially to outsiders—as to exactly where he and his co-star hung their individual hats. *We cared for them.* Then, in a quote that has passed into infamy, Duchovny complained about his adopted home's "400 inches" of rain. He exaggerated, of course, but before you could say "up your umbrella," the entire cast had departed for warmer climes. Trust no one, indeed. Mind you, there was also the small fact of Duchovny's new bride, Tea Leoni, residing in L.A. These days? Vancouverites still watch reruns of *The X-Files*. But if the subject comes up in conversation, you'll endear yourself to locals by saying you don't think the current series has *quite* the same subtle lighting as it had in the old days.

How Vancouver defines the world... Two local authors originated terms that have become international. When Douglas Coupland penned a novel on the angst and woes of twentysomethings whose future lay only in McJobs, he inadvertently created a catch-all term that defined his age group: *Generation X*. Score one for Vancouver. Score two, when sci-fi author William Gibson, wandering along Granville Street, popped into a video game arcade and soon after coined the term "cyberspace."

Why addresses speak volumes... Where you live is shorthand for your lifestyle, bank account, and ambitions. The old rich favor Shaughnessy, a spider's web of tree-lined streets where stone walls and velvet lawns surround immense mansions, some of them built by the First Families of Vancouver in the early part of the 20th century. Mock Tudor is the dominant architectural style. If you're gay, you usually gravitate to the West End. Nobody knows the percentage of West End same-sex couples who paint their apartments in next year's colors and display this month's *Wallpaper* on the glass-topped coffee table, but it must be high. Invariably called "Kits," Kitsilano is south of the city across Burrard Bridge. A "Welcome to Kitsilano" sign tells you that you've arrived. DINKs (double income, no kid couples) buy into the condos and townhouses, while students and the working young rent the apartments that have been carved out of gabled and front-porched Edwardian homes. The hippies and artists from the Summer of Love are long gone, although you'll still spot the occasional long-haired hold-out. Between Kits and UCB (University of British Columbia) is Point Grey, much favored by ambitious young couples who fund their horrendous mortgages by renting rooms to students. To live around Commercial Drive used to mean you were Italian, and, to a large extent, it still does. But intermingled with shops selling fresh mozzarella and ravioli are Starbucks locations and stores selling rasta clothes, representative of the cool young crowd that now lives here. A bit about real-estate speak. In Kitsilano, a home "north of 4th" (4th Avenue) rates higher on the prestige scale, as does "west of Denman Street" in the West End. Upper Shaughnessy has more cachet than Lower and, across the Lions Gate Bridge, West Vancouver considers itself several cuts above North Vancouver, while British Properties, both geographically and socially, looks down on everyone else.

What's a Vancouverite's favorite put-down?... In England, people snicker about "Essex girls." In New York, they put down the "bridge and tunnel crowd." Every city has a 'burb it pokes fun at. In Vancouver, it's Surrey. "What's the definition of culture in Surrey?" "A porcelain gun rack." "Why does a Surrey girl wear hoop earrings?" Don't ask. You've probably heard them all before, except it was some other place being victimized. The truth? Surrey is a vast, flat suburb, east of Vancouver and south of the Fraser River, some of it rolling, farm-dotted countryside, some of it dreary stretches of shopping malls and cheek-by-jowl tract housing. Some of it's attractive, some of it's awful—just like anywhere else.

When should I dress up?... When Montrealers or Torontonians first move here, jaws drop at the dress code outside business hours—or, rather, the lack thereof. In summer, shorts will take you almost anywhere. You can wear jean cut-offs to the beach; linen shorts to lunch at Il Giardino. A discreet "black tie" on an invitation is often totally overlooked, except at the handful of la-di-da fund-raising balls on the social calendar. Few places in Vancouver demand that a man wear a jacket and tie. A casket is one of them. About the only time people do dress up and have fun is on opera opening nights. Beads, baubles, suits, silks—bring 'em out (although you still won't feel out of place in your chinos).

Where can I park?... Most main streets ban parking during crush hour, and especially in the 3 to 6pm time slot. Sorry, but even with out-of-town license plates, you'll definitely be ticketed, and probably towed. Watch out for the metermaids and -men in the South Granville area: They're especially vitriolic. On the bright side, parking enforcers are so busy keeping the main arteries clear that if your money does run out on a side street, you'll probably have a longer grace period. Meters apply seven days a week between 9am and 8pm.

Who or what was Woodward's?... Once upon a time, there was a department store called Woodward's, owned by a local family and famous for its "$1.49 Days." Many residents still have a Pavlovian reaction to the term and, without prompting, will sing you the $1.49 radio commercial with its unique and catchy musical hook. Also unique, and an annual treat for well-behaved kiddies, was a look at Woodward's animated Christmas windows, followed by a listen to the Talking Christmas Tree and a short spell on Santa's lap. The basement grocery department was famous for its imported goodies. Alas—now gone, all gone. A victim of changing times and specialty stores, Woodward's permanently closed its doors in the mid-'90s. Talk of turning it into social housing—much needed locally—has gradually faded away, and the store now stands forlornly boarded up on a squalid block of Hastings Street that was once the hub of fashionable shopping.

Who or what is/was/is/was Eaton's?... Once upon a time, there was a department store called Eaton's, owned by a Toronto family and famous for its catalog, whose underwear pages were the equivalent of *Playboy* for several generations of pubescent Canadians. It was affectionately known as Uncle Tim's by the old-timers, after founder Timothy Eaton. In 1999, Eaton's went bankrupt, leaving large empty spaces in shopping malls across the country, and an especially prominent one in Vancouver at the corner of Granville and Georgia streets. But, wonder of wonders, the venerable chain miraculously did a Bela Lugosi act and came back from the dead in 2000, when an American buyer swooped in, bought up the chain's assets, and reopened the Vancouver store in the same space under the same nationally sacred name. Of course the comeback didn't last, and today it's a Sears. Victoria's downtown Eaton's also reopened in *its* old home, then reclosed, and now it's known as The Bay.

Why are all those trailers parked by the curb down the street?... It might be around the Vancouver Art Gallery—a popular location—or in Robson Square, or Gastown, but it's guaranteed that sometime during your stay, you'll happen upon a movie shoot. Clues include ultra-slick star trailers, police cars with U.S. plates, bored guys wearing baseball caps, and, more subtly, the neon-colored signage at intersections that alerts crews which way to turn. Vancouver, however, rarely plays itself. Instead, it's stood in for Seattle, New York City, Hong Kong, Los Angeles, turn-of-the-century Boston, San Francisco, Detroit, and London. Why? It's three hours from L.A. (and in the same time zone); has a favorable exchange rate; and offers a pool of qualified talent both behind the camera and in the editing suite. The air is clean, the skies cinematically blue. All keep business booming. Vancouverites may mutter about the big trucks on the street, but few turn down the hefty fees that movie crews will sometimes pay for a few days' use of their home. The **B.C. Film Commission** (tel 604/660-2732, 375 Water St.) is so used to people asking what's being shot right now, and who's in it, that the company issues a free information sheet. You don't even need to go up to the offices; just pick up a copy downstairs in the lobby.

Where have all the flowers gone?... The answer, my friends, is blowing in the wind chimes. Like their counterparts to the south who invaded San Francisco, all self-respecting Canadian hippies drifted west. Since there is nothing much beyond the Rockies in the way of major urban centers except Vancouver, it became, by default, Canada's heart of hippiedom. Its epicenter was the corner of 4th Avenue and Burrard Street; today there's a surfboard shop where the whole foods store once stood.

Never mind: Kits has kept its street cred as the place to go for enlightenment; it's just that the epicenter has moved a few blocks west and south to West Broadway. Within a couple of blocks, you'll find a half-dozen stores offering aromatherapy, herbal remedies, wind chimes, and infinite ways to cleanse your inner self, as well as several vegetarian restaurants.

What in the hell is a "monster house"?... It's a local catchphrase for the "archi-torturous" style that invaded the city in its glory days of the '80s and early '90s. With money flooding in from overseas, builders razed modest cottages and replaced them with the mini-Versailles that they believed would appeal to immigrants. Unquestionably impressive, but aesthetically suspect, what were soon derided as "monster" homes swiftly invaded upscale neighborhoods. By the time residents began to protest that bylaws were being bent in many directions, it was too late. These ersatz Taras and White Houses are every-where, distinguished by double-height windows (some-times encircled with engraved swans or foliage), front doors that wouldn't look out of place at Buckingham Palace, and concrete lions on the gateposts—and all on 60-foot lots.

Pardon me, but is that the Colosseum?... Love it or loathe it, you have to admit the main branch of the Vancouver Public Library has a certain...familiarity. Yup, you got it. It's based on the Colosseum, and ever since it opened its doors in 1993, Vancouverites have loved it unconditionally. What's not to love? A cov-ered arcade with a coffee shop, pizza place, and deli lets students hitting the books take a break. The library itself is equipped with dozens of carrels and thousands and thousands of books: Nothing's hidden away in storage.

Where can I buy booze?... Not in supermarkets, not in grocery stores, and most definitely not in gas stations— all the various levels of government keep a tight rein over those sinful alcoholic substances. Outside of going to a bar, your only source of gin is an official liquor store, though you can buy beer and wine from private stores such as **Darby D. Dawes Cold Beer and Wine Shoppe** (tel 604/731-8750, 2001 MacDonald St.), which stays open until 11pm every night. Even on Sunday.

Where's the fourth floor?... In some new Vancouver hotels, you'll notice there isn't a fourth floor. The reason? Four is a very unlucky number in Chinese numerology (it sounds like the Chinese word for "death"), so—given the number of Asian visitors to this Pacific Coast city—builders cannily "omit" the fourth floor, for the same reason that you'll rarely see a thirteenth floor in many other towers.

How did the Lions get their name?... Looming beyond the city are two mountain peaks, the Lions, which in turn gave their name to the famous Lions Gate Bridge, built in 1938. But they've enjoyed other, less stately, monikers over the years. Unfamiliar with lions, the Squamish native peoples called the two "chee-chee-yoh-ee" which means "twins." Close, but no cigar, said early pioneers, who called them "The Sisters" and (foreshadowing the David Lynch TV show?) "Twin Peaks." Raunchier settlers, however, looked at the perky double mounds and named them "Sheba's Breasts." Fortunately, viewed from a certain angle, the peaks did have a definitely leonine look, and before long, they were known worldwide as "The Lions." Whew.

Why does Vancouver have world-famous pipes?... Not the plumbing variety, not the type you smoke, but *bagpipes*. British Columbia still has a strong Scottish flavor from the thousands of immigrants who headed west in the late 19th century. In fact, lumped together, the McAdams, McCormacks, and all the other "Mc"s and "Mac"s take up about 60 pages in the Vancouver phone directory. Robbie Burns Day is celebrated, at least one butcher sells haggis year-round, and guys in plaid skirts are a frequent sight in parades and at events. Playing the bagpipes is taken quite seriously here. In fact, the Simon Fraser University Pipe Band has won the title of Best in the World at the World Pipe Band Championships in Glasgow three times in recent years. No other band outside of Scotland has achieved the honor more than twice. Those who love the sound proudly trumpet the news. Those who don't tell a joke: "What's the definition of a gentleman?" "Someone who knows how to play the bagpipes." Pause. "And doesn't."

Where can I get a proper cuppa?... A place as huge, old, and buttoned-down as Victoria's **Fairmont Empress**

Hotel *must* have a few skeletons in its closet, right? Well, not exactly—but we're here to let you in on a few nifty secrets about this *grande dame* on Vancouver Island. First, you don't even need to be a guest to partake of its tea and crumpets. Even the luxurious sitting rooms, including the amazing Palm Court (those crystal chandeliers cost a mint) and Crystal Lounge (check out the Tiffany glass dome), are open to the public. Just remember there's a dress code of sorts and that reservations for the busy afternoon high tea are a good idea. Actually, you don't even need to be human to get into the Empress: A cougar once wandered into the hotel garage to spend a night before the oh-so-mildly-surprised staff caught on. (There's no report on what rack rate she was able to negotiate.) Famous people have stayed here too, including the newly married Pat Nixon and her yet-to-be-disgraced hubby Dick, the then-king of Siam (no, it wasn't Yul Brynner, wise guy), and Bob Hope. He actually had the temerity to whack some golf balls around on the front lawn, but we don't recommend you follow suit—unless you want to end up in Victoria's pokey. So what are you supposed to do with all this declassified knowledge? Try some of it on the bellhop or reservation clerk if he gives you some serious attitude.

What's this about a bathtub race?... Vancouver Islanders have a rather wry sense of humor about what constitutes fun. (Bear in mind that these folks are largely the descendants of soccer fans.) Consider some of their less-publicized annual events. The annual **Bathtub Race,** held in July, is a good example: Nobody in his or her right mind would hop into a motorized bathtub in Nanaimo to brave the heaving Strait of Georgia, yet scads of gonzo locals heroically take the plunge year after year. Most of the crafts spring leaks and go down, and their captains must be plucked from the briny deep, but at least one tub makes it all the way around the 35-mile circuit to win the coveted Silver Plunger. Just north of Nanaimo, Parksville Beach sees two annual events requiring little (okay, no) athletic ability: a massive **World Sandcastle Competition** that attracts artistically minded contestants from around the globe each July, and the very British **World Croquet Championships** in August. Springtime's ritual **Pacific**

Rim Whale Festival may sound commercial, but it's actually a loosely organized series of mostly local events in Tofino and Ucluelet held to fete the annual swim-by of the world's largest mammal.

accomm

1

odations

"If we can't export the scenery, we'll import the tourists," declared railroad boss William Cor-nelius Van

Horne in 1885. Having spanned Canada with the Canadian Pacific Railway, he shrewdly went on to build grand hotels all along its route. With visionaries like that in its past, it's no wonder that Vancouver is plentifully supplied with hotel rooms—over 10,000 rooms in the downtown core alone. But 'twas not always so. For a good stretch of the recent past, Vancouver relied on the rash of lodgings built for (drum roll) that epoch-making six months in local history, the World's Fair of 1986, also known as Expo '86. After that, pretty much nada happened. But tourism sped ahead, so eventually beds got to be in heavy demand. Right now, however, the hotel picture is lively, with new spots opening up right, left, and smack-dab in the center of downtown. Some are huge and glitzy; others are small boutiques; still others are multimillion-dollar makeovers of hostelries that you wouldn't have looked at twice. As in any major city, the deeper your pockets, the softer your pillow. Rock stars and their entourages book into the five-bedroom extravaganza at the **Four Seasons Hotel**, which comes complete with a patio big enough to host barbecues. At the other end of the spectrum, impoverished students at the bus station get a free lift to the **American New Backpackers Hostel**. Price of a bunk there? A retro $10 a day. The standard among top hotels is high—in fact, Vancouver is the only Canadian city to boast three AAA five-diamond hotels: the **Four Seasons Hotel**, the **Sutton Place Hotel**, and the **Pan Pacific Hotel**. But even RVers get a place that's better than average: the Capilano Mobile RV Park, which sits on the Capilano River right under the Lions Gate Bridge across from Stanley Park.

Expo '86 also brought the idea of bed-and-breakfasts to the city—and wow, has it been successful. While staying in a private home isn't necessarily cheaper than staying in a hotel, it does give you an insider's view of life in Vancouver. And, far from just providing a mattress and a meal, many owners now include frills like aromatherapy oils, à la carte breakfasts, and a civilized glass of sherry before you head out for dinner. Robes, ironing boards, and hair dryers are standard in the top echelon of hotels. Below that, you'll have to call housekeeping if you have a sudden urge to iron your suit or dry your hair. Newer places with any class at all assume you'll be carting your laptop along and provide the appropriate hookups.

Winning the Reservations Game

Just because Vancouver is awash with new hotels doesn't

mean you can float into town and take your pick. Tourists, conventioneers, celebrities—all those bods add up. If you do show up in town with nowhere to drop your bags, go directly to **Tourism Vancouver**'s TourismInfo office (see Diversions) at the foot of Burrard Street. Staffers there will pull every trick they know to find you a place to rest your head (and a bonus—if you're planning to visit Whistler or Vancouver Island, they'll book you a room there too). One caveat: Remember, the bureau folks can only recommend properties that belong to their members. Also, if the International Association of Bee-keepers or whoever has descended en masse, you may have to get creative. Instead of that intimate little B&B in the woods you envisioned, you may find yourself downtown at a corporate mega-hotel paying a hefty dollar; it's smarter to book ahead or have a list of backup options at the ready. Keep in mind that rates reflect demand. In July or August, the city is a tourism magnet, often crammed to the gills, and you'll pay top rates. If it's November, and rooms are empty, negotiate. Begin by asking for a corporate rate, and dicker from there. In general, you'll get the best deals between October and April, what Tourism Vancouver calls "the entertainment season," because that's when the theater scene swings into high gear. If you come in cruise season, between May and September, it'll cost you more, and space is tighter. Festivals and major events can also fill up the city. Three-day weekends in the United States have an echo effect here—check out all those Washington and Oregon license plates around town making the most of the low Canadian dollar.

Is There a Right Address?

So it's your first time here and you're bent on absorbing every sight in town beginning with the mountains? Then spring for a downtown hotel on the waterfront with a view of the peaks and the harbor. In town on business? A central location makes sense. You won't be stuck for choice, and you'll find a couple of places only a heartbeat from Vancouver's convention center at Canada Place next to the cruise ship terminal. Got a cultural agenda? Check into hotels around Vancouver's entertainment area on the eastern fringe of the central hub. Like every city, of course, Vancouver has its share of hotels that are homes to the city's druggies, indigents, and insect life (rooms advertising special rates by the week or month are one tip-off), but most of these hotels from hell are concentrated east of the downtown core, so make like Dionne Warwick and walk on by. If your goal is some peace and quiet, you'll be happiest near Stanley Park, or on the North Shore—the neighborhoods of North Vancouver and West Vancouver just across the Lions Gate Bridge—with nature right at your doorstep. But bear in mind that Vancouver isn't a vast rambling city like L.A. or London—other neighborhoods are accessible from wherever you stay, and unless you've booked a room that's really away from it all, such as West Vancouver, you'll find you can walk to most places.

Taxes

Rooms are subject to a 10 percent tax, as well as a 7.5 percent federal goods and services tax. Ask at the hotel front desk for an application form and, provided you're a nonresident and the sum is more than $14 (which means you've forked out $200), the government will give you your GST (Goods and Services Tax) money back.

The Lowdown

Howard Hughes slept here... Hotels in Vancouver keep quiet about who's stayed where, but we do know that the guy who lent new meaning to the word "eccentric" checked into the tall tower of the **Westin Bayshore** near Stanley Park with his flunkies in 1971 and stayed there four months—until, so the story goes, the Canadian tax people got wind of him. Both Audrey Hepburn and Sophia Loren unpacked their elegant bags at the tony **Four Seasons Hotel** downtown. The dark and comfortable Gerard Lounge—the Polo Lounge of the north—at the très chic **Sutton Place Hotel** is a favorite spot for eyeballing stars like Gwyneth Paltrow, Mel Gibson, and John Travolta. Citing "guest confidentiality," staff won't confirm that they actually *stayed* here—which of course is one reason why the stellar like to unpack their bags at this swank hotel. Down by the water, the ritzy **Pan Pacific Hotel**'s Pacific Suite ($3,000 a night) has seen Robin Williams, Robert de Niro, Joan Collins, and Cindy Crawford. Its Jacuzzi looks large enough to contain a champion sumo wrestler, though the in-suite kitchen apparently lacks a little something—Luciano Pavarotti requested special Lagostina pots when he wanted to whip up some pasta here. By the way, don't think you'll find yourself shoulder-to-shoulder with the famous just because you're both staying at the Pan—most celebs discreetly use the staff entrance and elevator.

Rooms with a view... Get out your Nikon. Viewed from city central, that mix of white-capped mountain skyline, glinting water, and forested Stanley Park is a sight so irresistible that it makes even Vancouverites go weak in the knees. Make sure to request a north-facing room if you want the whole kit and kaboodle, although the water-and-sunset views from westerly rooms rate a close second. Obviously the higher the floor, the wider the vista—that's what Prince Charles, Pavarotti, and Elizabeth Taylor must have figured when they all (individually, we hasten to add) checked into the luxurious **Pan Pacific Hotel.** Joined to the Vancouver Trade and Convention Centre inside Canada Place—whose distinctive roof is designed to resemble billowing white "sails"—the hotel pokes right out into Vancouver Harbour, giving its guestrooms a front row center view. The SeaBus zips back and forth, little floatplanes land under your nose...you could spend half the day just watching the action from your room. The view starts right in the lobby, through a vast eight-story atrium, complete with a waterfall and totem poles. Gawk at the harbor panorama through the giant windows in the lounge and the Five Sails restaurant. The Pan Pacific has made just about every "best" list there is— it's one of the city's five-diamond delights (as is the Five Sails restaurant). Originally built in time for Expo '86, it was completely refurbished in 1998 with Italian fabrics and marble. Rooms feel richy-rich but hues are subtle enough not to detract from what's happening outside. Guestrooms don't start 'til the eighth floor, so you're guaranteed unobstructed sightlines, even from some of the bathrooms. While Canadian Pacific owns the **Waterfront Centre Hotel** across from Canada Place, it's not in the chain's usual Scottish Baronial architectural mold (check **The Fairmont Hotel Vancouver** and you'll see what that means: a green copper roof topping a gray stone building with parapets and carvings). The hotel walks a nice balance between friendly and formal (note the mix of casual gear, cruise wear, and business suits in the lobby), but with that view, that's fine with us. While major development on this stretch of the water is relatively new, the **Westin Bayshore** further west has been a city fave since 1960. To put it kindly, the hotel was dated, and its Trader Vic's restaurant (now just a mai tai memory) was so cheesily Polynesian, it was almost hip. But the main tower was renovated in 1996, and by summer 2000 a massive face-lift updated the hotel's main building. It has only one drawback—downtown is a goodly hike from here along the concrete canyon of Georgia Street. Most guests "commute" on the free shuttle bus. Redecoration means rooms look modern. They're spacious too, and you'll get vistas from all of them, either of peaks, harbor, or cityscape, but for the numero uno winners, tell 'em you want to go as high as you can in the tower. For jaw-dropping views further east, ask for a suite on the 30th or 31st floor at the **Westin Grand**.

Back to the past... Once upon a time, way before there was a Starbucks on every corner, Vancouver walked to the beat of a slower drummer. Trolley cars trundled along streets lined with gingerbread-trimmed mansions, and the place to stay in town was the **Fairmont Hotel Vancouver**. Proof that knocking old buildings down is nothing new around here, this is the third Hotel "Van" to be built where Georgia and Burrard streets meet—the first one in 1887, the second, much bigger, in 1916, and the newest, and largest of all, in 1939. Today, she's a magnificent old broad with her green copper roof, carvings, and stone skirts sweeping the sidewalks of two of the city's best-known streets. This lady has *presence*. In the mid-'90s, Canadian Pacific treated her to the equivalent of a full-body makeover, returning the chandelier-hung lobby to its former glory (and replacing a couple of dismal restaurants with jazzy new ones). Though the hotel is huge, the guestrooms feel homey (in a wealthy lawyer sort of way), and service is right on the ball. A block away, opposite the Vancouver Art Gallery, is the **Crowne Plaza Hotel Georgia**—not a name that exactly rolls off the tongue. But most locals still call it the Hotel Georgia, which is what it's been since it opened in 1927. After sinking into a sad decline, it got a top-to-toe makeover in 1998, restoring the lobby's ornate woodwork, colorful tile, and sweeping staircase (Scarlett O'Hara would feel right at home). Guestroom furnishings are more modern, and rooms now look fresh and attractive; those on the south side provide a terrific view of the art museum. Take afternoon tea in a lounge at the side of the grand lobby to dwell upon its vintage charms. Many of the staff members have been here forever, and their dedication shows. You'll get four-and-a-half-star service here at three-star rates; pay $30 more for an Executive Club room and you'll net continental breakfast and weekday evening receptions. By the way, the executive floor lounge was once a guestroom where the King went beddy-bye—yes, Elvis slept here. (Could that overweight seagull that regularly alights on the windowsill be a reincarnation?) What was formerly the distinctly downmarket Niagara Hotel is now the **Ramada Limited Downtown Vancouver** (another clunker of a name) and has been spiffed up at enormous cost inside and out. Sketches of old-time Vancouver decorate rooms furnished in serene browns and fawns. It's close to the shopping core, and it even has some views (ask for the fifth or sixth floor at the back). Room service is not available, but they do put out a breakfast bar each morning. By the way, the "Limited" in the name is one of those boring corporate things, and certainly doesn't refer to the facilities, or the length of your stay.

Let me call you sweetheart... Honeymooners, illicit lovers, or staid old marrieds who want to jump-start things all go gooey-eyed when they get to the **Wedgewood Hotel.** This tranquil boutique spot is just off the main Robson Street drag but it feels remarkably more secluded, like a serene corner of Paris or Rome. With blue canopies over the sidewalk, and a fireplace and flowers in the lobby, this is romance big-time. Each room, laid out with antique-style furniture, has a small balcony that overlooks the formal plantings of Robson Square, as well as the Law Courts (a salutary reminder of what happens when love curdles). The European feel of the place stems from Greek-born owner Eleni Skalbania, who enlivens the whole hotel with her passion for antiques. Just across the Lions Gate Bridge in West Vancouver, the **Park Royal Hotel** drips with vines and stands in lush English-style gardens that border on the Capilano River. Decor is gently nostalgic: Some rooms have brass beds and wingback chairs. Trust us, you won't be the only couple trysting there—it's a tried-and-true spot for romance whether you're honeymooners or an old married twosome. On the same side of the water, north on mountain-bound Capilano Road, is **ThistleDown House**, a five-bedroom B&B. Decorated with mementos, this rambling old Arts and Crafts house scores highly with newlyweds. Complete with gardens to ramble in, antique-furnished rooms to envy, and hosts who are almost embarrassingly generous about dishing up afternoon tea with homemade European pastries, or pouring a decanter of port or sherry—it's like being in a Merchant–Ivory movie.

Getting down to business... Opened in spring 1999, the all-suite **Sheraton Le Soleil** is right in the heart of the business district, a block from Howe Street ("stockbroker country") and the monuments to commerce on Burrard Street. Rooms offer only peekaboo views of the mountains, but who has time to look anyway? The decor is exuberant and baroque, quite un-chainlike. With its gilded sun motifs and fake leopardskin cushions and ottoman, the smallish lobby has a quasi-Versace look; upstairs, gold and crimson color schemes and overall sumptuousity make the suites' bedrooms and living areas appear small for what you're paying (although mirrored walls help). But the bend-over-backward service compensates—bottled water and fruit waiting in your room, Godiva chocolates resting on your pillow, Aveda products lining the bathroom, and housekeeping when you want it. No on-site health club, but you can get a discount pass to the spiffy new YWCA Fitness Centre next door—a good place to work off the calories you're bound to take on while eating at Oritalia, the hotel's highly rated restaurant. Stay at the **Westin Bayshore** and you can lope off into Stanley Park instead—even staid business types appreciate the thought of wilderness jogging trails and boats docked right outside their windows. A free shuttle bus overcomes the distance from downtown meetings. Built in the 1960s, its landmark tower was totally renovated in 1996. Its main building got a brand-new update in the summer of 2000, including high-speed Internet access in guestrooms, double the convention space, a redesigned lobby for meeting and greeting, and an underground parking garage. The $35 million face-lift is intended to make the Westin Bayshore front row center with the briefcase brigade. With its double-height chandeliered lobby, the **Hyatt Regency** feels like a train station, with a constant flow of people coming and going; with 645 rooms, it's the largest hotel in the city. The Burrard Street location is handy for doing business, which, combined with its size, makes this a major hit with the convention crowd. It's only a couple of minutes' walk from the convention center. Rooms are spacious—you can't fault the decor, but you won't remember it either—there's a decent health club, a small outdoor pool, and, if the skies open (what, in Vancouver? Never!) you can get to a shopping mall and the SkyTrain without going outdoors. The humongous new **Westin Grand** suite hotel, downtown across from the public library, courts business travelers by providing dedicated suites with fax, copier, printer, and ergonomic chair—it's sorta like sleeping at the office. If you're nailing down a deal from your room at the **Pan Pacific Hotel**, tell them you want one that's equipped with computer and video camera so you can link up with your backers in Tokyo or Turin. CEOs and other corporate VIPs will appreciate the Pan Pacific's luxe decor and killer views; mere drones and drudges may not be able to swing its room rates on their measly per diems, which is a pity, given its handiness to the convention center.

Spoil yourself rotten... Is money no object? Then spend away on the five-bedroom, two-story penthouse at the summit of the **Four Seasons Hotel** downtown. Movie types and rock stars usually stay here, but it would be a perfect spot for a family vacation—the kid's bedroom is a little one's dream (there's even a car-shaped bed to sleep in). Typically, Four Seasons hotels have grand and gorgeous entrances, but not this one. Arriving by car, you have to kind of sidle in a side entrance, then take an escalator before you hit the lobby area; pedestrians can enter through the Pacific Centre, the attached shopping mall, cruising through the designer department of Holt Renfrew on their way to the lobby, which is itself usually filled with chic types weighed down with shopping bags full of Armani and Jil Sander. Big, lush, sumptuous, with a fine health club and indoor/outdoor pool, this Four Seasons has won every travel award worth having. The restaurant looks a bit somber from the outside, but it has an outstanding, regionally focused menu that makes critics and oenophiles drool in their Chateau Pétrus. If you want to go someplace downtown in the evening, just ring for the complimentary limo. Across the street at the Asian-flavored **Metropolitan Hotel**, every room has been carefully designed to get its *feng shui* just right, but those with big bucks can gain extra serenity (as if they needed it) by booking into the Tai Pan suite. You may recognize it from the Mel Gibson/Goldie Hawn flick *Bird on a Wire*; its amenities include a retractable six-foot movie screen, surround sound, and DVD player—and that's just the downstairs. Pampering is the key word on the Entrée Gold floor at the **Waterfront Centre Hotel** across the street from Canada Place. Concierge service, cocktails, complimentary breakfast, a lounge: All the pluses make it worth the extra investment. Gardeners may want to ask for a third-floor terrace room, which looks out on a 2,000-square-foot sylvan expanse filled with herbs, flowers, and veggies that make their way into the hotel's cuisine. Chef Daryle Ryo Nagata will also rustle up a soothing herb tea if you're struck down by insomnia or a headache.

Thick of the action for skinny wallets... Don'tcha love tourism industry euphemisms? When the small **Kingston Hotel** says it's "European style," it actually means the bathrooms are down the hall (in almost all cases) and the TV—a fairly small one at that—is in a lounge off the lobby. What the heck! Brief touchdowns in your room to change from your daytime jeans to your nighttime duds are all you need when Robson Street and Pacific Centre are just round the corner. While this octogenarian, granite-faced building wears its age lightly, room decor won't win awards for creativity. A couple of blocks away, the **St. Regis Hotel** is another former down-on-its-lucker much improved by big whacks of money. The rooms are pleasant enough for the price, if mundane in design, and those at the front can be noisy; the tiny elevator can mean waits if others are checking in or out. Neither hotel has room service, but both include a serve-yourself Continental breakfast in their modest room rates.

Artful decor... A needle-shaped spire helps make the mirrored, needle-pointed **Sheraton Wall Centre Hotel** the tallest building in Vancouver; so does the fact that it stands on a small rise of land. Downtown, Yaletown clubs, False Creek: It's a few blocks from everywhere but really close to nothing. Depending on your taste, you'll find the old-meets-new decor either quirky or fascinating. Rooms themselves are run-of-the-mill design, but poke around the public areas and you'll come upon 18th-century Indian chests, funky screens, Persian rugs, and hand-blown glass. The **Listel Vancouver** on Robson Street does them one better: It has designated two of its floors—close to half its rooms—as individual galleries. We're not talking amateur efforts either—the original and limited edition art on display bears signatures from the likes of Helen Frankenthaler and Z.Z. Wei, and it's all for sale.

For culture hounds... The **Comfort Inn Downtown** takes itself so un-seriously, it actually has a Director of Fun on staff. A former rooming house, the hotel is right in the middle of what used to be a crummy part of Granville Street. Have no fear, it's being gentrified so fast you can feel your head spin. Art deco-ish, honey blond decor adds more than a whiff of class; it feels like a spot that Fred and Ginger might have checked into. Today, you're more likely to bump into entertainers, musicians, fashion buyers, and entrepreneurs—definitely not your IBM crowd. Perks here include a Continental breakfast buffet, access to VIP lineups at the "in" clubs, and—if you want it—a personalized itinerary. There's a club in-house and access to Yaletown's nightlife. If jazz is more up your alley, the **Listel Vancouver** nabs the city's hottest performers for its O'Doul's Restaurant and Bar. Lovers of the high Cs can catch Opera Breve while they chow down every Sunday during the summer (every other Sunday the rest of the year). Made up of recent music grads, this new company performs offbeat opera while you dine. Lauded as "seamlessly chic" by a major design 'zine, the Listel Vancouver's hip, art-driven decor attracts a clientele to match.

Spread out, suite-ie... Suite hotels are a major hit in Vancouver. For downtown glam and glitz, the **Sheraton Le Soleil**, with its buzzing red and gold decor, is hard to beat. Although its suite rooms aren't the largest, top-notch service and classy amenities make up for it. Across from the main branch of the library, the **Rosedale on Robson** towers above the revitalized eastern downtown area. The muted decor is nothing to write home about, but the location is ace if you want to go shopping for cool

THE LOWDOWN | ACCOMMODATIONS

clothes in Yaletown, take in a game at BC Place Stadium, or see some theater at the Vancouver Playhouse or Queen Elizabeth Theatre. The hotel's on-site convenience store is, well, a real convenience. The nearby **Westin Grand**—so-called because it's shaped like a grand piano—announces itself with a swooping flight of entrance stairs, which can look a little daunting after a trans-Pacific flight. Relax, go beyond them, and you'll see a bank of elevators. Decor? It's like borrowing the apartment of your hip but conservative cousin. Too new to have found its identity in the Vancouver hotel hierarchy, this humongous spot wants to be all things to all people—special business-traveler suites draw that crowd on weekdays, while the Westin Kids Club attracts families on weekends. Reserve a suite on an upper floor if you want a seagull's-eye view of the city. Yearning to get away from downtown into the hub of the hip West End? The **Coast Plaza Suite Hotel of Stanley Park** is the place to slap down your credit card, especially if you've brought the kids. It's super close to Stanley Park and the beach.

When you need to stay on, and on, and on...

Owned by the Sutton Place Hotel, **La Grande Residence** does the long-term thing (the minimum stay is one week) in posh mode. Suites are big—even the smallest one-bedroom is over 500 square feet—and all have balconies, and kitchens large enough to whip up a three-course meal. The big plus here is you get to use the hotel's pool, Jacuzzi, and sauna (there's a charge if you want to pump iron). Pretending to be a Vancouver resident comes easy at the **Rosellen Suites**, where you're not merely in the West End, you're in its most desirable area close to Stanley Park. Most locals have never even heard of it, but guests in the know (especially folks in the movie industry) come back year after year, attracted by the neighborhood's trees, flowers, and tranquillity; the hipness of Denman Street nearby; and the good-sized suites (three-day minimum stay). Because this is mostly a residential area, you're only a walk away from groceries, a liquor store, and corner stores close by. No on-the-spot amenities but you do get free passes to a local health club and rates that drop the longer you stay.

Take a slow boat to China... Downtown, on Howe Street, what is now **The Metropolitan Hotel** leapt into life some years back as North America's first Mandarin Oriental Hotel, then morphed into a Delta before assuming its present name, but the sense of Asian heritage still pervades (the hotel even hands out a self-guided tour of Chinatown). Two black stone lions, known as "foo" dogs, guard the entrance; you'll see Chinese guests rub the lions' foreheads for luck on their way in or out. Hand-carved from camphor wood, a massive gilded temple screen stands in the lobby, and that gleam is 24-karat gold. Rooms are serenely elegant, and if you feel remarkably well balanced, it's hardly surprising: The entire hotel was built according to *feng shui* principles. Minutes from the airport, the **Radisson President Hotel and Suites** stands in the midst of the "new" Chinatown, a 20-minute drive south from the city in the suburb of Richmond. With its glittering mirrored facade and a main stairway lit with tiny lights, it could have been airlifted straight from Hong Kong or Kuala Lumpur. Next door, the huge Yao-Han Centre's T&T supermarket carries popular products from the Far East, like Naive shampoo and Follow Me toothpaste. You can snack on typical Asian "street food," watch a traditional Chinese tea ceremony, and crown your experience with a visit to an authentic Buddhist temple.

Stanley Park yourself here... The nice thing about Vancouver's climate is that it's rarely too hot or too cold for playing outside, so choosing a hotel close to outdoor activities is actually a logical idea. Boasting the best location for strolling, cycling, or in-line skating around the Stanley Park Seawall, the **Westin Bayshore** sits right on the Coal Harbour waterfront—the hotel has its own marina. Known for its drop-dead views, this '60s landmark has undergone a massive renovation, and none too soon. You'd better love Stanley Park to stay here—lively Denman Street (think sushi bars, swimsuit stores, and sidewalk cafes) is reasonably close but the hotel is a good hike from pubs, clubs, and major shopping, although the hotel does operate a shuttle bus to take the heat off your feet. Convention organizers often praise this one because of its size and distance from downtown distractions. Smaller altogether, but equally close to green spaces, tall trees, and colorful gardens, is the **Buchan Hotel**, tucked away on a peaceful side street in the residential West End. It's been there since the 1930s, decorated like a modest European inn with beamed ceilings and a brick fireplace in the lounge. No views, unless you ask for a room that looks out over a leafy urban mini-park. At these prices, don't expect big hotel luxury, and Marlboro men be warned, the Buchan was the city's first totally non-smoking hotel. A street or so over, across from a handsome heritage house, is the romantic **English Bay Inn** bed-and-breakfast. Owner Bob Chapin has put a lot of energy into his five rooms, festooning them with Ralph Lauren linens, antiques, and collectibles: Some have sleigh beds, one a four-poster, and three look out onto a small, peaceful garden. It's a world of grandfather clocks, fainting couches, and breakfast in a Gothic-style dining room. If you'd rather assemble your own breakfast from all the options on busy Denman Street, kitchens come with the pleasantly furnished, balconied rooms at the **Coast Plaza Suite Hotel of Stanley Park.**

Other oddball B&Bs... Just ten minutes from downtown over in West Vancouver, **Chickadee Tree Bed & Breakfast** offers weary travelers a cozy haven. You can set up camp in one of the two self-contained suites in the main house, or go for full-blown privacy at the separate "outback cottage," which can sleep up to eight and has its own fully appointed kitchen. Soak your troubles away in the heated swimming pool or indoor hot tub, or sweat them out in the sauna. The cedar and glass buildings are stunning, and so are the woods that surround them. A great place for long-term stays. Forty minutes south of the city in Ladner, swans glide by **The Duck Inn**, a delightful cottage right on the water amidst an enclave of floating homes. The inn has its own dock, and a view of water and mountains. A separate living area adjoins the bedroom, which boasts an eiderdown feather bed atop the mattress, a down duvet, and decor that's distinctly "duck-y." Home-smoked salmon for breakfast too. Definitely not for anyone who wants to go clubbing 'til 3am—the biggest thrill here is to take a canoe out and catch the sunset, which can be awesome indeed. Back in town, busy Oak Street is only a few steps from **Ten Fifteen West Sixteenth Avenue**, a gorgeous Arts and Crafts bed-and-breakfast hidden away in attractive gardens. It's owned by two former Hong Kongers, one English, one Asian, which explains why breakfast can be just about anything you like, from bacon and eggs to exotic noodles. Real linen sheets, brass name-card holders on each door, headed notepaper—the mood is '30s colonial. Check out the collectibles too, especially the campy toast-rack in the cabinet to the left of the fireplace.

Peachy beach locations... Scuffing your toes in the sands of English Bay watching the sky turn apricot and amethyst is a pretty nice way to wind up the day. The place that puts you closest is the Virginia creeper–covered **Sylvia Hotel**, a classic old dame just across the road from the water and two blocks from Stanley Park. Named after the architect's daughter, the Sylvia started life as an apartment building in 1912 and hung onto its charm over the years, even as it morphed in the 1930s into a hotel (where, in 1954, the first cocktail bar in the city opened). Room decor is pretty basic, and don't expect high-tech amenities— it's staid, it's totally out of any trendy loop, but you'll genuinely be steps from the beach. Book well ahead if you want to get in—this place is an institution. Talk to any not-yet-wealthy-but-getting-there Vancouverites and the name "Point Grey Road" is bound to be dropped— winding along the West Side, right on the water, this residential street is the city's "golden mile." For a pittance (relatively speaking) you can get the same panorama a few blocks east where Point Grey Road becomes less-luxurious Cornwall Avenue. The **Kenya Court Guest House** is a friendly bed-and-breakfast with million-dollar views from its large suites and rooftop deck. The place has nothing to do with Africa except that the original owner once lived there. How is it decorated inside? Hardwood floors, Persian rugs, and traditional furniture—antiques in some cases—mean comfort that's on the elegant side. Each of its five suites has its own kitchen, or you can shop for take-out deli food locally, eat at a nearby French bistro, or head downtown—which is all of five minutes away.

Off the beaten track... So long as you can adjust to the rhythms of the Lions Gate Bridge (Tip number one: Avoid rush hour), you can settle yourself cozily on the North Shore and swing like a pendulum between downtown life and raw nature. A picturesque 1920s bed-and-breakfast in North Vancouver, **ThistleDown House** is right across the street from the wilderness trails of Capilano Canyon, yet civilized enough to serve afternoon tea and sherry surrounded by antiques and keepsakes. Set in a lovely English garden, the small **Park Royal Hotel** is a hop and a fast skip across a main artery to the easygoing seaside route that winds along the beaches and parks of West Vancouver. Its classic furnishings and calm ambience defuse urban stress in minutes. Brought your binoculars and bird book with you? See if you can get into **The Duck Inn**, a charming riverfront bed-and-breakfast in Ladner. It's a 40-minute drive from downtown, but where else do swans swim past your front door?

Family affairs... This city is kid-friendly, and so are its hotels. Anywhere with a heated outdoor pool scores highly, such as the chic but relaxed **Waterfront Centre Hotel** or the elegant modern **Pan Pacific Hotel**, on the waterfront right next to the convention center. The restored old dowager **The Fairmont Hotel Vancouver** is so fond of youngsters, it even has toddler-sized robes. Folks are friendly, rooms are large, and kids will think the glamorous lobby is way cool. Don't let the hushed, chic lobby and deluxe bedrooms at the **Four Seasons Hotel** fool you—this chain treats its youngest guests wonderfully, even dishing up an amazingly tasty children's menu, which lists such culinary delights as Whamburgers and Whizburgers. The huge **Westin Grand**, in the revitalized eastern downtown across from the public library, has a special Westin Kids Club involving things like free sodas and newsletters; its suites give youngsters plenty of room to scatter their stuff around in. Like, Da-a-a-d, we wanna go shopping—so settle them in downtown at the hip and design-conscious **Listel Vancouver** or the **Sutton Place Hotel** with decor so classically French it wouldn't be out of place in a chateau and they can have their run of Club Monaco, Armani A/X, and everything else on Robson Street. Note that more junior votes will probably go to the Sutton Place, thanks to its restaurant's Chocoholic buffet, which sets out its calorie-laden pies, tarts, and tortes Thursday, Friday, and Saturday evenings.

Where the towels are marked "his" and "his"...

The West End has one of the largest gay populations in North America—nobody's going to give you a hard time if you walk up to the check-in desk with a same-gender partner. But if you want the real inside dope on gay-oriented clubs and nightlife, consider the **Royal Hotel** on Granville Street, which proudly boasts a gay concierge and gay staff. It's been recently renovated; the trendily sponged tawny faux painted walls are to die for. The Royal offers a wide range of room types with clean, modern, and surprisingly low-key decor. What's more, the very reasonable room rate includes a map of gay Vancouver and a complimentary cocktail in the pub next door. In case you don't get the point, the Royal's promotional brochure shows a buffed bod with visible tan lines exhorting you to "stay gay." It's almost anticlimactic that the hotel is also straight-friendly. Across Granville Street, 'round the corner on Nelson, the art deco-chic **Comfort Inn Downtown** put out the welcome mat for you and the guy or gal in your life when it was known as the Dakota; check to see if it still does.

For bodacious bods... Keeping those abs flat and those pecs convex takes more than a stroll around the shops. Sporty types praise to the skies the glossy **Pan Pacific Hotel**'s lush health club, with its squash and racquetball courts and excellent weight training and workout equipment; only trouble is, there's a charge to use it, although doing a length or two in the outdoor heated pool is free. **The Fairmont Hotel Vancouver** gets raves too for its equipment and pool, surprising modern amenities in this renovated grande dame downtown. A fitness center, squash courts, and a sexy indoor pool are all draws at **The Metropolitan Hotel**. If body work means pampering rather than pumping iron, check yourself into the **Century Plaza Hotel and Spa** on Burrard Street. Staff members answer the phone "Century Plaza Hotel and Spa," which shows you the importance of the facility in the hotel's scheme of things. The hotel is nice enough—a 30-story tower a quarter-century old whose rooms had a recent makeover in rich, classic colors. But the spa is exceptional—a draw for visiting celebs, as well as local sybarites. You could spend days here having people work over every inch of you—mud wraps, lemon ginger scrubs, an all-over faux tan with the same product used on *Baywatch*. What the heck, go for the "Body Care Complete"—a 4-hour extravaganza that includes exfoliation, a "rose petal plunge" (spaspeak for a hydrotherapy massage bath), a lengthy massage, and a manicure and pedicure in the Throne Chair.

Serious budget-shavers... Staying at the Y is one of the first recourses for budget travelers. Close to Yaletown and the theater district, and just across from BC Place Stadium, Vancouver's **YWCA Hotel/Residence** has more panache than most YMCAs, thanks to its up-to-date design and wider choice of accommodations, which range from rooms with tubs to singles with a bath down the hall, or dorms with space for you and four buddies. Low rates mean you don't get TV (unless you're in a room with a private bath) but a trio of TV lounges can supply a daily fix. All rooms have small fridges (just the place to stash the gin and vermouth). Kitchens are shared, and you can rent pots and pans. No exercise facilities on the premises but if you feel the urge, the YWCA Health & Wellness Centre, a 15-minute walk across town, provides a swimming pool, gym, steam room, and whirlpool. You gotta be kidding—ten bucks a *night*? Yup, that's the room rate at the **American New Backpackers Hostel**— deals like that still do exist. Granted, the place is about as quiet as a frat house, and often no one answers the phone (leaving you to listen to a recorded message playing "Hotel California" for the umpteenth time) but you can't beat the price. It's dorm rooms mostly, with a few singles (accessed through the dorms, just so you don't get spoiled with too much privacy), and a handful of doubles. Bring your own linen unless you're renting a double. Heaps of Aussies, Brits, and Europeans frequent it. The utilitarian furnishings are a yard sale mishmash, and the kitchen is chaos, but there's a TV lounge (with sofas lined up cinema-style), a pool table, and a small Astroturfed roof area where the crowd hangs on sunny days. Give the staff notice and they'll pick you up free at the bus station or airport. Rides back when you leave are a modest 10 bucks. If what you want is a killer beach just down the road, a wilderness park, tennis courts, and one of the ultimate Vancouver views, see if you can score a bed at **Hostelling International Jericho Beach**. Showing little evidence of its barracks origins, its dorms and private rooms are hugely popular with hostelers, even if it does take a half hour by free shuttle bus to get downtown. But hey, where else can you wander out on a jetty and watch the evening sun turn the office towers to gold? Back in the West End, its sister, the unimaginatively named **Hostelling International Downtown,** is big and light, with tons of amenities, including the free shuttle to Jericho Beach and the bus station; split a visit between the two and you'll get the best of both worlds. (The downtown hostel is practically hotel quality.)

Cleared for take-off... A horrendously early flight or an interest in bird-watching are two possible reasons why you might want to bed down near Vancouver's airport (which is, after all, only a 20-minute drive from the city). Or maybe you've just flown in from Paris or Tokyo and want to rest before the hair-raising drive to the Whistler ski slopes. Not far away, right on the Fraser River, the **Delta Vancouver Airport Hotel & Marina** is mostly geared to the business crowd and others making quick hops in and out of Vancouver. It's big and efficient, with innocuously designed rooms, but it does offer scads of meeting space and a business center with all the bells and whistles. Even closer—it's actually built over a terminal—is Canadian Pacific Hotels' latest baby, the **Fairmont Vancouver Airport**, which debuted in fall 1999. The overall style is West Coast contemporary (think lots of slate, stone, and hardwood) in the public areas. Rooms are modern without being sterile, their windows triple-glazed to keep out the roar of overhead 747s. This hotel has a nifty high-tech room system—you can set your thermostat, lighting, and TV station as you like it. It all shuts off when you leave the room, only to switch on when you walk back in the door. The Entrée Gold floor offers the usual perks, except you don't get shutter-style bathroom windows, as you do on the other floors, that let you watch TV from the comfort of your tub. Considerably farther away from the airport, in the center of Richmond, the mirrored **Radisson President Hotel and Suites** offers Asian surroundings and Chinatown ambience, plus a fast remedy for dismal airline food—its restaurant serves some of the best dim sum in the city.

THE LOWDOWN | ACCOMMODATIONS

Here, Rover! Good dog... Though they don't advertise the news widely, most Vancouver hoteliers will make dogs and cats feel at home. In fact, the downtown **Sutton Place Hotel**'s V.I.P. (the "P" stands for Pet) program takes care of them better than some places treat guests. Room service will send up a gourmet dinner of grilled Alberta beef T-bone steak or seared fresh tuna filet topped with caviar in a porcelain dish. In the water bowl? Evian! Turn-down service includes treats, a weather service, and bedtime storybook. Walking and massage services are extra. At the top-drawer **Four Seasons Hotel**, the concierge will take Rover on a walk for you. If you do opt to accompany your golden retriever on his morning stroll, however, grab the shower cap out of the wastebasket and stick it in your pocket. Vancouverites get very upset if you don't scoop.

Bunking down on Vancouver Island... Just a hop, skip, and a ferry ride from Vancouver, this island has oodles of places to stay. You'll find most of them in the touristy hamlet of Victoria. It's easy to find a bed, although summer brings visitors in droves, so you'll want to book as far ahead as possible for the best choice. This used to be an expensive town to stay the night in, but increasing numbers of backpackers and families on vacation have upped the options, and now there's everything from barebones dorm rooms to top-floor luxury. Starting at the very bottom of the price range are two youth hostel–style accommodations downtown. **Hostelling International Victoria** and **Ocean Island Backpackers Inn** offer pretty much the same thing: lots of bunk beds. Hostelling International's building is very central and historic-looking, but also a bit worn—and there are no double rooms in summer. The newer Ocean Backpackers goes a little looser on the rules. If you need a motel or hotel, the **Strathcona Hotel** is the ultimate cheapie pick: a tower of budget rooms and bars in which to blow the money you saved. The nearby **Admiral Inn** is equally lowbrow but also quite acceptable. Mid-range choices, mostly B&B's tucked within the confines of saner residential streets, abound. Try **Andersen House B&B** for interesting architecture, good chow, and lovely rooms. To get a lot more atmo (for a lot more money), check into **Abigail's Hotel,** an extremely friendly and romantic place of flowers, fireplaces, whirlpools, and the like. There are plenty of other expensive options in town, too, like the **Delta Victoria Ocean Pointe Resort** with its magnificent harbor views. Finally, if you're *really* wanting to splash out (as the English say), get yourself to either of two impressive resorts, one up-island and one across-island—both the height of luxury in these parts. **Sooke Harbour House** and the **Aerie Resort** each feature top-flight restaurants (see Dining), stunning natural settings, Jacuzzi tubs, and lots more. You'll feel about a million miles away from society.

The Index

$$$$$	over $300
$$$$	$200–$300
$$$	$100–$200
$$	$50–$100
$	under $50

Abigail's Hotel. Mid-priced to expensive small hotel located just off Victoria's Inner Harbour. Plenty of sweet honeymooner-type touches like flowers, hot tubs, and the like.... *Tel 250/388-5363 or 800/561-6565. 906 McClure St. $$$$*
(see p. 38)

Admiral Inn. Small, unassuming choice close to the harbor action. Cheap yet friendly.... *Tel 250/388-6267 or 888/823-6472. 257 Belleville St. $$$* **(see p. 38)**

Aerie Resort. Super-luxurious, secluded resort of plush fabrics, gorgeous views, and creature comforts.... *Tel 250/743-7115. P.O. Box 108, Malahat. $$$$* **(see p. 39)**

American New Backpackers Hostel. Cheapest beds in town, and the location is great for sightseeing. Co-ed and single-sex dorms, a few singles and doubles. Rooms at the front can be noisy. Free pickup from bus station or airport.... *Tel/fax 604/688-0112. 347 W. Pender St., V6B 1T3. Bus 4. 80 beds. $* **(see pp. 20, 36)**

Andersen House B&B. Classy bed-and-breakfast. Four rooms featuring hot tubs, antiques, garden views, and nice design touches. Superb breakfasts.... *Tel 250/388-4565. 301 Kingston St. $$$* **(see p. 38)**

Buchan Hotel. Leafy West End surroundings and proximity to Stanley Park make this peaceful old-timer popular. No restaurant. Parking a block away.... *Tel 604/685-5354 or 800/668-6654, fax 604/685-5367. 1906 Haro St., V6G 1H7. Bus 5. 65 rooms. $$$* **(see p. 31)**

Century Plaza Hotel and Spa. All rooms are suites in this renovated 30-story tower close to downtown, famous for its luxe spa. Restaurant, pool, parking.... *Tel 604/687-0575 or 800/663-1818, fax 604/687-6103. 1015 Burrard St., V6Z 1Y5. Bus 22. 236 studios, 1-bed suites. $$$* **(see p. 35)**

Chickadee Tree Bed & Breakfast. Forget museums—spend your days in the heated pool, sauna, and hot tub, or strolling through the surrounding woods at this gorgeous West Vancouver B&B.... *Tel/fax 604/925-1989, e-mail lowalker@direct.ca. 1395 3rd St., West Vancouver V7S 1H8. 2 suites, 1 cottage. $$$* **(see p. 32)**

Coast Plaza Suite Hotel of Stanley Park. Lively West End location close to both the beach and Stanley Park. Good-sized rooms, all with balconies. Restaurant, health club with pool, squash courts, parking.... *Tel 604/688-7711 or 800/663-1144, fax 604/688-5934. 1763 Comox St., V6G 1P6. Bus 5. 99 rooms, 168 suites. $$$$$* **(see pp. 30, 32)**

Comfort Inn Downtown. A major face-lift in art deco style has made this old-timer a real winner. Located in a cool neighborhood. Restaurant, parking.... *Tel 604/605-4333 or 888/605-5333, fax 604/605-4334. 654 Nelson St., V6B 6K4. Bus 8. 100 rooms. $$–$$$* **(see pp. 29, 35)**

Crowne Plaza Hotel Georgia. Serious money was spent restoring this 1927 landmark to its former glory. Dedicated staff. Restaurants, live jazz, fitness center, parking.... *Tel 604/682-5566 or 800/663-1111, fax 604/642-5579. 801 W. Georgia St., V6C 1P7. Granville SkyTrain Station. 313 rooms. $$$$* **(see p. 24)**

Delta Vancouver Airport Hotel & Marina. Out near the airport, but a pretty riverfront setting. Restaurants, fitness studio, pool, parking.... *Tel 604/278-1241 or 800/268-1133, fax 604/276-1975 or 888/315-1515. 3500 Cessna Drive, Richmond, V7B 1C7. Shuttle bus from airport. 415 rooms. $$$$* **(see p. 37)**

Delta Victoria Ocean Pointe Resort. Luxury digs, plus sublime views of the Victoria waterfront. Lightning-fast Net access in the rooms is a welcome bonus.... *Tel 250/360-2999 or 800/667-4677. 45 Songhees Rd. $$$$$* **(see p. 39)**

The Duck Inn. Riverfront cottage B&B 40 minutes from central Vancouver.... *Tel/fax 604/946-7521. 4349 River Rd., W. Ladner, V4K 1R9. You need a car. 1 room. $$$* **(see pp. 32, 34)**

English Bay Inn. Charming old-fashioned B&B in a peaceful part of the West End.... *Tel 604/683-8002 or 866/683-8002, fax 604/899-1501. 1968 Comox St., V6G 1R4. Bus 5. 5 rooms. $$$* **(see p. 32)**

The Fairmont Hotel Vancouver. Built in 1939, this grande dame has an impressive lobby and rooms but is best known for friendly service and kindness to kids. Restaurants, health club, indoor pool, parking.... *Tel 604/684-3131 or 800/441-1414, fax 604/662-1929. 900 W. Georgia St., V6C 2W6. Bus 5. 513 rooms, 43 suites. $$$$$* **(see pp. 23, 24, 34, 35)**

Fairmont Vancouver Airport. Luxurious lodging right over the airport terminal—you can check in right at the airport. Lots of slate, stone, and wood. Restaurant, health club, pool, parking.... *Tel 604/207-5200 or 800/441-1414, fax 604/248-3219. 3111 Grant McConachie Way, P.O. Box 23798, Richmond, V7B 1X9. 392 rooms. $$$$$* **(see p. 37)**

ACCOMMODATIONS | THE INDEX

Four Seasons Hotel. Highly rated for its impeccable service—they'll even walk your dog. The surroundings are semi-formal, linked directly to upscale shopping. Fine-dining restaurant, indoor pool, excellent health club, parking.... *Tel 604/689-9333, 800/268-6282 (Canada), or 800/332-3442 (U.S.), fax 604/684-4555. 791 W. Georgia St., V6C 2T4. Granville SkyTrain Station. 385 rooms, including 67 suites. $$$$$* **(see pp. 20, 22, 27, 34, 38)**

Hostelling International Downtown. Big, bright facility in the heart of the West End with mostly co-ed or single sex dorm-style accommodation (a few doubles). So good, it's practically a hotel. Joining the Canadian Hostelling Association gets you a deal on rates.... *Tel 604/684-4565 or 888/203-4302, fax 604/684-4540. 1114 Burnaby St., V6E 1P1. Bus 6. 239 beds. $* **(see p. 37)**

Hostelling International Jericho Beach. Crackerjack location steps from a beach, park, and tennis courts, but a half-hour from downtown. Co-ed or single sex dorms, some private rooms.... *Tel 604/224-3208 or 888/203-4303, fax 604/224-4852. 1515 Discovery St., V6R 4K5. Bus 4. 285 beds. $* **(see p. 36)**

Hostelling International Victoria. Very centrally located, if somewhat cramped, "official" dormitory complex. Don't expect privacy, but do expect to meet fellow travelers from the world over.... *Tel 250/385-4511. 516 Yates St. $* **(see p. 38)**

Hyatt Regency. Vancouver's biggest hotel under one roof, often awash with conventioneers. Connected to SkyTrain Station. Restaurants, outdoor pool, health club, parking.... *Tel 604/683-1234 or 800/532-1496, fax 604/689-3707. 655 Burrard St., V6C 2R7. Burrard SkyTrain Station. 645 rooms. $$$$* **(see p. 26)**

Kenya Court Guest House. Reservations are a must if you want to get into this spotless B&B right by Kits beach. Big suites and a rooftop deck.... *Tel 604/738-7085. 2230 Cornwall Ave., V6K 1B5. Bus 22. 5 suites with kitchens. $$–$$$* **(see p. 33)**

Kingston Hotel. No private bathrooms, no room service, no

TV—but you do get your own phone, and the downtown location very close to Robson Street makes this B&B a good deal for the money.... *Tel 888/713-3304 or 604/684-9024, fax 604/684-9917. 757 Richards St., V6B 3A6. Bus 5. 56 rooms. $$* **(see p. 28)**

La Grande Residence. Handsomely furnished luxury suites owned by Sutton Place Hotel (see below) with full-size kitchens, steps from the downtown hub. Minimum 1-week stay. Restaurant, pool, health club, parking... *Tel 604/682-5511 or 800/961-7555, fax 604/682-5513. 855 Burrard St., V6Z 2K7. Bus 22. 162 1- and 2-bedroom suites. $$$$* **(see p. 30)**

Listel Vancouver. In-the-thick-of-it Robson Street location gives this art-filled, design-savvy hotel an edge. O'Doul's restaurant often has live jazz music performances.... *Tel 604/684-8461 or 800/663-5491, fax 604/684-7092. 1300 Robson St., V6E 1C5. Bus 5. 130 rooms and suites. $$$* **(see pp. 29, 34)**

The Metropolitan Hotel. Decor with an Asian touch means serenity but the Met still has a definite buzz. Restaurant, terrific sports facilities including squash courts, valet parking.... *Tel 604/687-1122 or 800/667-2300, fax 604/643-7267. 645 Howe St., V6C 2Y9. Granville Station SkyTrain. 197 rooms. $$$$$* **(see pp. 28, 31, 35)**

Ocean Island Backpackers Inn. Newly opened hostel is much better outfitted than the other one in town, more laid-back, and pretty well-positioned to boot.... *Tel 250/385-1788 or 888/888-4180. 791 Pandora St. $* **(see p. 38)**

Pan Pacific Hotel. Arguably the best all-round location in Vancouver, right on the waterfront with died-and-gone-to-heaven views. Neighboring convention center often means lots of guests wearing name tags. Restaurants, outdoor pool, good health club, parking.... *Tel 604/662-8111, 800/663-1515 (Canada), or 800/937-1515 (U.S.), fax 604/685-8690 or 604/662-3815. 999 Canada Place, V6C 3B5. Waterfront Station SkyTrain. 504 rooms. $$$$$* **(see pp. 20, 22, 23, 27, 34, 35)**

Park Royal Hotel. Flourishing gardens, manicured lawns, and a river give this West Vancouver hideaway an intimate upscale European quality, close to Stanley Park and beaches. Restaurant, free parking.... *Tel 877/926-5511 or 604/926-5511, fax 604/926-6082. 540 Clyde Ave., West Vancouver, V7T 2J7. West Vancouver Blue Bus service. 30 rooms. $$$* **(see pp. 25, 34)**

Radisson President Hotel and Suites. Huge, mirrored hotel at the hub of the new Chinatown in Richmond. Restaurant, fitness center, pool, free parking.... *Tel 604/276-8181 or 800/333-3333, fax 604/276-8136. 8181 Cambie Rd., Richmond, V6X 3X9. Bus 421 (car preferable). 184 rooms. $$$$* **(see pp. 31, 37)**

Ramada Limited Downtown Vancouver. What was once a tacky hotel has been completely transformed. Upside, a breakfast buffet. Downside, valet parking necessary. No restaurant.... *Tel 604/488-1088 or 888/389-5888, fax 604/488-1090. 435 W. Pender St., V6B 1V2. Bus 22. 80 rooms. $$$* **(see p. 25)**

Rosedale on Robson. All rooms here are suites, and this place is close to the city library, theaters, GM Place, and BC Place Stadium. Don't forget those Yaletown night spots, either, which are very close at hand. Restaurant, pool, health club, parking.... *Tel 604/689-8033 or 800/661-8870, fax 604/689-4426. 838 Hamilton St., V6B 6A2. Bus 5. 275 1- and 2-bedroom suites. $$$$* **(see p. 29)**

Rosellen Suites. West End location and residential ambience make this a quiet choice. No restaurant, passes to local gym and pool, parking. Minimum 3-day stay required.... *Tel 604/689-4807 or 888/317-6648, fax 604/684-3327. 2030 Barclay St., V6G 1L5. Bus 5. 30 suites. $$$$* **(see p. 30)**

Royal Hotel. Renovated West End hotel definitely geared to the gay crowd, but straight-friendly too. No restaurant, parking.... *Tel 604/685-5335 or 877/685-5337, fax 604/685-5351. 1025 Granville St., V6Z 1L4. Bus 8. 82 rooms. $$–$$$* **(see p. 35)**

Sheraton Le Soleil. New, upbeat spot in the middle of financial and shopping district featuring excellent service. Restaurant,

fitness facility next door, valet parking.... *Tel 604/632-3000 or 877/632-3030, fax 604/632-3001. 567 Hornby St., V6C 2E8. Granville Station SkyTrain. 122 suites. $$$$*
(see pp. 26, 29)

Sheraton Wall Centre Hotel. Needle-pointed mirrored hotel provides the best views in the city. A bit out of the way but still only 5 minutes' walk from Robson Street shopping and people-watching. Restaurant, health club ($10 charge), pool, parking.... *Tel 604/331-1000, 800/663-9255 or 800/325-3535, fax 604/897-7200. 1088 Burrard St., V6Z 2R9. Bus 22. 455 rooms, 39 suites. $$$$* **(see p. 28)**

Sooke Harbour House. Native art, tremendous views, thick duvets, and everything else you could possibly want for a no-expense-spared, nobody-can-find-you romantic getaway.... *Tel 250/642-3421. 1528 Whiffen Spit Rd., Sooke. $$$$$*
(see p. 39)

St. Regis Hotel. Renovated old-timer on busy downtown street offers ace deal for central location.... *Tel 604/681-1135 or 800/770-7929, fax 604/683-1126. 602 Dunsmuir St., V6B 1Y6. Granville Station SkyTrain. 72 rooms. $$–$$$*
(see p. 28)

Strathcona Hotel. One of the cheapest true hotels in downtown Victoria, and not half bad for the price. But if you like peaceful nights, go elsewhere: At night, this place is party central.... *Tel 250/383-7137 or 800/663-7476. 919 Douglas St. $$* **(see p. 38)**

Sutton Place Hotel. Sophisticated rooms here attract big-name movie stars, plus anyone who wants to be close to downtown action. Restaurant, health club, pool, parking.... *Tel 604/682-5511 or 800/961-7555, fax 604/642-5513. 845 Burrard St., V6Z 2K6. Bus 22. 359 rooms. $$$$$*
(see pp. 20, 22, 34, 38)

Sylvia Hotel. Staid 1930s ex-apartment building at the edge of Stanley Park, and no longer a well-kept secret. Reserve well ahead if you want a room, let alone a seaside view. Restaurant, parking.... *Tel 604/681-9321, fax 604/682-3551. 1154 Gilford St., V6G 2P6. Bus 6. 119 rooms. $$–$$$*
(see p. 33)

ACCOMMODATIONS | THE INDEX

Ten Fifteen West Sixteenth Avenue. Colonial elegance is the ambience at this tranquil B&B.... *Tel 604/730-0713, fax 604/730-9997. 1015 W. 16th Ave., V6H 1S7. 2 rooms. $$$* **(see p. 32)**

ThistleDown House. Romantic old Arts and Crafts B&B just across the Lions Gate Bridge in North Vancouver, civilized without being stuffy.... *Tel 604/986-7173 or 888/633-7173, fax 604/980-2939. 3910 Capilano Rd., North Vancouver, V7R 4J2. Bus 247, or SeaBus and Bus 236. 5 rooms. $$$* **(see pp. 26, 34)**

Waterfront Centre Hotel. Views, outdoor pool, and rooftop herb garden are just some of the reasons folks stay here. Restaurant, health club, parking.... *Tel 604/691-1991 or 800/441-1414, fax 604/691-1999. 900 Canada Place, V6C 3L5. Waterfront Station SkyTrain. 459 rooms, 30 suites. $$$$$* **(see pp. 23, 28, 34)**

Wedgewood Hotel. Hands-on European ownership means the mood is more like a private home than a hotel. Antique-adorned rooms with balconies overlook the plaza, greenery, and waterfall of Robson Square. Restaurant, fitness room, valet parking.... *Tel 604/689-7777 or 800/663-0666, fax 604/608-5348. 845 Hornby St. Bus 5. 89 rooms. $$$$* **(see p. 25)**

Westin Bayshore. Boats dock right outside, Stanley Park is the backyard...small wonder the Bayshore attracts out-of-towners. A top-to-toe renovation was completed in summer 2000. Ask for a tower room if you want mountain views that don't quit. Restaurants, pool, health club, parking.... *Tel 604/682-3377, 800/937-8461, or 800/228-3000, fax 604/687-3102. 1601 W. Georgia St., V6G 2V4. Shuttle bus to downtown. 325 rooms. $$$$* **(see pp. 22, 24, 26, 31)**

Westin Grand. Shiny new luxury chain hotel across from public library, close to theaters. All rooms are suites. Restaurants, pool, health club, parking, and incredibly friendly to kids.... *Tel 604/602-1999 or 888/580-9393, fax 604/647-2502. 433 Robson St., V6B 6L9. Bus 5. 207 suites. $$$$$* **(see pp. 24, 27, 30, 34)**

THE INDEX

ACCOMMODATIONS

YWCA Hotel/Residence. The good old "Y"—except that this is brand-new, with a cool design, and handy for Yaletown clubs. Discounts for students, seniors, and members.... *Tel 604/895-5830 or 800/663-1424, fax 604/681-2550. 733 Beatty St., V6B 2M4. Bus 15. 155 rooms. $$–$$$*
(see p. 36)

THE INDEX

ACCOMMODATIONS

Downtown Vancouver Accomodations

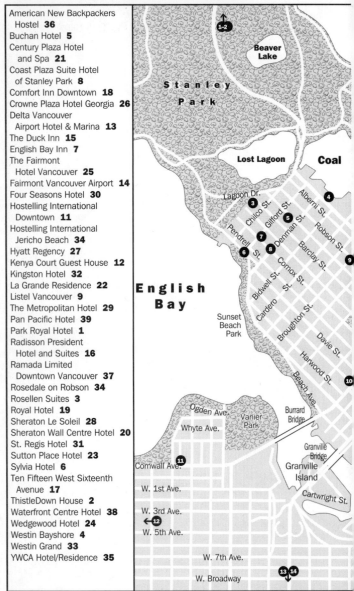

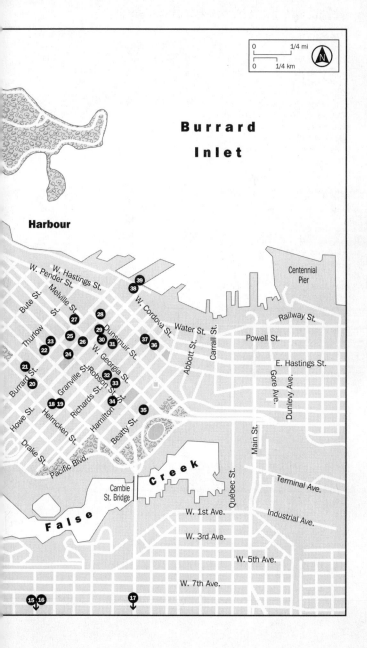

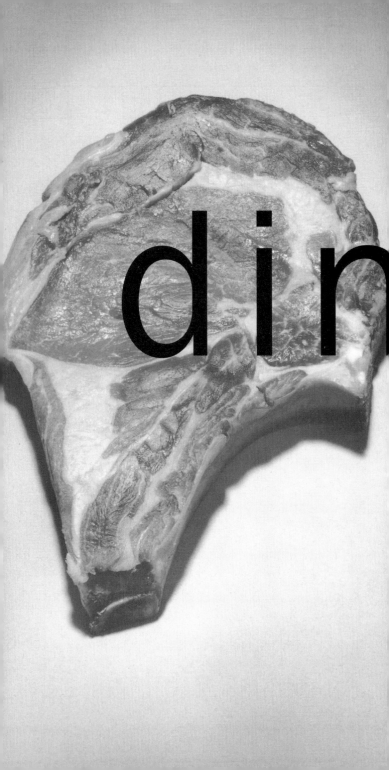

ing

Vancouver has
become the
mother lode of
Pacific Rim cross-
fertilization—
Pan-Med,
Tropical Asian,

Northwest Bistro, Pacific-Asian...new brand names for fusion techniques are coined as fast as you can say them. New restaurants pop up almost weekly, star chefs are poached by big-name New York dining institutions, and out-of-town critics send out slavering dispatches. Twenty years ago you could count the number of desirable Vancouver restaurants on the fingers of one hand, but the city now has some 3,000 establishments. Sometimes you've got to wonder if anyone in Vancouver eats at home anymore. Certain blocks of Fourth Avenue, Commercial Drive, and Robson Street are lined with one dining spot after another, and all over town competition is brutal. Either you cut it, or you're out of the culinary picture, fast. Result? Even at budget bistros, the fare is good enough to grace the tables at a top-name restaurant. Why the big food boom? First off, Vancouver benefits from the incredible bounty of fresh fish, fruits, and vegetables that flourishes throughout British Columbia. Second, the ol' "Triple S" lifestyle—(occasional) sun, sea, and sand—attracts, and keeps, first-rate chefs trained in two- and three-star Michelin restaurants in France. Third, there's the influence of the city's signficant immigrant population, ushering in Malaysian, Thai, Japanese, Indian, Italian, French, Portuguese, Spanish, and Greek cuisines. Finally—and locals hear it from visitors all the time—there's the value factor. Restaurants here are cheaper than almost anywhere else in North America; compared with Europe, they're downright bargains. You can eat like a king in Vancouver, without emptying the royal coffers in the process.

Only in Vancouver

Go local—enjoy West Coast Dungeness crab, buttery salmon, fresh lamb, heritage tomatoes, and berries of all sizes and tastes. Or choose international, dining on such exotica as Persian yogurt, herb gnocchi, or tangy hot-and-sour soup brimming with fat prawns and lemongrass. Vancouver is such a culinary melting pot that "foreign" food practically counts as local anyway; the Asian influence especially is so pervasive that Chinatown stalls are stocked with traditional Asian produce grown right here in British Columbia by local farmers.

How to Dress

Vancouver is very casual. There's hardly any place prissy enough to demand a jacket and tie. Smart-casual (which means no jeans) will get you in even some top-name places. If it's outdoors and it's summer, shorts and Rockports are almost de rigueur.

Getting the Right Table

Ideal spots to park your carcass: by the fireplace at **Chartwell,** next to the window at **RainCity Grill,** in the front room at **Villa del Lupo.** No begging or pleading needed: Just ask when you reserve. If a place won't take a reservation, don't take it personally—sideswiped by too many parties of six who never showed up, some small restaurants refuse point-blank to reserve tables anymore. To make sure you get into a popular spot, either sit down no later than 6pm or prepare to wait in line. As serious foodies know, chefs' weekends are usually Sunday and Monday. If it really matters to you whether the top toque is on duty in the kitchen, skip those nights. Tuesday, when the kitchen talent is at its freshest, may be the best culinary night of the week.

Where the Chefs Are

In such a food-obsessed city, naturally some chefs have become media personalities. Here's the scoop if you want to hold your own as a foodie. Think of it as a family tree: Tuscan restaurateur Umberto Menghi made waves in the late 1970s with his authentic Italian food. He now drives a Ferrari and owns umpteen restaurants in Vancouver (among them **Il Giardino di Umberto**) and in Whistler, plus a cooking school in Tuscany that's a pit-stop for the hoi polloi. Menghi's maitre d' John Bishop opened his own place, **Bishop's,** in the '80s, where he has cooked for Boris Yeltsin, former President Bill Clinton, and Robin Williams, among others. Another former Menghi maitre d', Sami Lalji, now maitre d's at his own eponymous Indo-fusion spot, **Sami's.** The French thread originated with Michel Jacob, the quiet perfectionist who runs the highly acclaimed **Le Crocodile.** His sous-chef Rob Feenie went on to open **Lumière,** which raised the bar even higher. In summer 1999, Feenie's chef de cuisine, Frank Pabst, left to open **Pastis.** And on it goes. Forget surnames: It's "Umberto," "John," and "Michel," if you want to be in the loop.

The Lowdown

Go on, spoil yourself... Robert De Niro, Jacques Pepin, Glenn Close, and just plain folks all head for **Bishop's—**

and everyone gets the same friendly treatment from the warm and attentive staff. When Bishop's first opened on a quiet block of 4th Avenue, the gorgeously serene decor—a roomful of colossal bouquets and original art— was like nothing else in town. It's been copied since, but no one has yet been able to match it. The cuisine, flavorful and finely tuned, is equally terrific. Chef Dennis Green prefers to cook with regionally produced foods, whatever is in season—he even visits a produce farm on his day off to check on his chard and carrots. Try the rack of lamb or huge scallops in a lime-spiked sauce roofed with potato pancakes. Salads and soups are reliably ace, as is "Death by Chocolate," a seemingly lethal dose of chocolate terrine splattered with raspberry coulis. Reservations are a must, although you may luck into a table midweek if you arrive early in the evening. Book too if you want to get into **Lumière,** a few blocks south, which some folks would go so far as to call the best restaurant in Canada. In simple (some say austere) surroundings, chef Rob Feenie takes an equally unfussy approach to his French-inspired prix fixe and multi-course tasting menus (waiters will patiently guide first-timers through the more unusual dishes). Try poached foie gras with dried pear and ginger jam, or tangerine sorbet with hibiscus jus—the purity of the flavor is startling. Feenie's kitchen even offers that rare thing, vegetarian gourmet dishes that are truly gourmet. There's just one caveat: The dining room's acoustics are average, making the room a little noisy for quiet conversation.

Where to seal the deal... Downtown, it's **Chartwell,** at the Four Seasons. Somber wood paneling, a fireplace, and a mature clientele make this luxe spot feel like a posh British men's club—"Another port, Buckley?" you expect to hear in the air—but this staid ambience is in sharp contrast to the highly contemporary West Coast cuisine that chef Douglas Anderson serves up. Prosciutto-wrapped wild salmon and Asian-marinated duck with a blackberry-licorice sauce are just a couple of possibilities. He's a nut for local ingredients—the desserts here are visual dynamite. And the service, especially from maitre d' Angelo Ciccone, is far more affable than the surroundings suggest. Across the street, **Diva at the Met** draws a feistier crowd. The restuarant is actually part of the Metropolitan Hotel (hence the name), but its entrance is separate. Sit way at the rear of this serenely modern, terraced room if you want to canoodle with your sweetie in privacy. Settle in midway, across from the open kitchen, if you want to catch the pan action from chef Michael Noble. Go for smoked black cod done any which way, followed by Noble's signature Stilton cheesecake. Bold, risk-taking, confident—that's his type of fare. Big-time movers and shakers bring their swagger to **Le Crocodile,** downtown just off Burrard Street. Warm yellow walls betray owner Michel Jacob's French heritage; so does the menu, which doesn't skimp on butter or cream. Best bets are the onion tarte and the calves liver with spinach.

Swiveling eyeballs... A couple of steps off Robson Street, and you're in **Joe Fortes**. Who's he? A famous local lifeguard who kept watch over nearby beaches in the early part of the century. With its wide staircase, brass rails, and big U-shaped bar, this hip watering hole is a favorite of ad-biz types, financial whiz kids, and major babes, all of whom actually seem to *like* the fact that it feels more like New York City than Vancouver. A martini or two and some freshly shucked oysters are just what you need to fuel the libido. Apart from meeting the love of your life, fish is the draw here, whether sea bass, salmon, mahimahi, or snapper. Mega money hangs out at **Il Giardino di Umberto**. Located south of downtown, toward False Creek, the restaurant lives up to its name, which is Italian for "garden." Il Giardino has a lushly landscaped courtyard that's arguably the best place in town for lunch on a summer day—*if* you can wheedle a table away from all the ladies (and gents) who lunch. The warmly painted restaurant is modeled after a Tuscan country house. Expect lyrical pasta and antipasto platters bursting with scarlet peppers, black olives, meats, and cheeses; exceptional game and meat dishes satisfy those who want something more substantial. It'll cost you, especially if you order the specials.

Watching the ships sail by... For a city that's so in love with its setting, Vancouver is remarkably light on waterfront restaurants. Pride of place goes to **The Five Sails,** at the end of Canada Place downtown in the Pan Pacific

Hotel. When sunset turns the mountains pink, the lights of the North Shore shimmer like gold dust, and it's truly magic. The decor is a tad mundane, though it trumpets *deluxe* all the way, with big comfortable seats and weighty linens. But never mind, because the stunning West Coast food—especially the sea bass or rack of lamb—more than compensates. Across town, snag a table at **C,** on False Creek, and you're overlooking a world of white pleasure boats, tanned roller-bladers, and sunlit high-rises. Praised for offering the best seafood in Canada, C is truly top-notch—you'll kick yourself if you miss it. Try the West Coast dim sum lunch, which packages scallop and Ahi tuna in a spring roll and includes chicken satay with a hoisin peanut sauce, or C's taster box of abalone tempura, salmon gravlax, and other delicious morsels, which arrives at your table on miniature wooden shelves. For a fresh perspective, head for West Vancouver and plan to arrive early at the **Beach House at Dundarave Pier**—that way, you'll have time to wander along the jetty, ditch your shoes, and wiggle your toes in the sand before you eat. The well-heeled, mostly neighborhood clientele enjoys outrageous views of Point Grey from the large deck and windows. Don't postpone it just because you're waiting for sunshine—the Beach House is even better on rainy days when ships are ghostly gray images and the lonely foghorn booms. Ahi tuna with miniature spring rolls or sea bass with a curried green apple crust is typical of chef Sonny Mendoza's West-meets-East flavors. On sunny afternoons, do what Vancouverites do and squeeze onto the patio at **Bridges Restaurant** on Granville Island. The food is nothing special (nachos, burgers, and similar casual fare), but there's no better spot on a summer day to watch the ferryboats chugging across the water and kayaks gliding by. It's times like these that make out-of-towners decide to pull up stakes and move west.

Under the Mediterranean sun... Maybe it's because of Vancouver's dreary winters, but Mediterranean-themed restaurants have caught on around here in a big way. Out near UBC, **Provence Mediterranean Grill** is run by the Quaglias, the most glamorous mom and pop you'll ever see: the darkly handsome Jean-Francis and the gorgeous and warm Alessandra. It's popular with the UBC and

Point Grey crowd—professors, students, and young families all zero in on the huge display of antipasti (a bitta this, a bitta that). One must-order is the pizzalike *pissaladiere*, its long-cooked onion filling tic-tac-toed with anchovies, olives, and grilled veggies. The simple honey-colored setting is a quiet background to the buzz. Just east of there, **Quattro on Fourth** has a mood, room, and (most definitely) menu that ooze with Italian generosity. The warm, glowing colors; tiled floors; a vine-draped veranda; and edibles as a major design element make it resemble a luxurious, familial dining-room air-lifted straight from Tuscany. The fare? It's hard to go wrong here (unless you get into too much grappa) but the pasta "for Italians only" (that's what it says on the menu) is especially fabulous. Downtown, **El Patio**'s butter-yellow walls are another antidote to gray skies, though on nicer days its rooftop patio makes a great place to eat al fresco (try to snare the table under the trees). The amiable hosts have created an upbeat bar atmosphere, one that even lone females can feel comfortable in. The paella's terrific, and so are the tapas, especially the *patatas bravas* (roasted potatoes in a fiery sauce). **La Bodega,** close to the north end of the Granville Street Bridge, is a real Spanish *cava* with red-checked tablecloths and specials chalked on a paella pan big enough to feed the chorus of *Carmen*. The tapas menu is similar to El Patio's—calamari, *patatas bravas*, and chorizo attract the regulars, who wash it down happily with sangria. Those with braver palates may want to sample some of the daily specials that wander into the uncharted territory of rabbit, blood sausage, and organ meats. Continuing around the Mediterranean, **Habibi's**, on West Broadway, is run by another hip young mom-and-pop ensemble who is passionate about the Lebanese food that arrives at your table. Homey touches here include family photos and pictures of the old country. Dishes are authentic (the marinated goat cheese is outstanding) and, even better, rock-bottom priced—around $6 apiece at last look. What's more, the warm service here would do many a four-star restaurant proud. If you're down at Granville Island, make your way to **Apollonia**, a real Greek family restaurant run by a real Greek family. *Dolmades* (stuffed grape leaves), souvlakia, prawns with feta cheese, a wowser of a roast lamb (the house specialty)—everything is recommended, especially the Cretan specialties brought by owners Harry and Thea Prinianakis from their homeland.

If you're tooling around the Davie Street area downtown, stop in at **Stepho's Souvlaki Greek Taverna** for giant-size servings of lusty Greek classics like roast lamb, Greek salad, and great chicken souvlakia—this place is home for the young, hungry, and impoverished. Recent renovations mean more space and less likelihood of a line. Note that they'll only take reservations for groups of five and up.

Raw naked fish... To say Japanese restaurants are popular around here is an understatement. They're usually good, even the cheap ones—and even the priciest have Tokyo tourists blissing out over the bargains. Most have the standard menu of sushi, sashimi, tempura, teriyaki, and udon dishes, but often you'll see specials listed on the wall—that's where the gastronomic adventures are. Salmon, octopus, and sea urchin are often from local waters, but wherever its seafood hails from, sushi here is dependably fresh. In the West End, Denman Street alone has three sushi joints right next door to each other. They're all reliable, cheap, hectic—and, at the small and invariably jam-packed **Musashi**, once in a while, the staff distribute free bowls of deep-fried shrimp heads to nibble on. Don't knock 'em 'til you've plucked up the courage to try 'em. Crunchy, savory, and surprisingly good. If you find yourself in the Cambie Street neighborhood, try **Hachibei**, a homey little place, simply furnished, where the specials give you an inkling of what home-cooked mama-san Japanese food tastes like. Noodle dishes warm you to your toes on a drizzly day, the sushi is fresh and tasty, but the most interesting flavors are among the specials with their side dishes of homemade pickles. On Robson Street, **Gyoza King** is frequented by homesick Japanese, who cure what ails them with the authentic gyoza (semicircular meat- or veggie-stuffed dumplings), sushi, and specials. The walls are dark—lists of specials make up most of the "decor." Be patient if there's a language problem. **Tojo's** on the West Side is the most serious player in town, the sort of place where you take visiting rich uncles—and hope they'll pick up the tab. You may find yourself chowing down next to a famous face. Sit in the spare modern room and gaze out at the city and mountains, or nab a seat at the sushi bar as loyal regulars do, and ask the superbly creative Tojo himself to feed you. Sushi may be garnished with fresh cherry blossoms, or it might incorporate decidedly western greens from local farms. You never know until you show up.

Is that Tom Cruise over there?... Probably not, but with all the movies being shot here, chances are better that you'll see a real live celeb in Vancouver than they would be in Elbow, Saskatchewan. **Fleuri,** at the Sutton Place Hotel, draws more than its fair share of famous out-of-towners. Ironically, locals don't like having to walk through the hotel lobby to get there (they're funny that way), and the ho-hum decor of the traditional dining room isn't enough of a draw for them. A pity, because chef Michael Deutsch's cooking more than merits the trip. The menu changes seasonally, but his tuna and lamb dishes are invariably electric. B.C. ingredients, Asian spices, and European know-how add up to signature dishes like oolong tea–steamed sea bass in a lemongrass and coconut broth, or crab cakes with avocado salad and tomato coulis. Yum. What? No famous faces? Stick your head into the dark, comfortable **Gerard Lounge** next door, where you may have better luck sighting a star. Even if you don't, the bistro chicken, thin-crusted pizzas, and martinis will compensate. Along Robson Street, **CinCin** is always in the news for another Big Star sighting. Otherwise, the crowd is urban hip (without being obnoxious). Even if you don't luck into Gwyneth Paltrow, you'll tuck into hearty Tuscan-style cuisine, veal chops, and house-made sausages from the wood-burning oven and grill. Sunshiney hues and rustic trattoria mood are a tailor-made backdrop for playing "Let's pretend we're in Italy." Food celebs make a point of visiting **Vij's,** just off South Granville. Marrying Western food and East Indian spices in a highly original (but not super-chili-heated) way, chef Vikram Vij offers such inventive fare as wine-braised goat on rapini, an addictively pungent green, and lamb chops in sweet potato curry. Dishes are exquisitely presented, service is first-rate (Vij formerly worked with the attentive John Bishop), and the space—once you score a table—is small but warmly welcoming. Its chief features are a massive door and a rotating artwork exhibit that often includes jewellike collages.

Decor with a twist... Papa Hemingway would have felt at home in **Havana**, on Commercial Drive, with a Cuban restaurant, theater, and gallery all in the same room. With its artfully scarred walls and vintage photos and prints, the restaurant attracts all genders, shapes, and styles—jeans, nose-rings, Birkenstocks, anything goes. A base of *sofrito* (a mix of onions and peppers) underpins the meat and fish dishes, and the enormous Cubano sandwiches alone are worth the trip. A little farther south is food for the mind at **Bukowski's.** Extracts of poems from the late Charles Bukowski (and other writers) are under the glass table-tops. Photos of Hemingway, Faulkner, and similar talents known to enjoy a drop or two dress up the yellow walls, and the funky bar stocks aged Cuban rums. The joint's not nearly as grungy as it should be, given its patron saint (Bukowski was a legendary barfly and bottom-dweller) but the intellectual action ranges from live music to poetry readings, and the food is a cred-itable version of what's called "global fare"—"Barfly" chicken salad, pastas, "Post Office" artichokes, steaks, satay sticks—if you know your Bukowski, you'll get the references. Bicycles on the wall are the main design element at **Sami's**, tucked away in the corner of a strip mall on West Broadway. Service is great, and the fare is inventively Indo-fusion—and, at eleven bucks a dish, a steal. Try the lamb vindaloo made with whole shanks, and preface it with chilled mango soup—killer. Downtown, **The Crime Lab** (so-called because that's what its building used to be) serves wine in lab beakers and gives amusing names like D.O.A. and Autopsy to its martinis. A snug little two-story place, its decor is restrained and modern: dark purple, silver, black, and black-and-white photos. Cramming it are the young and hip, as well as serious foodies who rave over what comes out of the minuscule kitchen. Try chili-rubbed halibut wrapped in a banana leaf, for instance, or a "bouillabaisse" of the local catch in a miso broth. On the West Side, the **Nyala Ethiopian Restaurant**'s col-lection of art and artifacts puts you in the mood for the spicy Ethiopian specialties, served on *injera* (a pancake-like bread). No dishes, no cutlery (a dish-washer's dream)—prepare to eat with your fingers, scooping the zesty curries onto your bread.

With six, you get egg roll... Eat in Chinese restaurants
every night in Vancouver for a year, and you'd still only
sample a fraction of the dishes that have sailed here
from across the Pacific in the past couple of decades.
Bustling **Hon's Wun-Tun House** first saw the light of
day in Chinatown but now has several branches,
including one on Robson Street—ideal if you're staying
in the West End and have an urge for good, inexpensive
Chinese in a clean-lined setting just like you'd find in
Hong Kong. Of nearly 300 menu items, a fave is
#222—shrimp balls, fish balls, and noodles swimming
in a hearty broth. Goose it with a drop or two from the
bottle of flame-red chili oil on each table. Create your
own Combination A by adding an order of the restaurant's signature dish: savory little dumplings called "pot-
stickers." The more upscale (but still affordable) **Sun Sui
Wah** is handy if you're trawling for antiques on Main
Street. Weekends, it's a zoo, a roiling mass of grandmothers, impeccably dressed women Krazy-Glued to
cell phones, and kids in baseball caps. It has sparkier
decor than most Chinese eateries, focused around the
giant canvas kitelike sails that hang over the dining
room. Go for dim sum, a diner-participation sport that
requires you to flag down the various serving carts, each
one stacked with small bamboo baskets or steel
containers containing luscious portions of various foods
to choose among (pounce on the *har gow*, fat and juicy
shrimp dumplings). For a few bucks apiece, you can also
order little dishes pan-fried to order in an open kitchen.
The specialty here is the roast squab, served head and
all. As in any upscale Chinese eaterie, you can eat cheap
on steamed rice or noodles, or go whole hog with live
seafood, or shark's fin soup, thereby upping your bill
well into three figures. Diners are mostly Chinese
(always a good sign) at **Grand King Seafood Restaurant,**
on West Broadway, where the food consistently wins
awards for subtlety and finesse. Seafood dishes and
winter melon soup are winners. The room is unexcep-
tional, but those steaming bowls and platters are the
reason everyone's here.

Vegging out... Vegetarians will think they've died and gone
to heaven, especially in Kits, the former center of hippiedom. Folks who want to trip right back into the love-bead

era will love **The Naam**, with its rustic ambience, beards, braids, and service so laid-back it's virtually nonexistent. Ignore the bee-pollen cookies and go for the burritos; plates are piled to the point where alfalfa sprouts fall off. In winter, it's cozy as a cabin; in summer, there's a tiny garden patio. Beach types flock into **Planet Veg,** on the periphery of Kits Point, for husky roti rolls, flavored tortillas stuffed with spiced potato, or chickpeas and eggplant, or—ask for the Katmandu—cabbage and other veggies. This is a take-out fuel stop primarily, though there are 16 seats if you want to feed while you read the community posters attached to the sponge-painted yellow and burgundy walls. More deep-pocketed herbivores head farther west into Kitsilano for **Lumière**'s eight-course vegetarian tasting menu. Star chef Rob Feenie may kick it

They really, really like their spinach here

Yes, vegetarianism is gaining ground everywhere, but in Vancouver it's ingrained in the lifestyle. Chinese Buddhist cuisine not only omits animal products, it nixes garlic and onions, too. All the more reason to admire the skill of the chefs at **Buddhist Vegetarian Restaurant** *(tel 604/683-8816, 137 E. Pender St.), who transform soy protein into texturally accurate shrimp or chicken. Lately, chefs have acknowledged that a vegetarian gourmet isn't an oxymoron. The highly revered* **Lumière** *(tel 604/739-8185, 2551 W. Broadway) was the first to launch a vegetarian tasting menu, and* **C** *(tel 604/681-1164, 1600 Howe St.) has now followed suit.*

off with luscious white and green asparagus with morels and sherry jus, going on from there in an upscale gourmet vein. Lovers of waterfront dining also drop in at **C** for seven courses of inventive stuff—arugula and roasted garlic risotto, artichoke carpaccio, and the like—with nary a drop of animal in it.

Southeast Asia tour of duty... Vancouverites are bonkers over chili peppers, lemongrass, Thai basil, and the whole gong-banging parade of Asian ingredients. At the Malaysian **Banana Leaf**, amid potted plants, pictures of tropical seas, and ceremonial masks, expats from Kuala Lumpur and Penang tuck into platefuls of *char kuey teow* (sweet-tasting noodles mingled with bits of egg, onion, and meat). Of the slew of Thai places in town, **Montri's Thai Restaurant,** on West Broadway, wins our vote as the best in town for its finesse, the subtle layerings of flavor, and the fact that the heat isn't dumbed down for non-Asians. Visiting foodies make the trek to **Phnom Penh,** in Chinatown, for Vietnamese and Cambodian cuisine. Like most restaurants in this neighborhood, the setting is forgettable—which is fine because the food's definitely not. Order garlic chili squid, memorable prawn dishes, and the great hot-and-sour soup. An out-of-the-way location doesn't seem to hurt **Delhi Darbar,** on Main Street—those who love their Asian food find their way here for curries and *dosas* (sorta crisp pancakes with spicy innards), not to mention the "Bombay snacks" on Saturdays. Try *batatawada*—deep-fried spicy potato balls—or puffed wheat-flour wafers called *paani-puri,* and don't miss the mango lassi, a delectable yogurt-based drink. The service is warm, and the place is quietly elegant.

Candlelight and romance... Across from Robson Square, **Bacchus Ristorante** is a sumptuous place to whisper sweet nothings. Draped curtains, heavy linens, Murano glass lighting fixtures carted home from Venice by owner Eleni Skalbania, a spectacular bar that's practically an entire, beautifully lit wall of bottles—it's luxe deluxe, and the West Coast cuisine is a knockout. Try chef Cameron Caskie's crispy rough eye rockfish with a sage and verjus butter, chardonnay-steamed clams and white bean mash, or wine-mushroom tart with pheasant confit and carmelized onions. Every evening, Bacchus features a classic of French cuisine: Wednesday is cassoulet night, Friday is bouillabaisse. If you smoke, ask to be seated in the "cigar room." (It's illegal to smoke in the restaurant.) On a rainy night, stroll along the cobblestoned streets of Gastown and wind up at **Raintree at the Landing**. Exposed brick walls (it's a heritage building), humongous beams, a wood-burning fireplace, and candles: This place has warmth in spades, not to mention a drop-dead view of the harbor and imaginative regional treats like fresh halibut with Dungeness crab butter. Take-out gourmet fish 'n' chips is a summer specialty here. Vancouver's downtown streets were once lined with charming turn-of-the-century homes; one of the few remaining now houses **Villa del Lupo,** a set of intimate rooms painted in warm Tuscan colors where it just seems natural to hold hands. The food's flavors are big and rich, with wine-braised lamb osso buco as the signature dish. Sometimes a West Coast influence creeps in (pasta is crowned with alderwood smoked salmon and caramelized jumbo scallops) but mostly the seasonal dishes are heartily, richly Italian. Note that the focaccia you'll be offered doesn't come free. For French cuisine with élan, head for the West Side and **Pastis,** where chef Frank Pabst (formerly at the highly rated Lumière) creates French-inspired fare at this upscale and attractive bistro. Like many young chefs, Pabst "evolves" his menu to showcase the best of what's local and fresh. A standout is the oven-dried tomato tart with goat cheese, caramelized onions, and tapenade. Service manages to be both friendly and nearly faultless.

Before or after the show?... One option is tapas before, and a few more after. Handy for the Fifth Avenue movie theater complex and ragingly popular (but definitely not in the pre-movie snack category), is **Moustache Café,** a place whose glowingly warm colors, and big open kitchen, are matched by outstanding meals. Call the food served here "Mediterranean with a twist," which is foodie-speak for dishes like salmon with piperade and a saffron, raisin, and pine nut tabbouleh. Don't go here for a quiet spot of romance: The room, when full, as it often is, can be noisy. Downtown, pre-theater dinners are an on-again, off-again happening—call around. Lively **Diva at the Met** and the more sobersided **Chartwell** usually offer them, both with the sort of upscale cuisine that complements a cultural night out. After a night of clubbing in Yaletown, head along Davie Street to **Bin 941,** and join the young and trendy who shoehorn themselves into this pocket-sized tapas spot with what may be the tiniest tables in town. But there's nothing small about the flavors: East-West crab cakes come with a burnt orange chipotle sauce and charred baby bok choy; lamb loin T-bones are sold by the piece.

Beyond the witching hour... Taking in a midnight drag show or late-night improv definitely limits your dining options in this 'burg. Open 24/7, **Benny's On Broadway** on West Broadway does bagels in various ways; the upstairs seating area on the mezzanine has more atmosphere simply because the ceiling is lower. Downstairs is noisier, but wood tables and plenty of free reading material mean it's still a cozy and fun place to hang out. Sidewalk seating, under the quirky wrought-iron canopy, is coveted even late at night when nothing much happens in this mostly residential area, especially by dog owners who settle in after that 1am walk for a nightcap. **The Bread Garden** on South Granville Street serves quiches, salads, and homey desserts. Simply designed, with a casual West Coast feel—like the food, in fact—this is the sort of spot where you can order a sandwich to go or to take over to one of the tables. Downtown, post-clubbing, try to elbow your way into **Bin 941** for some nouveau tapas.

Best of the lunch bunch... Downtown, either the top-drawer French **Le Crocodile** or men's-clubby **Chartwell** will spoil you rotten while you sell that screenplay or nail that deal. The sinfully creamy onion tarte at Le Crocodile or just about any of chef Doug Anderson's seasonal dishes at Chartwell will make it worth your while, even if the deal falls through. If you've shopped 'til you dropped at Holt Renfrew, haul your bags into **900 West** in The Fairmont Hotel Vancouver, where the emphasis is firmly on regional cuisine and the wine list is terrific (come here for dinner if you want to sample a flight of wines). High-ceilinged, with a nothing view of the breezeway, the somewhat formal room gets much of its energy from the lively bar, the lounge beyond, and chef Dino Renarts's verve-y menu. Grilled lobster is partnered with veal tenderloin, thyme and brown butter gnocchi, and a beurre blanc speckled with pink peppercorns and trout caviar: the ultimate surf 'n' turf. For dessert, the cannoli filled with white chocolate mascarpone is a killer. From Granville Island, it's a hop and a skip to **The Pacific Institute of Culinary Arts**, where tomorrow's culinary bright lights train. The plainly furnished room overlooks condo buildings and—far more fun to watch—students learning the intricacies of classical French cuisine. You get to eat their homework, meaning three-course lunches, beautifully prepared, for less than $20. Okay, so the service is sometimes a tad off-key; at these prices, it's worth it. Service is never an issue at the luxe **Il Giardino di Umberto** where, in the garden, with a bowl of exemplary pasta in front of you and something chilled and white in a glass, it really does feel like you're under the Tuscan sun.

Kid stuff... Having your kids in tow needn't mean endless golden arches. Try the West Side's **Provence Mediterranean Grill**, for instance, where a single antipasti is just the right size for a kid—and there's always child-friendly pasta. Funky decor, heavy on oversized fruit and parrots and chirpy servers make **Earls** ideal for the kindergarten and older crowd. There's one in the thick of things on Robson Street; the North Shore branch is conveniently close when you've been roaming the rain forest. The menu walks a neat line between mass market—fries, chicken wings, wood-oven pizzas—and grills and fusion pastas that moms and dads will enjoy. The chain even has its own wine labels from Chile—and they're not bad for the price. Upscale **Fleuri** in the Sutton Place Hotel downtown requires good table manners, but you may be able to tempt kids to put up with it for the sake of the Chocoholic Buffet on Thursday, Friday, and Saturday evenings—and thus win yourself a chance to sample chef Michael Deutsch's innovative cuisine. It may be a mite sophisticated for small fry. Enlightened parents let them skip the meat and potatoes, and "just this once" make a meal of nothing but chocolate. And of course, if they've gotta have a burger, go the whole nine yards at delightfully retro **White Spot**, particularly the West Broadway drive-in branch, where carhops will bring kid-meal Pirate Packs to your car, along with the famous Triple-O burgers.

Breaking the fast... On weekends, the crowd snakes out the door at **Sophie's Cosmic Cafe,** in Kits. The decor is best described as garage sale in gridlock. It's neither knowingly hip nor a hippie holdover; it's just meant as outrageous fun. Meals are filling—you may need a jog on the nearby beach to work off the huevos rancheros and other platters afterward. Blackened chicken penne and tostada salads are both good bets, and the fries with garlic aioli are awesome. There's far more panache at **Ecco il Pane,** on West Broadway, where regulars tend to be the laptop-and-Beemer crowd. Wrought iron, floral fabric, classical motifs, and creamy walls make this Kits hangout classy without being stuffy. It's a bakery, too, and the best breakfast here is the simplest: thick slices of toasted house-baked bread with homemade preserves. The chocolate and cherry buns are sin incarnate; less caloric (and just as tasty) is the *rustica*, an Italian breakfast scone, its dough generously speckled with raisins and fennel seeds. Actors, artists, and other locals troop in to **Tomato Fresh Food Café,** on Cambie Street, where the freshly squeezed power juices and homemade-meets-healthy breakfasts are as colorful as the walls. It's funky old diner meets Crayola box, with the scarlet-and-yellow decor a background to local art that's usually just as vivid. Perennial faves are a toothsome vegetarian chili, grilled salmon, and a truly delicious rotisserie chicken served Mom-style with mashed potatoes and veggies.

Robson Street action... Japanese, Indian, Italian: Take your pick from dozens of places on this hyperactive street. **CinCin**'s outdoor deck is a popular observation post, where the Tuscan-style cooking makes for a very agreeable meal, lunch or dinner, either a few antipasti or the whole nine yards of starter, something from the grill, and dessert. Cross Denman Street to find a quieter residential neighborhood where **Tapastree** offers a tranquil patio, an upbeat clientele, and exceptional tapas—the chicken livers and duck confit are killer. Get a kick out of the goofy arm-shaped light fixtures. Or, for a really wild ride, bleach your hair and dip into **Gyoza King** for Japanese-style dumplings; if the server doesn't speak much English, just point 'n' pay.

Simple salmon... Boston has clams, New York has steak, and Vancouver has salmon—and so, at some point, do most people who come here. Chefs whirl in circles, each trying to come up with an approach more inventive than the next. Set in what looks like a giant seaside cottage, **The Fish House in Stanley Park** showcases the efforts of ebullient chef Karen Barnaby, who prepares salmon pastrami style (never mind that she's had to explain to locals what pastrami is)—spicing it, slicing it, and serving it with bagels and cream cheese. Office workers escape here for lunch; at nights, it's a great end to a day on the beach or in the park. Wind up with Barnaby's earthshaking chocolate volcano cake. Close to downtown, Canada's West Coast aboriginal heritage is celebrated at **Liliget**

Feasthouse. The only First Nations restaurant in the city, its serene downstairs space showcases aboriginal art and artifacts. Alder-grilled wild sockeye salmon tastes the way it's been cooked for thousands of years (grilled over wood), as do the colossal potlatch platters of seafood. For fish plus stupendous views of the entire city and the waters of Howe Sound, head out to the **Salmon House on the Hill** in West Vancouver. They serve salmon done every which way, most memorably grilled over alderwood. The intriguing decor here is long on native artifacts, but the real draw is that mind-blowing view.

Known for their noses... Flinty Sancerre or fleshy Chardonnay? If you subscribe to *Wine Spectator*, you'll have a fine time cruising the city's wine lists. Those with deep pockets can check out the wine selections downtown at wood-paneled **Chartwell**, with Douglas Anderson's inventive West Coast cuisine, or the romantic fireplace-and-flowers French ambience of **Le Gavroche**. Also downtown, this establishment pairs the wines with French-meets-West-Coast fare. At **RainCity Grill**, close to English Bay, the wraparound view is a bonus to the wide selection of wines by the glass (and food-pairing suggestions for the uninitiated). The menu capitalizes on fresh seasonal ingredients. Grilled salmon comes with a salad of beans, squid, and spicy chorizo, and the Fraser Valley veal loin is paired with a "hash" of summer veggies. Watching the sun set over the bay from this warmly decorated room is as Vancouver as it gets. George Baugh, whose nose is famous in oenophilic circles, is co-owner of Armani-elegant **Piccolo Mondo**, so it's no surprise that he's stocked his cellar to complement the top-rate northern Italian food that comes from the kitchen. Try the seafood soup or risotto...heck, try anything here. The service is surprisingly warm, given the sleek look of the place. Downtown's **Diva at the Met** is the only restaurant in town to carry wines from Vancouver Island's much-praised Venturi Schulze Vineyards. Across in West Vancouver, at the quietly elegant **Beach Side Café**, locals pick the brains of sommelier Mark Davidson on what will work best with the duck, tuna, or other examples of chef David Foot's renowned fusion food. Five minutes west, the **Beach House at Dundarave Pier** appeals to the local, well-heeled crowd with a list long on medium and high-end Californian wines. Local labels and Old World wines are also well represented. Sommelier Michael Moller at the fine harbor-view restaurant **The Five Sails** has put together another fine list, strong on reds and scotch.

Where to mess up your shirt... Former Vancouverites go misty-eyed at the thought of **White Spot**'s "Triple O" burgers, which have been a local legend for some 60 years. The secret is Triple O sauce, a condiment somewhere between mayo and chili sauce. Worth the hype? Your call. Outlets abound, but the most time-warpy place to sample it is at the drive-in on West Broadway—turn on your headlights and out comes the carhop. City cops and seniors make up most of the clientele, so don't anticipate rockin' the rafters if you do go inside.

Attitude is everything... For a real cultural experience, head for Commercial Drive in East Vancouver and grab a seat in the **Calabria Bar.** The decor here is stratospheric kitsch—you've never seen so many marble statues—but the cappuccinos are good, the sandwiches are hearty, and you can practice your Italian. If you need an antidote to Vancouver's prevailing niceness, go for **The Elbow Room,** a crowded West End coffeeshop where the main attraction is the deliberately rude commentary that arrives with your coffee It's the staff schtick, and a big reason people come here, even celebs. Your appearance, sexual preference, and hang-ups are all are up for discussion. For dollops of Gen-X angst, slink into the gothic **Subeez Cafe,** on Homer Street at the edge of Yaletown, where you'll find massive candles, a sound system cranked to the max, and a menu chalked on the wall in a type size too small for all but the youngest eyes. Food spans the globe: cashew chicken curry, linguine with pesto, a hot seafood salad made with local fish, and Asian flavors; they're all up for grabs. Flipness equals hipness at **Delilah's,** in the West End, where drag queens, the gay crowd, and locals all schmooze over martinis and the prix fixe two- or five-course menu. Write out your own order for West Coast fusion dishes like tuna carpaccio, tempura prawns, or tri-mushroom fettucine. Low ceilings, plush velvet banquettes, and Tiffany-style lamps make the mood glam and intimate—but certainly not clique-y.

Biting off a chunk of Victoria... You can find everything from lowbrow eats to high falutin' dining in Victoria. This is a sea town populated largely by English expats, so if you really want an authentic experience, head to one of their fish 'n' chips joints or pubs. Nobody does the finny thing better than **Barb's Place**, right on the docks of the Inner Harbour about a half mile west of the Empress Hotel. For pub grub, you've got plenty of choices, though downtown offerings tend mostly to cater to tourists; try the more upscale brewpubs **Swans** or **Spinnakers** [see Nightlife], both serving healthier-than-you-think cuisine alongside their dynamite beers. The city also sports a surprising number of cafes and bistros, great for light lunches or dinner splurges. Everyone raves about the **Herald Street Caffe**—with its chef's inventive takes on the local fish, meats, and fruits—and tucked-away **Rebar** for its light vegetarian lunches. Also don't miss the compact Chinatown, packed with options from budget to upscale; **Don Mee Seafood** is a good starting point for freshly fried fish and shellfish and knockout dim sum at decent prices. Finally, if you want to drop a bundle and impress your significant other, hightail it out of town to the **Sooke Harbour House** (about 25 miles west of Victoria, via Highway 14) or the **Aerie Resort Dining Room** (15 miles to the north on Highway 1). These two joints, both attached to resorts [see Accommodations], are considered the island's very finest; each serves up scrumptious, expensive meals in dining rooms looking out onto woods or water.

Best places to get tea'd off in Victoria... Everybody knows London is the center of the universe, but Victoria must be a close second. Could it be all those Brit expats who've resettled here? No doubt—and they've duplicated the British experience right down to afternoon high teas, which have become nearly ubiquitous in Victoria hotels. The grandpappy of them all, of course, is that served in **The Fairmont Empress Tea Room.** We're talking a full, all-you-can-nosh course of scones, sweets, and more for 30 bucks—plus your pick of the finest teas in the world, served at the perfect temperature in the Queen's silver. Don't even *think* about wearing an anorak, shorts, or jeans, though; this is one room in normally casual B.C. where you can—and will—get ejected for messing with the dress code. The Empress is far from the only game in town, however. Do some comparison shopping by heading for the oh-so-English Oak Bay neighborhood on the ocean a few blocks south of downtown; here, the **Windsor House Tea Room** boasts stupendous water views, fine service, and much-better-than-average desserts, while the overrated **Blethering Place Tea Room** is a less-worthy alternative in the same general environs. (It's notable more for its aging Brit tourist crowd than its tea.) Back in the central district, the **James Bay Tea Room** (which is not really anywhere near James Bay) is a working-class kind of tea place, the polar opposite, cost-wise and otherwise, of the Empress. Think of it as a place where your English soccer fan might go for a quick cuppa leaf and some Yorkshire pudding or other greasy chow. **Murchie's Tea and Coffee,** less brazenly Anglophile than the rest, nevertheless sports the broadest selection of quality teas on the island, plus some primo java and everything from snacks to sandwiches.

The Index

$$$$$	over $50
$$$$	$40–$50
$$$	$30–$40
$$	$20–$30
$	under $20

Price categories reflect the cost of an entrée plus appetizer and dessert, not including drinks, taxes, and tip.

Aerie Resort Dining Room. Top-notch dinner menus and splendid views of the water and mountains.... *Tel 250/743-7115. P.O. Box 108, Malahat. $$$$$*
(see p. 70)

Apollonia. Homey Greek restaurant near Granville Island serving great lamb, stuffed grape leaves, souvlaki, and the like. Charming hosts.... *Tel 604/736-9559. 1830 Fir St. Bus 4 or 50. $$* **(see p. 57)**

Bacchus Ristorante. Chef Cameron Caskie maintains house tradition of serving modern B.C. cuisine in luxe Venetian surroundings. Great bar.... *Tel 604/608-5319. 845 Hornby St. Bus 5. $$$$$* **(see p. 63)**

Banana Leaf. Authentic Malaysian cuisine from upbeat waitstaff. Try the noodles.... *Tel 604/731-6333. 820 W. Broadway. Bus 9. $$* **(see p. 62)**

Barb's Place. The city's best fish and chips, doled out in a no-frills setting right on the water.... *Tel 250/384-6515. 310 St. Lawrence St. $* **(see p. 70)**

Beach House at Dundarave Pier. Hangout for le tout West Vancouver. Food is good, often terrific, the wine list is

famous, and you can't fault the view.... *Tel 604/922-1414. 150 25th St., West Vancouver. Take a cab. $$$$*
(see pp. 56, 68)

Beach Side Café. Serene neighborhood restaurant with fine fusion cooking and a great wine list to accompany it.... *Tel 604/925-1945. 1362 Marine Dr., West Vancouver. Take a cab. $$$$*
(see p. 68)

Benny's On Broadway. Round the clock bagels popular with the movie crowd.... *Tel 604/731-9730. 2505 W. Broadway, plus other locations. Bus 9. No MC or AE. $*
(see p. 64)

Bin 941. Micro room, macro flavors in 20-something tapas hangout. Stays open late for the need-some-munchies club crowd.... *Tel 604/683-1246. 943 Davie St. Bus 6. No AE. No reservations. $$*
(see pp. 64, 65)

Bishop's. Superb West Coast cuisine, elegant surroundings, and flawless service earn kudos year after year.... *Tel 604/738-2025. 2183 W. 4th Ave. Bus 4. Reservations essential. $$$$$*
(see p. 53)

Blethering Place Tea Room. Maybe not as great as they *think* they are, but at least you'll hear plenty of real English accents.... *Tel 250/598-1413. 2250 Oak Bay Ave., Oak Bay. $$*
(see p. 71)

The Bread Garden. Pre-made pastas, quiches, desserts, and salads to eat on the spot or take out. Part of a chain, but only this outlet is open 24 hrs.... *Tel 604/736-6465. 2996 Granville St. Bus 8. $*
(see p. 65)

Bridges Restaurant. Score a seat on the waterfront patio and order nachos. Note that the second-floor restaurant costs more.... *Tel 604/687-4400. 1696 Duranleau St. Granville Island. Bus 51. $$$*
(see p. 56)

Bukowski's. Cerebral decor, sensual global food on the East Side, and live entertainment, often of the spoken variety.... *Tel 604/253-4770. 1447 Commercial Dr. Bus 20. $$*
(see p. 60)

C. Top seafood restaurant with sybaritic vista of sailboats and beautiful people.... *Tel 604/681-1164. 1600 Howe St. Take a cab. $$$$* **(see pp. 56, 62)**

Calabria Bar. Classic Italian cafe crammed with classical Italian statues.... *Tel 604/253-7017. 1745 Commercial Dr. Bus 20. No credit cards. $* **(see p. 69)**

Chartwell. Gentleman's club atmosphere, stuffy lunchtime clientele, but stunning food.... *Tel 604/689-9333. 791 W. Georgia St. Granville Station SkyTrain. $$$$$*
(see pp. 53, 54, 64, 68)

CinCin. Wood-burning oven produces delectable grills, pizzas.... *Tel 604/688-7338. 1154 Robson St. Bus 5. $$$$*
(see pp. 59, 67)

The Crime Lab. Intimate two-story restaurant decorated with mug shots and fingerprints..... *Tel 604/732-7463. 1280 W. Pender St. Take a cab. $$$* **(see p. 60)**

Delhi Darbar. Excellent Indian cuisine, profoundly subtle in flavor.... *Tel 604/877-7733. 2120 Main St. Bus 3 or take a cab. $$$* **(see p. 63)**

Delilah's. Exotic clientele (of the drag queen and entertainer variety), terrific martinis, and a prix fixe menu ($21 or $33.50) in the West End.... *Tel 604/687-3424. 1789 Comox St. Bus 6. Reservations for groups of 6 or more. $$$–$$$$* **(see p. 69)**

Diva at the Met. A busy business crowd frequents this buzzy Howe Street spot located inside the swanky Metropolitan Hotel. One of the city's best restaurants; don't leave without trying chef Michael Noble's knockout Stilton cheesecake..... *Tel 604/602-7788. 645 Howe St. Granville Station SkyTrain. $$$$*
(see pp. 54, 64, 68)

Don Mee Seafood. Great dim sum and seafood, most of it at a surprisingly reasonable price. Families can save a bundle by ordering combo plates.... *Tel 250/383-1032. 538 Fisgard St. $$* **(see p. 70)**

Earls. Popular local chain hits all the right buttons—good value, cheery service, and crowd-pleasing pizza and pasta fare.... *Tel 604/669-0020. 1185 Robson St. Bus 5. $*

(see p. 66)

Ecco il Pane. Wood-burning oven and setting straight from Tuscany; delicious breakfast breads and homey Italian lunches. West Broadway location doubles as bistro Thurs–Sat nights.... *Tel 604/739-1314. 2563 W. Broadway. Bus 9. Also tel 604/873-6888. 238 W. 5th Ave. Bus 15. No AE. $$*

(see p. 66)

The Elbow Room. Coffee, sandwiches, breakfast, but known for the deliberately acid service.... *Tel 604/685-3628. 560 Davie St. Bus 6. Reservations for groups of 6 or more. $*

(see p. 69)

El Patio. Sunny Mediterranean spot with friendly after-work bar crowd.... *Tel 604/681-9149. 891 Cambie St. Bus 2. $$*

(see p. 57)

The Fairmont Empress Tea Room. Hands-down, the most authentic, starchiest cup of tea in Canada. Make advance reservations for the afternoon "high tea," a Victoria tradition of sweets, snacks, and endless cups of the good stuff.... *Tel 250/384-8111 or 800/441-1414. 721 Government St. $*

(see p. 70)

The Fish House in Stanley Park. At this seaside spot, chef Karen Barnaby takes a generous approach to flavors.... *Tel 604/681-7275. 2099 Beach Ave. Take a cab. $$$*

(see p. 67)

The Five Sails. Postcard view of harbor and mountains, enchanting at night, in the Pan Pacific Hotel. Sea bass and rack of lamb to drool over.... *Tel 604/891-2892. 999 Canada Place. Waterfront Station SkyTrain. $$$$$* **(see pp. 55, 69)**

Fleuri. Sparkling originality in the kitchen helps mask ho-hum hotel setting.... *Tel 604/642-2900. 845 Burrard St. Bus 22. $$$$$* **(see pp. 59, 66)**

Gerard Lounge. Cozily lit bar is celeb fave for bistro food such

DINING | THE INDEX

as fancy pizzas and chicken.... *Tel 604/682-5511. 845 Burrard St. Bus 22. $$$* **(see p. 59)**

Grand King Seafood Restaurant. Popular West Side Chinese spot, where the cooking is a cut above the norm. Seafood dishes are a specialty.... *Tel 604/876-7855. 711 W. Broadway. Bus 9 Boundary. No AE. Reservations recommended. $$–$$$* **(see p. 61)**

Gyoza King. Funky hole-in-the-wall is second home for Japanese students.... *Tel 604/669-8278. 1508 Robson St. Bus 5. $* **(see pp. 58, 67)**

Habibi's. Lebanese dishes pulse with authentic flavor. Exceptionally warm service.... *Tel 604/732-7487. 1228 W. Broadway. Bus 9. No credit cards. No reservations. $* **(see p. 57)**

Hachibei. Mom-style Japanese food in a cozy neighborhood spot just west of Cambie Street. Specials are a steal.... *Tel 604/879-3357. 778 W. 16th Ave. Buses 15, 17. No AE. No reservations. $* **(see p. 58)**

Havana. Real Cuban cuisine in high-energy Commercial Drive atmosphere. Theater and art gallery too.... *Tel 604/253-9119. 1212 Commercial Dr. Bus 20. No AE. $$* **(see p. 60)**

Herald Street Caffe. Extremely popular hot spot among locals, for both the eclectic food and the company. Brunches are a specialty.... *Tel 250/381-1441. 546 Herald St. $$* **(see p. 70)**

Hon's Wun-Tun House. Classic Chinese restaurant chain with dependably good food, an encyclopedic menu, and a cast of local characters.... *Tel 604/688-0871. 108-268 Keefer St. Bus 22 Knight. No credit cards. Also tel 604/685-0871. 1339 Robson St. No AE. $* **(see p. 61)**

Il Giardino di Umberto. Heavenly Tuscan cuisine, served in a vine-draped garden.... *Tel 604/669-2422. 1382 Hornby St. Bus 22. $$$$$* **(see pp. 53, 55, 65)**

James Bay Tea Room. Possibly the lowest-brow "tea room" in town, this is closer to pub grub than white-gloves.... *Tel 250/382-8282. 332 Menzies St. $$* **(see p. 71)**

Joe Fortes. Major meet-market for the upwardly aspirational.... *Tel 604/669-1940. 777 Thurlow St. Bus 5 Robson. $$$–$$$$* **(see p. 55)**

La Bodega. Dimly lit, cozy tapas restaurant near Granville St. Bridge.... *Tel 604/684-8814. 1277 Howe St. Bus 6. $$* **(see p. 57)**

Le Crocodile. Nearly faultless French/German cuisine from respected chef Michel Jacob.... *Tel 604/669-4298. 909 Burrard St. (entrance on Smithe St.). Bus 22. $$$$* **(see pp. 53, 55, 65)**

Le Gavroche. Traditionally romantic French restaurant serves Gallic-meets-West Coast cuisine. Legendary wine list, especially for Burgundy and Bordeaux lovers.... *Tel 604/685-3924. 1616 Alberni St. Bus 5. $$$$* **(see p. 68)**

Liliget Feasthouse. Authentic First Nations cuisine such as grilled salmon served in the West End.... *Tel 604/681-7044. 1724 Davie St. Bus 6. Reservations recommended. $$$–$$$$* **(see p. 67)**

Lumière. Chef Rob Feenie is fanatical about the fresh ingredients that go into his modern French table d'hôte and tasting menus, $55–75.... *Tel 604/739-8185. 2551 W. Broadway. Bus 9. Reservations essential. $$$$$* **(see pp. 54, 62)**

Montri's Thai Restaurant. Subtle spicing and layered flavors make the Thai food here a standout, possibly the best in town.... *Tel 604/738-9888. 3629 W. Broadway. Bus 9. No AE. $$* **(see p. 63)**

Moustache Café. Right next door to the Fifth Avenue movie theaters. Menu gets applause for creativity and performance.... *Tel 604/739-1990. 2118 Burrard St. Bus 4. $$$* **(see p. 64)**

Murchie's Tea and Coffee. Locally famous tea and coffee

DINING | THE INDEX

importer also serves light meals and snacks in central location.... *Tel 250/383-3112. 1110 Government St. $*
(see p. 71)

Musashi. Hole-in-the-wall Japanese restaurant in the West End is a reliable source of good, cheap food.... *Tel 604/687-0634. 780 Denman St. Bus 5. Reservations accepted. $*
(see p. 58)

The Naam. Retro decor and alfalfa-sprout cuisine attracts former hippies and wannabes.... *Tel 604/738-7151. 2724 W. 4th Ave. Bus 4. $*
(see p. 62)

900 West. Flagship restaurant of The Hotel Vancouver. Decor somewhat chilly, but cuisine and service compensate.... *Tel 604/669-9378. 900 W. Georgia St. Bus 22. $$$$*
(see p. 65)

Nyala Ethiopian Restaurant. Predominantly Ethiopian cuisine, with live African music sometimes.... *Tel 604/731-7899. 2930 W. 4th Ave. Bus 4. $*
(see p. 60)

The Pacific Institute of Culinary Arts. Edge-of-Granville Island cooking school offers three-course lunches, $18, and dinners, $25, weekdays only. Monday, half price.... *Tel 604/734-4488. 1505 W. 2nd Ave. Bus 51. $$*
(see p. 65)

Pastis. The wild-mushroom tart with caramelized onions and the tapenade are typical of the French-inspired cuisine at this upscale bistro. Seasonal dishes reflect chef Frank Pabst's passion for fresh, regional ingredients.... *Tel 604/731-5020. 2153 W. 4th Ave. Bus 4. $$$–$$$$*
(see pp. 53, 64)

Phnom Penh. Award-winning Vietnamese and Cambodian cuisine.... *Tel 604/682-5777. 244 E. Georgia St. Bus 3 Main. No credit cards. Also tel 604/734-8898. 955 W. Broadway. Bus 9 Boundary. No Visa. $$*
(see p. 63)

Piccolo Mondo. Smart, sophisticated dining room and fine Italian food.... *Tel 604/688-1633. 850 Thurlow St. Bus 22. $$$–$$$$*
(see p. 68)

Planet Veg. Kits vegetarians line up for spicy, filling, and inexpensive Indian fare. A few seats in addition to the takeout.... *Tel 604/734-1001. 1941 Cornwall Ave. Bus 22. No credit cards. No reservations. $* **(see p. 62)**

Provence Mediterranean Grill. West Side bistro out near UBC. You can't go wrong with the antipasti or anything else.... *Tel 604/222-1980. 4473 W. 10th Ave. Bus 10. Lunch reservations only for groups of 5 or more. $$*
(see pp. 56, 66)

Quattro on Fourth. A chunk of Italy in setting and mood. Molto fun and macho flavors.... *Tel 604/734-4444. 2611 W. 4th Ave. Bus 4. $$$–$$$$* **(see p. 57)**

RainCity Grill. Dynamic West Coast food at the beach end of Denman Street. Follow the B.C. wine suggestions on the menu for a memorable meal before splendid bay views through the windows.... *Tel 604/685-7337. 1193 Denman St. Bus 6. $$$* **(see pp. 53, 68)**

Raintree at the Landing. Dining room looks out on Burrard Inlet; bistro is great escape after Gastown wanderings..... *Tel 604/688-5570. 375 Water St. Buses 3, 4. $$$* **(see p. 63)**

Rebar. Overpoweringly healthy vegetarian restaurant, juice bar, and gathering spot for local greenies.... *Tel 250/361-9223. 50 Bastion Sq., downstairs inside shopping complex. $* **(see p. 70)**

Salmon House on the Hill. Magnificent views and expertly prepared salmon make it worth the drive.... *Tel 604/926-3212. 2229 Folkestone Way, West Vancouver. Take a cab. $$$–$$$$* **(see p. 68)**

Sami's. Good value Indo-fusion food in a mini-mall on the West Side.... *Tel 604/736-8330. 986 W. Broadway. Bus 9. No AE. $$* **(see pp. 53, 60)**

Sooke Harbour House. Creative Pacific Northwest cuisine, served and eaten next to amazing long views of water, woods, and mountains. The chef is known for incorporating fresh flowers into the meals.... *Tel 250/642-3421. 1528 Whiffen Spit Rd., Sooke. $$$$$* **(see p. 70)**

Sophie's Cosmic Cafe. Yard-sale decor, homey hearty food at this longtime Kits fave.... *Tel 604/732-6810. 2095 W. 4th Ave. Bus 4. No AE. Reservations only for parties of 10 or more. $* **(see p. 66)**

Stepho's Souvlaki Greek Taverna. Lusty Greek classics in belly-filling quantity for young, hungry West Enders. You may have to wait.... *Tel 604/683-2555. 1124 Davie St. Bus 6. Reservations only for groups of 5 or more. $* **(see p. 58)**

Subeez Cafe. On the fringe of Yaletown, this cafe attracts fringey artistic folk.... *Tel 604/687-6107. 891 Homer St. Bus 5. No AE. $* **(see p. 69)**

Sun Sui Wah. Simple noodles to shark's fin soup, it's all here, including live seafood. On weekends, expect to wait in line or go early.... *Tel 604/872-8822. 3888 Main St. Bus 3 Main. $$* **(see p. 61)**

Tapastree. Popular modern tapas place near Stanley Park. Nice patio and strange interior decoration.... *Tel 604/606-4680. 1829 Robson St. Bus 5. $$$* **(see p. 67)**

Tojo's. Possibly the best sushi in town.... *Tel 604/872-8050. 777 W. Broadway. Bus 9. $$$$$* **(see p. 58)**

Tomato Fresh Food Café. Sprightly decor and healthy food.... *Tel 604/874-6020. 3305 Cambie St. Bus 15. $$* **(see p. 67)**

Vij's. Vikram Vij takes Indian food to a new dimension. Expect lines.... *Tel 604/736-6664. 1480 W. 11th Ave. Bus 8. No reservations. $$$* **(see p. 59)**

Villa del Lupo. Signature lamb shanks and cozy rooms in a heritage house—that's amore.... *Tel 604/688-7436. 869 Hamilton St. Bus 15 Cambie. $$$$* **(see pp. 53, 63)**

White Spot. "Triple O" burgers are a Vancouver classic at this burger chain.... *Tel 604/731-2434. 2518 W. Broadway. Bus 9. No AE. $* **(see pp. 66, 69)**

Windsor House Tea Room. The best of Oak Bay's tea rooms, serving high tea and good pub-style food.... *Tel 250/595-3135. 2540 Windsor Rd., Oak Bay. $$* **(see p. 71)**

82

Downtown Vancouver Dining

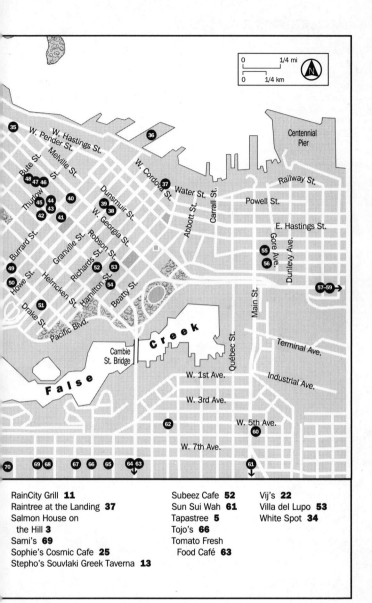

3

sions

If you yearn to
explore ancient
cathedrals and
palaces, don't
come to Van-
couver. It's a
young city,

barely a century old, and it only seriously got growing in the 1960s—which makes what *is* here, in the way of first-rate galleries and museums, all the more remarkable. Vancouver's most intriguing diversions draw from the city's strengths: natural beauty and a stewpot of peoples and cultures from all over the world. Tourist literature may yammer on about **Gastown**, which is undeniably quaint, but it pales beside native art from far-off misty islands in northern B.C., the yin-yang of industry and serenity that comprises **Chinatown**, the hip shops and cafes of **Yaletown**, or the majesty of Canadian geese in V-formation at the **George C. Reifel Migratory Bird Sanctuary**.

Getting Your Bearings

Finding your way around here is laughably easy. Barring the snooty **Shaughnessy** neighborhood, and a few other anomalies dictated by physical geography, the entire city is built on a grid system. Streets between **False Creek** and the **Fraser River** south of the downtown peninsula are numbered avenues (subtract 1,500 from any north-south street number, and that will give you a rough idea of the intersection to aim for). Most downtown streets are designated either "east" or "west"—think of **Main Street** as the boundary between them. If you do get lost, check where the mountains are—that's north, more or less. Set on its own peninsula, **downtown**—where you'll find most of the shopping and entertainment—consists of the business core, a shopping area centered on **Granville and Georgia streets**, and the residential **West End**. The big three to remember downtown are **Georgia, Hastings, and Robson streets**, all of which run east-west. Georgia Street winds up in **Stanley Park** at its western end, and, just east of downtown, turns into a highway that takes you lickety-split toward the stores and cafes of **Commercial Drive** on the East Side. **Hastings Street** continues east way into the suburbs and ends, in the west, at Jervis Street. **Robson Street**—which is often compared to Rodeo Drive, though not by residents—crosses downtown only. Running north to south between **English Bay** and **Coal Harbour**, **Denman Street** in the **West End** (the residential part of the downtown peninsula) will give you a good taste of Vancouver. On sunny evenings, its ice cream stores, sidewalk cafes, shoulder-to-shoulder crowds of shorts-clad pedestrians, and glimpses of the water make it feel like a seaside resort. Close by,

Stanley Park makes up roughly half of the downtown peninsula. Threaded with trails and ringed by the Seawall, this massive spread of nature is one of the city's prides. Two long fingers of water, **Burrard Inlet** and **False Creek**, hold downtown Vancouver between them. To reach Burrard Inlet from central downtown, go north on **Burrard** or **Granville street,** or any street in between. There's no waterfront as such, but a stroll along the "decks" of **Canada Place,** identifiable by its big white landmark sails, makes a fine stand-in. Burrard Inlet lies to the north, spanned by two bridges—the **Second Narrows Bridge** on the east side, and the **Lions Gate Bridge** from Stanley Park to the north shore, both of them prone to rush-hour tie-ups. The Lions Gate is the one you're more likely to take. Just three lanes wide—the center lane changes depending on traffic flow—it more or less marks the dividing line between **West** and **North Vancouver** (the communities visible across Burrard Inlet from downtown). South of downtown, heading toward False Creek brings you first to **Yaletown,** a former industrial area now refurbished into lofts and condos; it's downtown's hippest neighborhood, a happening area where you can pick up a lush leather sofa or designer jeans, then chill out with a beer at a brew pub. Parking is tight, though, so take buses or cabs. Beyond Yaletown, three bridges—**Cambie Street, Granville Street, and Burrard Street**—cross False Creek to the rest of Vancouver. Farther south, a series of bridges crosses the Fraser River, the two most used being the **Arthur Laing Bridge,** which leads to **Vancouver International Airport,** and the **Oak Street Bridge,** which leads to **Richmond** and eventually reaches the U.S. border. Three major highways feed into Vancouver from the Fraser Valley to the east: **Highway 1,** which is part of the **Trans-Canada Highway** (and also connects with **Highway 15,** an alternative route to the U.S.), and **Highways 7 and 7A,** which are mostly used by commuters from the eastern suburbs. Avoid them if you can, especially at rush hour. Unless you have a yen to see some of the more far-flung attractions, you won't need a car in Vancouver. Those brightly painted buildings underneath the Granville Street Bridge are on Granville Island, a "mustn't miss" mix of public market, stores, galleries, and theaters. Locals grouse about the city transit system, which can be packed tight at rush hour, but it's more than adequate for visitors. Besides, many of the sites you'll want to see are clustered together. The savvy will plan a day in this area, an afternoon in that one, and take in several attractions at once. Where to begin? **Tourism Vancouver** is a gold mine of free information, so stop at its main downtown office to load up on brochures and maps.

The Lowdown

Granville Island getaway... Sitting outside on a bench on Granville Island, coffee in hand, is a tough act to beat. Public market, public schmarket, it's a whole lot more than that. A century ago, this particular spot was just a couple of sandbars on the tidal flats in False Creek. Gradually it evolved into a 35-acre island made from fill dredged from the waters, becoming a booming industrial site with factories and machine shops that thrived until the mid-1940s. After a long decline, Canada's federal government intervened in the 1970s to bring this industrial wasteland back to life, with a new spiffed-up identity. The decrepit warehouses became homes for a public market, art school, galleries, theaters—a whole community. From the day it opened in 1979, the city took the island to its heart, and the relationship has gotten better with the years. In fact, Granville Island is a victim of its own success—with only one access road, getting there in prime hours can be a slow, tortuous process, especially on summer weekends. Aim first for the **Granville Island Public Market**, at the island's northwest corner. Housed in vast banner-hung former machine shops, it's a place of almost overwhelming profusion. Amble around, and you'll come upon international cheeses, homemade pastas, pea-size eggplants flown in fresh from Thailand, Okanagan-grown heritage apples: If you can eat it, it's here. For whimsical jewelry, hand-carved salad bowls, or exotic cushions, check the crafts at the tables in the central aisle, where artisans rent space by the day. Grab takeout Mexican or Ukrainian food (those are only two of your choices) or pick up a slab of grape-dotted *pane all'uva* at **Terra Breads**, and head outdoors into the waterside courtyard. Plenty of benches make this a perfect spot for a spur-of-the-moment picnic. Granville Island shops and galleries in the Net Loft, and elsewhere, are also definitely worth a trawl. Hand-knit sweaters, unique pottery, Japanese paper, kitchenware, and a shop selling nothing but beads: This is one of the city's best hunting grounds for non-tacky souvenirs. Armed with a map from the **Granville Island Information Centre**, you can check out the community of floating homes east of the market at the other end of the island; the Emily Carr Institute of Art and Design, where tomorrow's Rothkos and Rauschenbergs hone their skills; or the **Granville Island Sport Fishing and Model Ships Museum**. The center can also book seats for a theater performance right on the island. One caveat: If you brought the car, keep an eye on the time. Parking regulators swing by regularly, marking car tires with chalk, so they know how long you've been there. Plan B is to pay for parking in the covered garage; better yet, take alternative transportation—city buses (Bus 50 False Creek South) or the Aquabus, which every few minutes putters across the water from the south end of Howe Street.

Not one but two Chinatowns... Vancouver's many bilingual signs in Chinese and English over banks and restaurants attest to how many people who read Chinese now call the city home. The first Chinese came to the city in the 1850s to try their luck in the Fraser Valley gold rush; more followed to help build the Canadian Pacific Railway. Many settled around Main and Pender streets in Chinatown—take any of the buses along Hastings Street, and get off at Main Street. Street parking is problematic on weekends, but the parking garage at Keefer and Columbia streets usually has space. Once you're there, just follow your nose and your curiosity. Gilded dragons decorate streetlights and telephone boxes are pagoda-shaped, but you don't need these to tell you you're deep in another culture. A Chinese pharmacist weighs bark, dried leaves, and seeds (a popular cold remedy); a storekeeper arranges bundles of bright greens in tidy rows; an elderly woman hooks up a fish by its gills; glistening barbecued ducks and sides of pork hang in a window. Look in the shops, and you'll find finely embroidered linens and authentic cheongsams—slit-sided, high-necked (and definitely sexy) brocade dresses—to take home, but some of the best souvenirs are everyday pieces, like the functional cookware, its design unchanged in thousands of years, that you'll find at the back of larger grocery stores. Don't be shy about asking shopkeepers questions about their exotic stock, but only if business is slow. Ambling along Pender Street between Carrall and Main streets will take you past the Sam Kee Building (8 West Pender St.), the narrowest building in the world at just 2 meters (6 feet) wide, and past buildings, some with traditional recessed balconies, that date back to Chinatown's earliest days (look for dates inscribed on the facades). To delve even deeper into Chinese culture, visit the **Chinese Cultural Centre Museum and Archives**. Tools used by early gold miners, and games they played to pass the time, make it an intriguing look at the human side of Chinese-Canadian history. Images of Chinatown show you the streets outside as they used to be; not much has changed. Right next to it, the **Dr. Sun Yat-Sen Classical Garden** is a pool of tranquility, the first classical Chinese garden outside of China. No time? At least saunter through the Chinese-style walled park next door. It's a quiet enclave of whispering clumps of bamboo, tall evergreens, and rocks, with a Chinese pavilion, and pond. If you're hungry, try a bowl of *congee*—rice "porridge" bright with ginger and green onions—at **Gain Wah**. Ask for a side order of Chinese doughnuts to dunk. Jump-cut to modern Hong Kong, and the other, modern Chinatown that's sprung up to the south of Vancouver. Attracted by its proximity to the airport, many immigrants who arrived in the 1980s made their homes in the suburb of Richmond, which is now predominantly Asian—entire shopping malls, such as the **Aberdeen Centre**, were custom-built to make newcomers feel at home. Head for the epicenter at Cambie Street and No. 3 Road, a 20-minute drive from downtown (except during rush hour). The landmark to look for is the mirrored **Radisson President Hotel and Suites** [see Accommodations], where you can treat yourself to wonderful dim sum at the President Chinese Seafood Restaurant—even hardened gourmets weaken over the shrimp dumplings (*har gow*) and deep-fried chicken knees here. Next to it, in the **Yaohan Centre**, the supermarket is well worth a look, as is the food court specializing in authentic Asian street food. Take the elevator to the top floor, and you'll find a Buddhist temple complete with tea house. Across the street, **Aberdeen Centre** is intriguing, with its Taiwanese snack store—salted dried crabs, anyone?—and Chinese tea store, where the staff will perform an authentic tea ceremony for you. When these malls first opened, some locals grumbled that Westerners weren't made to feel welcome, though the language barrier was probably the main problem. That barrier still exists, but make an effort to communicate, and you'll be rewarded by an inside look at the Asian lifestyle.

Classical Gastown... Before you ooh and ahh over the cobblestoned paving, quaint streetlights, and leafy trees lining the oldest part of the city, be aware that they aren't original—a major makeover in the 1970s transformed this former skid row into a historic mall ripe for tourists. That said, Gastown is worth a visit, especially since it's an easy walk from downtown, starting a few blocks east of the convention center and ending more or less at Columbia Street. The main tourist attraction here is what's reputed to be the world's first steam-powered clock at the corner of Water and Cambie streets (built in 1977, it's hardly part of the city's long-ago past, and recently it's been revealed that steam doesn't actually *power* the clock; it's more for effect). Nevertheless, every 15 minutes visitors crowd around it, fingers on the shutter, waiting for the steam to erupt. Gastown's main drag, Water Street, is lined with tall turn-of-the-century buildings, many of them old hotels. Their high ceilings and wide-planked floors make them popular with today's architects and designers. Gastown's namesake—a gabby saloon keeper and ex-river pilot, "Gassy" Jack Deighton—is commemorated with a statue in Maple Tree Square at the east end of Water Street. Take a look at the Hotel Europe nearby at the junction of Water, Powell, and Carrall streets, a classic flatiron structure built in 1908, now apartments. From here you can wander into sleepy, ivy-clad Gaoler's Mews (12 Water St.); Gastown's first police chief chained up his prisoners here in the 1890s. To be honest, most of the stores cater to the bus and cruise ship tourists—this is souvenir T-shirt heaven—but there are some trendy boutiques on Cordova Street and other scattered shops selling antiques, contemporary furniture and furnishings, and artwork by First Nations designers: exquisite silver jewelry, masks, and bentwood boxes that may alone make the trip to Gastown worthwhile.

First Nations first... The **Museum of Anthropology** is a must-see on three counts: its brilliant exhibits, its awesome setting on the cliffs of Point Grey, and its remarkable building. You enter through an undistinguished front entrance, but it's an architectural tease—inside, the space soars into a vast light-filled area with a 15-meter (50-foot) glass wall that overlooks ocean and mountains. Northwest Coast First Nations art is the focus here—feast dishes, canoes, terrifying ceremonial masks, finely woven hats, totem poles carved with stylized eagles and bears—it's dynamite stuff that gives you some idea of how this region's natives lived and celebrated for thousands of years and, to some extent, still do. A standout is *The Raven and the First Men*, a massive work in yellow cedar by master carver Bill Reid, illustrating the Haida myth about the Raven discovering mankind concealed in a clamshell (kids usually giggle at the humans' rear ends poking out). Reid, who carved the magnificent jade canoe at Vancouver International Airport, also designed the huge bear that crouches in the museum's main area. Other musts are the Koerner Ceramics Gallery and the open stacks, where more than 15,000 objects are displayed by culture and use. Don't try to take it all in at once—focus on musical instruments, maybe, or games, or tools. The gift shop has an especially fine selection of Northwest Coast prints, carvings, and jewelry. Outdoors on the cliff top are two Haida bighouses and some more towering totem poles—in this fine setting of woods and water, they're many times more evocative than those tired Stanley Park totems that every tourist takes a snapshot of.

Art attacks... The majestic, pillared **Vancouver Art Gallery** guards the north end of Robson Square, its columned facade flying bright-colored banners promoting current exhibits, which can range from Japanese prints to Toulouse-Lautrec. Originally built as the Law Courts (go around to the Georgia Street side to see its original—and far grander—front entrance), the museum building has been reconfigured for art, with a huge glass dome that floods much of the interior with natural light. There are four floors of exhibits housing three or four different exhibits—none of them permanent. What you see when you go there could be Matisse, could be Munch, could be modern Native American art. Some pieces are on loan, but many are drawn from the gallery's own huge collection, a 7,000-strong assemblage of paintings, sculptures, and installations, with works ranging from David Hockney and Andy Warhol to Robert Mapplethorpe. Though the gallery does boast a Gainsborough, the focus is definitely on modern artists. Big-name Canadian artists like Jack Shadbolt and Gathie Falk aren't the only draw; the gallery may also have a Picasso or Magritte out on display. A permanent exhibit on the third floor highlights the works of Emily Carr, an early-20th-century British Columbian painter famed for her bold renditions of wild northern forests and native villages. (The Emily Carr College of Art and Design on Granville Island is named after her.) The simplicity and strength of her work powerfully evokes the region she loved—and has earned her international recognition. There's a cafe on site with an outdoor patio, but for a mind-blowing view of Robson Square, walk across to the modern Law Courts and find the **Law Courts Restaurant.** Overlooking a massive decorative pool, it's meant for lawyers and other legal staff, but anyone is welcome to eat here. The food isn't bad (sandwiches, pastas, and other mainstream fare), the price is a bargain for the quality, and you can't beat that downtown view. Another downtown gem is the **Canadian Craft Museum**, on Hornby Street, facing an enchanting but hidden public green space. Daylight floods into the airy open gallery, which houses changing exhibits that range from finely knit sweaters and needlepoint to beautiful pottery and filigree glassware. Be sure to take a look at the entrance desk, the work of Ontario furniture-maker and designer Gordon Peteran; knickknacks galore have been incorporated into its surface, all representative of different crafts. If you're into weaving or pottery, there are several galleries and workshops on **Granville Island**; galleries displaying oils and watercolors cluster along both sides of **South Granville Street** across the Granville Street Bridge from downtown, and emerging artists display their works around **Commercial Drive**. Check local newspapers such as the *Georgia Straight* to find out what's going on where. Over in North Vancouver, **Presentation House Gallery** displays historic black-and-white photos, avant-garde video installations, national and international exhibits—if it's been shot with a camera lens, there's a chance you'll see it here. Camera buffs still talk of the Ansel Adams show here some years ago. It's set in a green-painted, wood-frame Victorian building that has been in its time a school, city hall, and jail; it's only a short walk from the SeaBus terminal at Lonsdale Quay.

Fishy business... Go eyeball-to-eyeball with a mighty killer whale at the **Vancouver Aquarium** in Stanley Park. Be warned, sitting in the front row "splash zone" at a training session in the outdoor pool means a drenching when one of these huge mammals leaps and lands back in the water. Less rambunctious is the Pacific white-sided dolphin that shares space with the "killer," and the five gentle beluga whales who have a pool of their own. Indoors, displayed in regional settings, are thousands of fish as well as selected reptiles, birds, and mammals. A steamy jungle, complete with hourly thunderstorm, houses a sloth, giant freshwater fish, and scarlet ibis; sharks swim in a re-creation of an Indonesian reef. It makes for a fascinating few hours, though it may put you off sushi for life. If you're in town in late summer or early fall, you can witness an even more dramatic fish story on the North Shore: All that grade school stuff you learned about the salmon's life cycle comes to vivid life at the **Capilano Salmon Hatchery** (take the first road on the left after the Capilano Suspension Bridge). Come spawning season, the salmon return upstream to the waters where they originated; lean out over the weir and you'll see them trying for vertical take-off. Inside the hatchery, you get a close-up view of the fish as, one step at a time, they leap up fish ladders. Pretty banged-up by now, they soldier on till they arrive at last in the holding tanks. After that—sorry fellows, what happens next ain't pretty. Models and pictures provide deep background on the salmon's life cycle. Outside, rearing ponds hold the next doomed generation.

How does your garden grow?... Some of the priciest real estate in the western world lies within Vancouver city limits—and even so, great chunks of it are happily devoted to botanical gardens. Even in high season, you'll find a leafy corner to call your own at the **Van-Dusen Botanical Garden** on Oak Street, ranked among the world's top ten by *Horticulture* magazine. A former golf course, the sprawling 22 hectares (55 acres) is an undulating delight of lawns, trees, and perennial borders, with every plant and shrub clearly identified. Colored "leaves" painted on the pathways guide you along various walking routes, timed to take 20 minutes, an hour, or longer. Make a beeline for the deliciously scented fragrance garden, the formal rose garden, the Elizabethan maze, or the meadowlike Alma VanDusen Garden. Amble around the man-made lakes, and keep an eye out for the scattered sculptures by local and international artists. Even in the winter, this place is a joy. On the University of British Columbia campus, the **UBC Botanical Garden** is primarily a "teaching" garden, quieter in mood than the VanDusen and—at 28 hectares (70 acres)—even larger. Tomato plants, espalier apple trees—you'll see the productive side of a garden as well as the aesthetic side. The formal Physick Garden, laid out with herbs and medicinal plants, is especially intriguing. A spectrum of plants native to British Columbia are displayed, ranging from skunk cabbage on the coast to desert varieties; avid earth-tillers can explore the new plant varieties developed at UBC. South on Cambie Street is the entrance to **Queen Elizabeth Park** on Little Mountain, the city's highest point. Here, former quarries have been transformed into rock gardens lush with shrubs, flowers, cascades, and ponds, making the spot so picturesque, it's a favorite weekend site for wedding photos. At the peak of the mountain, a 43-meter (140-foot) Plexiglas dome covers the **Bloedel Conservatory**. It's literally a jungle in there, full of banana trees, raucous parrots, multicolored birds, gaudy flowers, and—a godsend on a chilly Vancouver day—warm and humid tropical warmth.

In search of old architecture... Most of Vancouver's original downtown architecture has fallen prey to the wrecker's ball, with one spectacular exception: **The**

Marine Building (555 Burrard St. at Hastings St.), an art deco gem. Built in the late 1920s in the same "waterfall" style as some of New York City's finest old skyscrapers, its giant needle soars skyward. A frieze of shells and sea creatures adorns its facade; wander inside and take a gander at its stained-glass window, tiled lobby, and ornate elevators—all just as they were in the flapper era. Just east along Hastings Street lies a group of historic sturdy graystone buildings crowned by a clock tower, mostly dating back to early 1900s. They used to be government buildings; now the main floor has been converted into swank Sinclair Centre (757 W. Hastings St.), home to some of the priciest stores in town. Across the Cambie Street Bridge, architecture buffs can wander through a similar "adaptation" at City Square (555 W. 12th Ave.), just across from Vancouver's art deco–styled City Hall. This side of the water is also home to Vancouver's oldest building, the **Old Hastings Mill Store Museum**, built in 1865, and one of the few structures that the fire of 1886 didn't touch. Inside this wooden one-story building, you'll come upon Native baskets, old photos, furniture, clocks—its collection is an engaging mishmash. Crossing back to downtown, check out **Roedde House Museum**, a charming restored Victorian home that's one of the city's best-kept secrets. (Say the name to most Vancouverites and you'll get blank stares.) Take the guided tour of the interior to get a snapshot of Vancouver daily life a century ago.

Global neighborhoods... English, French, Chinese, Hindi, Portuguese, Greek, German—you'll hear them all spoken on Vancouver streets, and not just by visitors. Right from its early beginnings, the city has attracted immigrants from around the world, most of whom settled where they felt most at home—meaning next door to others from their homeland. Even though its coffee shops and butchers now cohabit with offbeat stores and galleries, **Commercial Drive** on the East Side is still Italian to its core. It's well worth a wander, especially on a sunny Saturday morning with pauses every so often at a sidewalk cafe. A more concentrated Little Italy is located along **East Hastings Street** around Nanaimo and Renfrew streets You'll see poppas carefully selecting ripe peppers, mommas discussing the right cut of veal with the butcher, groups of guys noisily following a soccer game on TV straight from Italy—and you'll hear lots and lots of Italian spoken. Both areas cater to life Italian style, from cheese shops and bakeries to stores selling first communion dresses. The once-lively Greek neighborhood that centered on **West Broadway** between downtown and UBC has been reduced to a bank and a handful of stores, but at **Minerva Mediterranean Deli** you'll still see groups of middle-aged men, hatted and suited, sipping coffee together while their wives purchase olives and feta to the sound of recorded *bouzoukia* music. **The Parthenon** super-market has changed locations over its 30-year history, but it's still a favorite haunt for olives—especially the house-made spicy ones—feta cheese, and groceries from the European sun belt. Chinatown apart, your most vivid excursion into another culture is the Punjabi Market on Main Street between 48th and 51st avenues. Stately grandmothers in saris (often topped with western-style raincoats) sail galleonlike along the sidewalks, while teens check out the latest Bollywood videos. A clatter of spices scents the air; spangled and beaded silk saris dyed saffron, magenta, and vivid turquoise fill the windows. Look for wannabe fashion designers and trendoids poring through bales of fabric, or savvy shoppers investing in deluxely embroidered wedding saris, to have them recut into evening wear. Time your explorations around lunchtime, and you can refuel at one of the rock-bottom cheap restaurants; the vegetarian buffet at **All India Sweets** is a dependably tasty choice.

A park full of museums... You can cross off several attractions in one fell swoop with a visit to Vanier Park, just south of the Burrard Street Bridge. The **Vancouver Museum** (formerly the Centennial Museum), has an attractive cone-shaped roof that's intended to look like a traditional Native woven hat—but you'd never guess that unless someone told you. Once past the giant metal crab spewing water outside, you wander through a series of galleries, a walk through the city's history. History isn't sugar-coated here: Displays allude to the internment of Japanese-

Canadians during World War II, and photos show Granville Street—now a several-block stretch of porn and pawn shops—as it was in its neon-lit heyday as a theater district. Reconstructions let you peer in the window of an early fur trading post, or sail steerage class on an immigrant ship—a truly grungy way to travel. Check out the fully furnished rooms of a Vancouver home with its gingerbread-and-fretwork exterior; pore over artifacts portraying the "Britishness" (teashops and manicured gardens) of a city where the Queen's photo still hangs in every public school. If all this piques your curiosity about Vancouver's past, the **City of Vancouver Archives** lies just across the parking lot, with photographs of the old Vancouver usually on display (the archives hold thousands more, not to mention maps, books, and newspaper clippings you can root through). Far more captivating, though—especially for kids—is the Vancouver Museum's immediate neighbor, the high-tech **Pacific Space Centre**, which offers interactive displays and a thrilling space ride. A short walk across the park brings you to the triangular **Vancouver Maritime Museum**, an imposing totem pole beside it and a drop-dead view of the water and mountains stretching before it. Its prime attraction is the *St. Roch*, an RCMP two-masted schooner that made history in 1940–42 as the first vessel to go through the Northwest Passage west to east. It was also the first boat to circumnavigate North America. There's a haunting feeling aboard, with an Inuit tent on deck and Morse code tap-tapping away in the wireless operator's cabin, as if captain and crew had vanished suddenly, leaving everything just as it was. Elsewhere in the museum, keep your eyes peeled for Captain Vancouver's chronometer, a ship's biscuit from 1864— very wormy, analysis shows—and model ships carved from meat bones by prisoners of the Napoleonic wars. A resident model-maker builds museum-quality pieces, which are on display; some are for sale. If possible, avoid visiting here mid-week when school is in session and dozens of kids swarm aboard.

Reasons to go back to school... Classic and modern architecture, acres of unspoiled surrounding forest, a nude beach nearby, million-dollar views, plus several tourist attractions on-site—now this is what you call a campus. The **University of British Columbia,** invariably called UBC, is also vast and easy to get lost in. Best to drop in at the Student Union Building and take one of the regular scenic walking tours, held twice daily during the summer. If you want to do it on your own, be sure to take a map. The Tudor-style Cecil Green House with its flower-filled English gardens, and the Chan Centre for the Performing Arts, set among more greenery, are especially worth checking out. Talk about musical: The Chan Centre's Concert Hall is shaped like a cello and has an adjustable canopy that can "tailor" the space acoustically. Scientific types gravitate toward a free 90-minute tour around the **TRIUMF Research Centre** for a look at the world's largest cyclotron. Ramble around the stunning **UBC Botanical Garden**, or check out rocks and fossils (including a super dinosaur skeleton) at the **UBC M.Y. Williams Geological Museum**. A half-hour drive east in the suburb of Burnaby is the region's other big center of learning, **Simon Fraser University**, named after an early explorer and fur trader. Winding your way along the road that climbs Burnaby Mountain brings you to a vast panorama of craggy skyline, city towers, and harbor activity. As spectacular as its mountaintop setting is the university itself, a futuristic design by Arthur Erickson (parts of the campus have been used as locations for sci-fi flicks). As with UBC, your best bet is to join a tour or, tour map in hand, wander around on your own.

Hey, kids!... Fasten your seat belts for a ride into space at the **Pacific Space Centre** in Vanier Park (it shares an entrance with the **Vancouver Museum**, an excellent museum that's more for the history-minded). The Space Centre is an absolute blast, with multimedia shows, hands-on exhibits, a piece of the moon you can actually touch, and laser light and rock music shows at night in the planetarium. A space simulator jolts and lurches riders as it seemingly hurtles through the galaxy. Steps away, at the **Gordon Southam Observatory**, you can drop in and look at the stars through a half-meter (20-inch) telescope; on weekends if the sky is clear, volunteers can even help you shoot the moon with your own camera. One of the few buildings that didn't get dismantled after Expo '86's six-month run, a giant glittering "golf ball" at the end of False Creek now houses **Science World British Columbia.** A real city landmark, at night it looks like a giant illuminated dandelion puffball. The huge sculpture outside ticks, clangs, and boings as it sends a series of balls through funnels, around spirals, and down chutes, and that's just at the entrance to this fascinating place. Once inside, everyone's free to act like a kid—blow mega-sized soap bubbles; jump and wave your arms and legs as you "freeze" your shadow on the wall; use your feet to play a giant piano keyboard (like Tom Hanks in *Big*). The gift store is crammed with dinosaurs in every possible incarnation, and other neat stuff. For somewhat simpler pleasures, there's a petting zoo-cum-farmyard at Stanley Park [see Getting Outside] but if your children really want to spend time with animals, go to **Maplewood Children's Farm** in North Vancouver, where they can fondle bunnies, chicks, and other domesticated animals and birds. High-decibel first-grade cries of "Oh, cu-u-u-te!" rend the air as youngsters explore the joys of Goathill and Rabbitat, and city kids can even watch a real cow being milked ("Ooh, gr-o-o-ss!"). A half hour from the city, at **Richmond Nature Park**, you can hike on interpretative nature trails through peat bog and greenery (wear boots if it's been raining), then duck inside the Nature House to look at snakes and salamanders.

A B.C. time machine... For a real time-trip, head for **Burnaby Village Museum**, a half-hour drive east of the city and a century away in spirit. "Villagers" in turn-of-the-century costumes get on with their daily lives in more than 30 restored buildings—the smithy, the movie theater, the print shop, and the dentist's office all bustle with activity, but kids are drawn most to the ice cream parlor and 1912 antique carousel. Walk beside Deer Lake afterward, and take a look at the art galleries and waterfowl. You can easily make a day of it.

Mega-views... No doubt about it, Vancouver does have some ace scenery. It's worth taking your camera to **Queen Elizabeth Park**, the highest point in the city. If you want to do the full 360 degrees in one shot, head for what looks like a UFO atop Harbour Centre, and ride the exterior glass elevator to **The Lookout! at Harbour Centre Tower**. It's a pricey journey, but the ticket you buy includes a tour and a video, and lets you go back as many times as you want in a single day—if possible, drop by a second time for the spectacular nighttime view. Get a rotating look around Vancouver along with a drink or dinner at the **Cloud 9 Revolving Restaurant** on the 42nd floor of the Empire Landmark Hotel. Granted, the panorama is more memorable than the West Coast–style food, and be careful when you get up to go to the bathroom—finding your way back to your table can be disorienting. Riding suspended in the sky on the **Grouse Mountain Skyride** can give you almost too broad a view, but on clear days, it's dynamite. You'll get eagle-eye views all the way, plus skiing or hiking when you get there, depending on the season. Up at the top, take a gander at the *Born to Fly* video, which provides an eagle's eye view of southwestern British Columbia.

Asian garden retreats... Had it with too many flowers, and looking for more cerebral surroundings? On the western edge of Chinatown adjacent to the Chinese Cultural Centre is the **Dr. Sun Yat-Sen Garden**, a lyrical place of craggy rocks, flowing water, swaying bamboo, bridges, and traditional buildings. Built in the Ming dynasty style, it demonstrates how subtle variations in shape and texture can define a garden landscape. The first classical Chinese garden outside China, it was built using imported Chinese labor and materials. There's a charge to enter, but this serene escape from the cacophony of Chinatown is worth it, like instant Prozac after the chaos of Pender and Keefer streets. (The adjacent park, also enclosed and tranquil, is free.) Out at UBC, close to the Museum of Anthropology, is the peaceful **Nitobe Memorial Garden**, a traditional Japanese garden in which every tree, shrub, and rock has been deliberately placed with an eye to harmony. Plump *koi* glide across mirrorlike pools, and bridges span chuckling streams; flowering cherry trees make it magical in spring, but any time of the year it's a pleasure to visit. Go at either end of the day on a weekday, and you'll often have the whole place to yourself.

For the birds... Feathered friends by the thousands fly in and out of the **George C. Reifel Migratory Bird Sanctuary** on Westham Island, a mere 35 minutes from downtown (providing you avoid rush hour)— worth the journey if you're a bird-lover; otherwise, skip it. Grab a map when you enter, and wander through its windy, rural depths, along dyke paths with views of the Fraser River delta marshlands. Binoculars are a must, as is a birding book to identify different species—some 250 different varieties have been sighted here. There's usually migratory action in spring and fall. Closer to Vancouver, the lake at **Jericho Beach Park** on the West Side is a popular spot for spying water fowl.

For weirder tastes... Gruesome murders, a flourishing drug trade, sordid crimes—the seamy side of the city is laid bare at the **Vancouver Police Centennial Museum**. It's perhaps appropriately housed in the old Coroner's Court, around the corner from police head-quarters—a suitably unsavory area, just north of the city's grungiest corner at Main and Hastings streets. Inside the museum (note that the "guard" behind the glass partition is a dummy), the displays of historic uniforms can be a bit of a yawn, but there's plenty of more fascinating stuff on exhibit: counterfeit money, spiked baseball bats, blow-dart guns, opium pipes, fake IDs, lock picks, and an early model Breathalyzer called the Harger Drunkometer. Needless to say, this is a highly popular field trip destination for school kids. Tag on to a group if you want a no-holds-barred explanation of the city's criminal past. The attached Cop Shoppe sells such souvenirs as Vancouver Police Department T-shirts, badges, and pins. What do you get if you stash away 50 years of travel mementos? Visit the **Museum of the Exotic World** housed in a bright turquoise building on Main Street, if you really want to find out. Dead bugs, photos of native dancers, and other memorabilia fill two entire rooms in Harold and Barbara Morgan's home. Like any-body's vacation souvenirs, these bits and bobs lack resonance unless you were there, and the Morgans were—in Borneo, Egypt, Thailand, all those places marked with a red pin in the map on the wall. Get them to tell you some anecdotes.

Road runners and high flyers... Off the beaten track in Richmond, the **Trev Deeley Motorcycle Museum** attracts motorcycle fanatics with some 300 bikes on display, almost a third of them Harley-Davidsons; the oldest dates back to 1913, and every decade is represented after that. Among the rarities are a 1949 Whizzer moped, a Schwinn-made 1926 Excelsior Super X, and Indian brand bikes from the 1940s. If you're into bikes, you'll be in heaven. (P.S. If you've brought your Harley with you, the place to strut your stuff is the Starbucks downtown at the southwest corner of Robson and Thurlow streets. Mind you, neighbors have complained about the noise. Expect a clamp-down.) It takes even longer, at least an hour, to drive to the **Canadian Museum of Flight** at Langley Airport, but aviation enthusiasts make the trek to get a close-up look at a Sopwith Camel, a Tiger Moth, and other early aircraft. If you're really keen on flying machines, time your trip to B.C. to coincide with the Abbotsford International Air Show held in August.

Wide world of sports... Downtown inside BC Place Stadium is the **BC Sports Hall of Fame and Museum**, the largest of its kind in Canada. For jocks, or indeed anyone into sports, it's a gold mine of photos, medals, trophies, equipment used by famous athletes, and other memorabilia. A walk-through "Time Tunnel" telescopes 130 years of sport in B.C. Individual galleries expand on the monumental journeys of two local heroes: a cancer victim, the one-legged Terry Fox, who made his courageous run across Canada on a prosthetic leg; and wheelchair-bound Rick Hansen, whose Man-in-Motion global tour enlightened the world. If casting a fly into a trout stream is your idea of heaven, visit the **Granville Island Sport Fishing and Model Ships Museum**, a trove of antique lures, rods, and the world's biggest collection of Hardy reels, as well as a model of a giant halibut. A simulator lets you discover how it feels to reel in a trophy-sized salmon, and overlooking the water are finely detailed, large-sized model ships. In the UBC area, the former 1920s clubhouse of the University Golf Course is now home to the **BC Golf Museum**, where artifacts and memorabilia take you from golf's early days to the advent of TV and Saturday golf. There's information here about other courses around the province, and the good-sized library contains enough reading material, from 19th-century volumes to current publications, to keep you happy for days. There's even golf art for sale.

Many bridges to cross... Vancouver's been called "the village at the edge of the rain forest," and it's no exaggeration—half an hour north of the downtown office towers, you can be in what looks like real jungle. Giant plants, towering cedars—it's straight from an adventure movie, and more than a few have been shot hereabouts. But Disney country, this ain't; wander too far off the beaten path, and it's easy to get lost. Head for Capilano Canyon and follow the signs to the **Capilano Suspension Bridge**, 137 meters (450 feet) long, and swinging a scary 70 meters (230 feet) above the canyon, with whitewater tumbling over the rocks far below. It's undeniably a fun experience, but a fee is charged, and you'll be in plenty of tourist company. Vancouverites are more likely to direct you to **Lynn Canyon Suspension Bridge and Ecology Centre** to the east. It's shorter but just as high, the waters below just as roiling, and it doesn't cost you a dime. The ecology center, with its tons of info on native flora and fauna, is a bonus.

Let someone else do the driving... Vancouver is such an easy city to get around in on your own that anyone with half a brain can, well, find their way around on her own. That said, if you do want a quick fix of facts, sights, and anecdotes, you may as well line up with dozens of others and settle in for a bus tour. **Gray Line of Vancouver** is the biggie. A more fun way to get around is with the **Vancouver Trolley**

Company, whose bright red trolley cars trundle around town stopping off at all the usual attractions. Buy a ticket, and you can hop on and off when you want. Wanna skip the tourist traps, and see the more unusual sides of Vancouver? Gather some like-minded folk and contact **Captain Billy's Magical Tours**, whose six-passenger van will take you anywhere you like, within reason.

Sail away to see... Gleaming white as snow-covered cliffs, the vast cruiseliners parked at Canada Place attract little envy from the hordes of Vancouver commuters who sail back and forth twice a day on the **SeaBus** ferries between downtown and the North Shore. Mountains, harbor, seagulls, boats, floatplanes, cityscape: It's a terrific deal. When you hop off the SeaBus across the harbor, pop in to Lonsdale Quay Market. Time your trip right, and you can lunch on fresh-cooked Dungeness crab while you watch tugs chunter out into the water traffic. Rather than facing the traffic on Granville Island, downtowners catch one of the **Aquabus Ferries**, cartoonish water taxis that chunter across every couple of minutes. (From a distance, they look like bath toys.) **Granville Island Ferries** can also take you across. During the summer, both offer sailings farther afield. Lacking a floating gin palace of their own, locals play "let's pretend" on the **Harbour Cruises** paddlewheeler, which loops around Burrard Inlet during the warmer months. Wandering farther afield, **Paddlewheeler River Adventures** uses a 1980s sternwheeler built on authentic lines to take tourists along the Fraser River to New Westminster. Wildlife up close and personal is the kicker with **Starline Tours**, which sets out on sealion "safaris" to Steveston, south of the city, between March and May (the months you're most likely to see the critters). On all of these, you'll be rubbing elbows with others. For a far more serene experience, sign up with **Lotus Land Tours** for a kayaking day-trip. Even beginners are welcome on these.

Diverted in Victoria... Just a 90-minute boat ride from the Vancouver outskirts, Victoria makes one heckuva day trip or overnight stay. You'll probably arrive by ferry—it's cheaper than the small-plane shuttles from Vancouver, and the landing is right on the so-called Inner Harbour close to downtown. Hoof it a couple blocks to that big, ornate hotel called **The Fairmont Empress,** the perfect introduction to this very English city. It's pretty pricey to bunk down here, but thankfully the huge vaulted sitting rooms are free. Also don't miss the tearoom; afternoon high tea is a real treat, although it's not cheap, and you'll have to make reservations (see Dining). From here, you can take your pick of day trips, even though there are surprisingly few historic sights downtown. If you've got kids with you, be warned: The area is full of slightly tacky attractions with names like "Miniature World." Try to skip those and wander next door to the **Parliament Buildings,** where British Columbia's legislative business gets done, then on to the **Royal British Columbia Museum,** perhaps Canada's finest. Its hands-on exhibits are truly eye-popping, and the attached IMAX theater shows science and nature films on a panoramic screen from early in the morning until pretty late at night. If shopping's your thing instead, head north a couple streets to the Old Town and downtown districts, which sort of blend into each other. Both possess block after block of kitschy and genuinely interesting shops, restaurants, and bars. If you like parks, head south from The Fairmont Empress to tiny **Thunderbird Park.** It doesn't look like much at first sight, but its totem poles are more interesting than most, and in the summer you can watch carvers making new ones right in the park. Try to engage these guys in conversation; if you hit paydirt, you'll get a unique insight into their nearly lost craft. Even farther south, the larger and greener **Beacon Hill Park** is a good spot for a picnic or a stroll that will eventually bring you right to ocean views. There's even a children's farm here, where the little ones can pat farm critters they might otherwise never get to know up close and personal. Still not sated? You're just getting started, since much of the joy of Victoria lies *outside* the downtown area. Using the city's watery position to your advantage, hop on the bathtub-like **Victoria Harbour Ferries** to take a spin around the harbor. Even better, if you've got a few days and you *really* wanna catch the very best of Victoria, get yourself a car or hop on a bus and end up at popular **Butchart Gardens** some 15 miles northwest of the city. It's hard to believe this 50-acre wonderland of plants and flowers used to be a scarred old quarry. Make plenty of time for this visit (at least half a day), since there are thousands of varieties of exotic flowers, plants, and trees arranged in interesting gardens and configurations. There are even two top-flight restaurants in the gardens, though reservations in summer are a must. The nearby **Victoria Butterfly Gardens** are less spectacular but also easier to cover in a few hours—and cheaper. Back in Victoria, top off your visit with a walk through the amazing **Craigdarroch Castle,** built by a rich mining exec for his home-sick Scottish wife. It's a shame he didn't live long enough to enjoy it, though she did for many years.

Aberdeen Centre. You'd swear you were in Asia at this

The Index

DIVERSIONS | THE INDEX

suburban mall.... *Tel 604/270-1234. 4151 Hazelbridge Way, Richmond. Bus 421 (car is preferable).*
(see pp. 90, 91)

All India Sweets. Bargain Indian buffet is a handy pit stop when exploring the Punjabi Market.... *Tel 604/327-0891. 6507 Main St.* **(see p. 97)**

Aquabus Ferries. Cute little boats provide a fun ride from Granville Island to downtown.... *Tel 604/689-5858. 1617 Foreshore Walk, Granville Island. Boats run 7am–10pm daily. Admission charged.* **(see p. 105)**

BC Golf Museum. Golfing memorabilia in a restored club-house near UBC.... *Tel 604/222-4653. 2545 Blanca St. Buses 4, 10. Open noon–4pm Tue–Sat.*
(see p. 104)

BC Sports Hall of Fame and Museum. Memorabilia, arti-facts, photos, interactive exhibits, all for sports lovers.... *Tel 604/687-5520. Gate A, BC Place Stadium, 777 Pacific Blvd. S. Stadium Station SkyTrain, Bus 2. Open 10am–5pm daily. Admission charged.* **(see p. 103)**

Beacon Hill Park. A good green spot to spread out the picnic blanket. Or take your kid to the petting farm. Healthy walking distance from the harbor, too.... *No phone. Corner of Southgate St. and Douglas Blvd., reached from downtown by Belleville St. Open daily dawn to dusk.* **(see p. 106)**

Bloedel Conservatory. Tropical flowers, trees, and birds under a dome in Queen Elizabeth Park.... *Tel 604/257-8584. Queen Elizabeth Park, between 29th and 37th avenues, off Cambie Street. Bus 15. Open 9am–8pm Mon–Fri, 10am–9pm Sat–Sun (10–5 daily in winter). Admission charged.* **(see p. 95)**

Burnaby Village Museum. Restored turn-of-the-century village with costumed interpreters.... *Tel 604/293-6501. 6501 Deer Lake Ave., Burnaby. Bus 123. Open 11am–4:30pm daily. Closed Oct–mid-Nov and Jan–Apr. Admission charged.* **(see p. 100)**

Butchart Gardens. Amazing 50-acre wonderland of exotic flowers, trees, and plants.... *Tel 250/652-4422. 800 Benvenuto Ave., Brentwood Bay. Bus 75. Opens daily at 9am, closing times vary. $10–20 adults, $1.50–$10 children.* **(see p. 107)**

Canadian Craft Museum. Six major exhibits yearly (with gaps of a week or two in between) of pottery, glass-ware, textiles—the finest that hands can produce.... *Tel 604/687-8266. 639 Hornby St. Burrard Station Sky-Train. Open 10am–5pm Mon–Sat (until 9 Thurs), noon–5 holidays; also open noon–5 Sun Mar–Aug. Admission charged.* **(see p. 93)**

Canadian Museum of Flight. Large display of vintage aircraft.... *Tel 604/532-0035. Langley Airport. 5333 216th St., Langley. Open 10am–4pm daily. Admission charged.* **(see p. 103)**

Capilano Salmon Hatchery. Come to this North Shore resource in late summer and watch salmon take their final swim home, all in magnificent forest surroundings.... *Tel 604/666-1790. 4500 Capilano Park Rd., North Vancouver. SeaBus to Lonsdale Quay, and Bus 236. Open 8am–dusk.* **(see p. 94)**

Capilano Suspension Bridge. Stalwart tourist attraction high above the Capilano River canyon.... *Tel 604/985-7474. 3735 Capilano Rd., North Vancouver. SeaBus to Lonsdale Quay, and Bus 232. Open 9am–5pm (8am to dusk in spring/summer). Admission charged.* **(see p. 104)**

Captain Billy's Magical Tours. Quirky and personalized tours in a luxury van for groups of up to six.... *Tel 604/687-2220. 1423 Howe St. Admission charged.* **(see p. 105)**

Chinese Cultural Centre Museum and Archives. Background to today's Chinatown. Dr. Sun Yat-Sen Garden is next door.... *Tel 604/658-8880. 555 Columbia St. Bus 22. Open 1–5pm Tue–Fri, 11–5 Sat–Sun. Admission charged.* **(see p. 90)**

City of Vancouver Archives. Browse through old photos, clippings, and books about the city's early days.... *Tel 604/736-8561. 1150 Chestnut St. Bus 22. Open 9am–5pm Mon–Fri.* **(see p. 98)**

Cloud 9 Revolving Restaurant. Spinning view restaurant on top of the Empire Landmark Hotel.... *Tel 604/662-8328. 1400 Robson St. Bus 5. Dinner only.* **(see p. 101)**

Craigdarroch Castle. A piece of Scotland transplanted to an off-the-beaten-track neighborhood in Victoria: lots of carpets, swirling staircases, art, and statuary.... *Tel 250/592-5323. 1050 Joan Crescent. Open daily 10am–4:30pm. Admission charged.* **(see p. 107)**

Dr. Sun Yat-Sen Classical Garden. The first of its kind outside China, a serenely beautiful spot.... *Tel 604/662-3207. 578 Carrall St. Bus 22. Open 10am–dusk. Admission charged.* **(see pp. 90, 101)**

The Fairmont Empress. Huge, over-the-top hotel opened in 1908 by Canadian Pacific Railways and still one of the city's most interesting sights.... *Tel 250/384-8111or 800/441-1414. 721 Government St.* **(see p. 106)**

Gain Wah. Great congee, and other everyday Chinese fare, in the heart of Chinatown. Live seafood too.... *Tel 604/684-1740. 218 Keefer St.* **(see p. 90)**

George C. Reifel Migratory Bird Sanctuary. Follow trails, bring a bird book, and count how many varieties you spot. Annual Snow Goose Festival in November.... *Tel 604/946-6980. 5191 Robertson Rd., Ladner. Open 9am–4pm daily. Admission charged.* **(see pp. 86, 102)**

Gordon Southam Observatory. Stargaze though a telescope down by the beach at Kits Point.... *Tel 604/738-2855. 1100 Chestnut St. Bus 22 MacDonald. Call for hours. Open weekends if sky is clear and volunteers are available.* **(see p. 99)**

Granville Island Ferries. Scenic link between locations around False Creek.... *Tel 604/684-7781. 1804 Boatlift Lane, Granville Island. Ferries run 7am–9pm daily.* **(see p. 105)**

Granville Island Information Centre. Wanna know where to find the floating homes or the theater on Granville Island? Get a free map here and go exploring.... *Tel 604/666-5784. 1398 Cartwright St.* **(see p. 89)**

Granville Island Public Market. Pulsing with action, and brimming with good things to eat. Fabulously popular; avoid weekends midday.... *Tel 604/666-5784. 1689 Johnston St. Bus 50 or 8, then 51. Open 9am–6pm daily.* **(see p. 88)**

Granville Island Sport Fishing and Model Ships Museum.

If you're into either, you'll have a fun half hour here. Otherwise, skip it.... *Tel 604/683-1939. 1502 Duranleau St. Bus 50 False Creek South or 8 Granville, then 51 Granville Island. Open 10am–5:30pm daily, closed Mon Oct–Mar. Admission charged.* **(see pp. 89, 103)**

Gray Line of Vancouver. City tours by coach.... *Tel 604/879-3363 or 800/667-0882. 255 East 1st Ave. Tours run 9:15am–2pm. Admission charged.*
(see p. 104)

Grouse Mountain Skyride. North America's largest aerial tramway, only 20 minutes from downtown. Skyride ticket includes videos in Theater in the Sky.... *Tel 604/984-0661. SeaBus to Lonsdale Quay, then Bus 236. Open 9am–10pm daily. Admission charged.* **(see p. 101)**

Harbour Cruises. Quaint paddle-wheeler cruises Burrard Inlet during the summer.... *Tel 604/688-7246. #1 North foot of Denman St. $18/75-minute harbor cruise.*
(see p. 105)

Jericho Beach Park. Forest trails, wild birds, and wraparound views 10 minutes from downtown.... *Foot of Point Grey Rd. off 4th Ave. Bus 4.* **(see p. 102)**

Law Courts Restaurant. Share a sandwich with the legal fraternity, and a great view of Robson Square.... *Tel 604/684-8818. 800 Smithe St.* **(see p. 93)**

The Lookout! at Harbour Centre Tower. Glass elevator zooms up to the landmark "flying saucer," and a 360-degree view of the city.... *Tel 604/689-0421. 555 W. Hastings St. Waterfront Station SkyTrain, or northbound buses on Granville St. Open 8:30am–10:30pm daily in summer, 9–9 in winter.* **(see p. 101)**

Lotus Land Tours. Kayaking day trips explore the "wild" side of Vancouver.... *Tel 604/684-4922 or 800/528-3531. 2005–1251 Cardero St. May–Oct.* **(see p. 105)**

Lynn Canyon Suspension Bridge and Ecology Centre. The bridge, a heart-hammering experience, links you with clearly marked trails.... *Tel 604/981-3103. Peters Rd. off Lynn Valley Rd., North Vancouver. SeaBus to*

Lonsdale Quay, then Bus 229. Open dawn–dusk.
(see p. 104)

Maplewood Children's Farm. Domesticated creatures for little kids. If you're DINKs, don't bother.... *Tel 604/929-5610. 405 Seymour River Place, North Vancouver. SeaBus to Lonsdale Quay, then Bus 229, then Bus 215 or 212. Open 10am–4pm Tue–Sun (and holiday Mondays). Admission charged.* **(see p. 100)**

Minerva Mediterranean Deli. Greek groceries, plus foods to buy, take home, or eat on the sidewalk patio.... *Tel 604/733-3954. 3207 W. Broadway.* **(see p. 97)**

Museum of Anthropology. Award-winning cliff-top building houses the region's premier collection of Northwest Coast First Nations art. Totem poles and big houses outdoors.... *Tel 604/822-3825. 6393 NW Marine Dr. Buses 4, 10 UBC. Open 10am–5pm daily (until 9 Tue). Oct–mid-May: 11–9 Tue, 11–5 Wed–Sun. Admission charged.* **(see p. 92)**

Museum of the Exotic World. Vancouver couple's souvenirs from a half-century of global travels.... *Tel 604/876-8713. 3271 Main St. Bus 3. Open 1–4:30pm Sat–Sun. Admission charged (funds go to the SPCA).* **(see p. 102)**

Nitobe Memorial Garden. Re-creation of a classical Japanese tea garden on the UBC campus.... *Tel 604/822-6038. 1903 Lower Mall, UBC Bus 4, 10 UBC, then Bus 42 Chancellor. Open 10am–6pm weekdays March–Oct. Admission charged.* **(see p. 101)**

Old Hastings Mill Store Museum. The city's oldest surviving building is now a random collection of Native baskets, old photos, furniture, clocks; contents are an engaging mishmash. Down by the beach.... *Tel 604/734-1212. 1575 Alma St. Bus 4 UBC. Open 11am–4pm Tue–Sun mid-June–mid-Sept. Otherwise, weekends only 1–4pm. Suggested donation.*
(see p. 96)

Pacific Space Centre. Interactive space "exploration," a chunk of the moon, and a high-energy space ride.... *Tel*

604/738-7827. 1100 Chestnut St. Bus 22 MacDonald. Open 10am–5pm Tue–Sun, daily in summer. Admission charged. **(see pp. 98, 99)**

Paddlewheeler River Adventures. Board a sternwheeler for a cruise on the mighty Fraser River.... *Tel 604/525-4465. 810 Quayside Dr., New Westminster. $39.95/full day tour. June–Oct.* **(see p. 105)**

Parliament Buildings. Twin legislative buildings designed by the same architect who drew up the Empress; tours take place daily.... *Tel 250/387-3046. 501 Belleville St. Open daily 9am–5pm.* **(see p. 106)**

The Parthenon. Feta, olives, and groceries from around the Mediterranean draw regulars to this longtime fave supermarket in Kitsilano.... *Tel 604/733-4191. 3080 W. Broadway. Bus 9.* **(see p. 97)**

Presentation House Gallery. Changing exhibits of photos old and new, often of international caliber; also video installations, in a historic house.... *Tel 604/986-1351. 333 Chesterfield Ave., North Vancouver. Lonsdale Quay SeaBus. Open noon–5pm Wed–Sun, Thurs until 9. Closed Aug. Suggested donation.* **(see p. 94)**

Queen Elizabeth Park. Attractively landscaped park off Cambie Street, between 29th and 37th avenues. Site of Bloedel Conservatory.... *Tel 604/257-8570. Bus 15.* **(see pp. 95, 101)**

Richmond Nature Park. 40-hectare (100-acre) wilderness south of the city, with peat bog and nature trails.... *Tel 604/718-6188. 11851 Westminster Hwy., Richmond. For transit info, tel 604/521-0400. Open dawn–dusk. (Nature House open 9am–5pm, suggested donation.)* **(see p. 100)**

Roedde House Museum. Restored downtown Victorian home, a real charmer.... *Tel 604/684-7040. 1415 Barclay St. Bus 5 Granville. Guided tour only, 2–4pm Wed–Fri; also tea party tours. Call ahead to confirm. Admission charged.* **(see p. 96)**

Royal British Columbia Museum. Amazingly good collection of science and natural history exhibits, all designed to be as hands-on friendly as possible.... *Tel 250/356-7226 or 888/447-7977. 675 Belleville St. Open 9am–5pm daily. Admission charged.* **(see p. 106)**

Science World British Columbia. Hands-on exhibits and and the Alcan Omnimax Theater in the giant "golf ball" at the end of False Creek.... *Tel 604/443-7440. 1455 Quebec St. Main St. Station SkyTrain. Open 10am–5pm Mon–Fri, until 6 Sat–Sun. Admission charged.*
(see p. 100)

SeaBus. Part of the public transit system, this harbor "minicruise" between downtown and the North Shore is a must.... *Tel 604/521-0400. BC Transit head office, 13401–108th Ave., Surrey. SeaBuses run 6am–12:30pm Mon–Sat, 8am–11pm Sun. $2–3.* **(see p. 105)**

Simon Fraser University. The Burnaby Mountain-top campus is worth the trek for architecture and view.... *Tel 604/291-3397 (tours). Burnaby Mountain. Bus 135 daytime Mon–Sat, Bus 35 evenings, Sun, holidays.*
(see p. 99)

Starline Tours. Bring your camera on this water "safari" for a close-up look at sea lions.... *Tel 604/272-9187 or 604/522-3506, New Westminster Quay. Apr–Oct. Admission charged.* **(see p. 105)**

Terra Breads. Crusty baguettes, and terrific grape bread.... *Tel 604/685-3102. 1689 Johnston St. Bus 51. Also tel 604/736-1838. 2380 W. 4th Ave. Bus 4.*
(see p. 88)

Thunderbird Park. Small park near the Empress featuring both standing totem poles and works in progress.... *No phone. Corner of Belleville and Douglas sts. Open dawn–dusk.* **(see p. 106)**

Tourism Vancouver. Cool staff, scads of information—and they'll book rooms too.... *Tel 604/683-2000. 200 Burrard St. Waterfront Station SkyTrain.* **(see p. 88)**

Trev Deeley Motorcycle Museum. Road hog heaven.... *Tel 604/291-2453. 2375 Boundary Rd., Richmond. Open 10am–4pm Mon–Fri.* **(see p. 103)**

TRIUMF Research Centre. See the world's largest cyclotron. Call for times of free 90-minute tours.... *Tel 604/222-7526. 4004 Westbrook Mall. For transit info, call 604/521-0400.* **(see p. 99)**

University of British Columbia. Museums, gardens, architecture, and a drop-dead location on Point Grey.... *Walking tours info: tel 604/822-8687. Point Grey. Bus 4 or 10.* **(see p. 98)**

UBC Botanical Garden. A teaching garden first and foremost. Don't miss the Physick Garden.... *Tel 604/822-4186 or 604/822-6038. 6804 SW Marine Dr. Buses 4, 10 UBC, then 42 Chancellor (limited service). Open 10am–6pm daily. Admission charged.* **(see pp. 95, 99)**

UBC M.Y. Williams Geological Museum. Rock jocks can peruse 40,000 different types of crystals, minerals, fossils, and more. The star attraction is the skeleton of an 80-million-year-old dinosaur.... *Tel 604/822-2449. Geological Sciences Building. 6339 Stores Rd. Buses 4, 10. Open 8:30am–4:30pm Mon–Fri.* **(see p. 99)**

Vancouver Aquarium. Otters to octopi, if it swims, it's here. Best known for its killer and beluga whales.... *Tel 604/659-3474. Stanley Park. Open 9:30am–7pm late June–Labor Day. Rest of the year, 10–5:30. Open noon–5 Christmas, New Year's Day. Buses 135, 23, 25. Admission charged.* **(see p. 94)**

Vancouver Art Gallery. The city's premier gallery, which often hosts international touring shows of contemporary and historical art. Known for its Emily Carr collection.... *Tel 604/662-4700. 750 Hornby St. Bus 5 Robson. Open 10am–5:30pm, later on Thurs, Easter–Thanksgiving. Closed Mon in winter. Admission charged.* **(see p. 92)**

Vancouver Maritime Museum. The first boat to traverse

the Northwest Passage west to east is the big star at this waterfront museum.... *Tel 604/257-8300. 1905 Ogden Ave. Bus 22 MacDonald. 10am–5pm daily. Closed Mon early Sept–late May.* Admission charged.

(see p. 98)

Vancouver Museum. Lively introduction to Vancouver's history, plus a real Egyptian mummy. Allow plenty of time for poking around.... *Tel 604/736-4431. 1100 Chestnut St., Vanier Park. Bus 22. Open 10am–5pm Tue–Sun (daily Jul–Aug). Closed Christmas Day.* Admission charged.

(see pp. 97, 99)

Vancouver Police Centennial Museum. Weapons, illegal drugs, counterfeit money, and fake IDs—you'll learn plenty.... *Tel 604/665-3346. 240 E. Cordova St. Bus 3. Open 10am–3pm Mon–Fri, also 10–3 Sat early May–late Aug.* Admission charged.

(see p. 102)

Vancouver Trolley Company. Ride from one attraction to the next aboard a picturesque scarlet trolley car.... *Tel 604/801-5515. 875 Terminal Ave. $25 adults, $12 children.*

(see p. 105)

VanDusen Botanical Garden. Acres of lush landscaping.... *Tel 604/878-9274. 5251 Oak St. Bus 7. Open 10am–dusk daily.* Admission charged.

(see p. 95)

Victoria Butterfly Gardens. Lesser-known but still impressive collection of gardens, handily within a mile of the more-famous Butchart complex.... *Tel 250/652-3822. 1461 Benvenuto Ave., Brentwood Bay. Open 9am–5pm daily mid-May–Oct; 9:30am–4:30pm daily Nov–April.* Admission charged.

(see p. 107)

Victoria Harbour Ferries. Tiny ferries providing convenient transport from the Victoria docks to outlying points. Also offers scenic boat tours of the harbor.... *Tel 250/708-0201. Ferries run up to four times hourly 9am–9pm in summer. Runs weekends-only the rest of year; call for hours. Single rides $1.50–3, multiple-ride tickets $12–14.*

(see p. 106)

Yaohan Centre. Suburban shopping center is fast trip to modern Asia.... *Tel 604/231-0601. 3700 No. 3 Rd. Richmond. Bus 421 (car preferable).* **(see p. 90)**

getting

4

outside

Check out a city
map: At least half
of Vancouver's
downtown penin-
sula is colored
green, and that's
not counting

the even larger expanses of wilderness to the north and south, or the pockets of manicured public lawn that dot the rest of the city. This is Vancouver's backyard—and boy, do we use it. Downtown wage slaves on their lunch hour escape to sand as fine as sugar. Hoary old clichés about "the West Coast lifestyle" prove themselves real on a sunny day in May when you've been snowboarding down Grouse all morning, working on your tan until dusk, and are planning a wilderness hike for first thing tomorrow. Skiing, snowboarding, hiking, climbing, cycling, in-line skating, swimming, bronzing, playing golf or tennis, or just kicking back and watching a game of cricket—as any Vancouverite will tell you, we'll get outside at the drop of a hat.

The Lowdown

The green half of downtown Vancouver... A 400-hectare (1,000-acre) wilderness pushing up against the West End's apartment and office towers, **Stanley Park** is the flip side of downtown Vancouver. Calling it a city institution is an understatement. Forget the grumbles about getting stuck in traffic; citizens would present a human barricade if the authorities tried to widen the causeway that winds through this chunk of unspoiled forest. Even in rush hour (provided you keep your windows wound up against the car fumes), it's a chance to brush up against raw nature—and not just huge cedars. A much-cited Vancouver "moment" is the springtime sight of a harried morning commuter screeching to a halt to let a procession of mother duck and ducklings cross the road. But it's not all perfect. Enter the park from downtown, and you'll see a giant mural on the huge concrete wall of a dome-topped building to your left. Done in the style of a romance novel cover, this sylvan "eden" of trees and blossoms represents what you'd be seeing for real had this monstrosity not been built. Ignore it, stay in the right lane, and peel off on the road that winds its meandering, counterclockwise way for 8 kilometers (5 miles) around the park's perimeter. First up are pleasure boats moored in Coal Harbour that belong to members of the Royal Vancouver Yacht Club, and the Vancouver Rowing Club, and a cannon that booms out at 9pm each night. Call the rowing club if you're a member of a rowing, field hockey, or rugby club, or if your yacht club has a reciprocal arrangement, and ask about using its facilities. At Brockton Point, a narrow strip of land connects with Deadman's Island, once a Native burial ground. Keep going and you'll come to Brockton Oval, the site of much-photographed totem poles. Your call whether you stop to grab a snapshot. Those at the **Museum of Anthropology** [see Diversions] have a far more evocative setting. Speaking of attractions, at this point you're close to the **Vancouver Aquarium** [see Diversions] and **Malkin Bowl**, summer home to **Theatre Under the Stars** [see Entertainment]. Back on the road, you'll pass what appears to be a lookalike of Copenhagen's *Little Mermaid* statue. On the West Coast? Get real. It's the bronze *Girl in a Wetsuit*. Press on, and you'll see a giant hollow red cedar tree and Siwash Rock, said to be a young Native man whom the gods turned to stone. The road eventually circles back onto Georgia Street and the city, past **Lost Lagoon** with its central fountain where, in an odd Vancouver ritual, engineering students often deposit a VW bug. Splashes and rustles signal the abundant wildlife that lives around here: geese, herons, black swans, raccoons, squirrels, and, in the deep of night, guys eager to share brief but sensual moments with one another. While a swift drive around will show you the park's geography, it won't give you its flavor. For that, schedule some time on the **Seawall**, the wide promenade that rings the entire park. On sunny Sundays, it's a living frieze of tank-topped in-line skaters, seniors out for a stroll, couples with kids in strollers, cyclists, and dog-walkers—all feeling smug that they live in Vancouver. If the crowds or the sun starts to get to you, plunge into the cool, shadowy woods on one of the many hiking trails. Most guided tours include Stanley Park on their itineraries, but for help without hype, rent a self-guided audio tour on cassette or CD from **Ace Tours** (tel 604/730-2750). The hour-long tour covers 16 popular sites and is timed to match the speed that you'd normally take to drive, cycle, or in-line skate through the park. The cost is $10 plus a $3 deposit, refunded when you mail back the tour in the package provided. You can buy one at **Beach Corner Shop** (tel 604/688-7656, 1187 Denman St.), close to the park. Romantics can trot among the trees with **Stanley Park Horse-Drawn Tours** (tel

604/681-5115) in a two-person carriage, or join the hoi polloi in a larger, and cheaper, one.

Goin' for even more green... Stanley Park may attract the ink, and the tourists, but fame has its price. Expect paid parking everywhere, snail-slow traffic on weekends, and crowds. Far less known, just as impressive, and totally uncommercial, **Pacific Spirit Regional Park** is the one Vancouverites keep to themselves. And let's not forget size—at 763 hectares (roughly 1,800 acres), it's almost twice as large as its more in-your-face downtown brother. A cinch to get to by bus, bike, or car, this magnificent wilderness spanning Point Grey is right between UBC and the city. Terrain-wise, it's British Columbia in a nutshell: ravines, bog, forested plateaus, rocky beaches, tidal flats, evergreens, maples, and wildlife—it's a magical place to wander. Accompanied by the wind in the trees and the occasional cry of an eagle, hikers, joggers, dog-walkers, and horseback riders roam on a total of more than 50 kilometers (31 miles) of trails that wind, climb, and dip through the landscape. Routes are clearly marked, but it's still easy to lose your sense of direction. Pick up a free map at the **Park Centre** on West 16th Avenue, 400 yards west of Blanca Street. Smaller and far more "tamed" is **Jericho Beach Park**, which sits north of 4th Avenue where it meets North-West Marine Drive. What it lacks in size, it makes up for in charm. Trails wind past copses of birch trees, slopes ablaze with wildflowers, and a bulrush-fringed pond that's home to ducks and herons. Late August, armed with pails, locals amble along picking blackberries. When the temperature rockets, it's a pleasant escape from the blazing sun at nearby **Jericho Beach** (see below). You'll need a car or a bike, and a strong pair of legs, to reach **Iona Beach Park**, two skinny spits of land in the Fraser River just west of the sewage works—no worries, it's all perfectly clean, and all you'll smell is sea air. The **Iona Jetty**, a 4-kilometer (2.5-mile) pathway, is actually built on top of the pipes that direct the treated you-know-what into the sea. There's a separate road for cyclists. Even longer, and more rustic, the **North Arm Jetty** is edged with beaches. It's a fine vantage point from which to watch tugs, log booms, and planes flying in and out of the nearby airport. Both are known for their 360-degree views and abundant wildlife—more than 130 bird varieties have been sighted in these parts. If you're seriously into roaming the wilderness, the **Greater Vancouver Regional District** (tel 604/224-5739) can set you up with maps and information on these areas and more.

Islands to treasure… Gotta take in some of those neighboring islands when you're passing through Vancouver. Closest to home is **Bowen Island**, a scant 20 minutes by **BC Ferries** (tel 250/386–3431 or 888/223-3779) from Horseshoe Bay. It's $5.75 to $6 round-trip if you walk on. Don't bother to spring for a ticket for your car; most of the action is well within walking distance of the ferry terminal. Pick up a map, wander the streets, amble along the beach, and start thinking seriously about telecommuting. There's even less to do on **Barnston Island** in the Fraser River, but, if you've an afternoon to spare, it's a pleasant jaunt, especially if you bring your bike. For a close-up view of log booms, cow-dotted pastures, and herb farms, drive east on Highway 1, take the 176th Street exit north, and hang a right on 104th Avenue. Toot your horn, and the ferry will take you across for free. Further afield, an hour and a half's voyage puts you on huge **Vancouver Island**. The trip on **BC Ferries** (car and driver fare is about $45 one way, peak season weekends, less other times) from Tsawwassen to Swartz Bay (a half-hour south and north of Vancouver and Victoria, respectively) passes forested islands, and squiggles its way through narrow Active Pass—you may even spot a whale. The ferries plying this route are huge; some hold more than 2,000 passengers. In summer, head straight for the deck and pass the voyage absorbing sunshine and scenery.

Islands—the big one… Once you've ferried your way out to Vancouver Island, you might as well make a day (or, even better, several) of it. If you think Vancouver's got a lot to offer in terms of the great outdoors, then get a load of this place: It's the *greater* outdoors. From tiny fishing towns and soaring peaks and seals to salmon and dripping rainforests and bubbling hot springs, there's a little bit of everything for the outdoors-hungry. Close to Victoria, the offerings are tamer but more accessible. Check out **Mount Tolmie Park** (tel 250/744-5341, Mayfair Dr.), which offers easy walks in the residential Mayfair neighborhood near the University of Victoria, or **Mount**

Douglas Park (tel 250/744-5341, Cordova Bay Rd., Saanich), with loads of impressive views, trails, trees, and a stretch of rocky shoreline. Both make a terrific half-day respite from the crowds and cars and are open from dawn to dusk. Also in Saanich, the hilltop **Dominion Astrophysical Observatory** (tel 250/363-0001, W. Saanich Rd.) is great for its views of the city below—not to mention the two big telescopes aimed at the skies above, which the public is sometimes allowed to peer through. About 10 miles west of town, **Fort Rodd Hill** and its **Fisgard Lighthouse** (tel 250/478-5849, Fort Rodd Hill Rd., Colwood) offer some of the best views of Victoria's harbors. There's a visit-worthy museum in the lighthouse, and hiking trails run through fields down to tide pools. If that's *still* too tame for you, ditch the child's play and head cross- or up-island to three of the West Coast's most killer parks. **East Sooke Regional Park** (tel 250/478-3344), about 25 miles west of Victoria off Highway 14, has some pretty darned good hikes and beaches. It's a lot farther to **Pacific Rim National Park** (tel 250/726-7211)—about 90 miles north on Highway 1 and then another hundred miles west on Highway 4 to Tofino or Ucluelet—but well worth the trip. Once you reach this wild, oceanside park, you'll feel like you've reached the ends of the earth. A trail snakes along the spine of the sea cliffs, which make up most of the park. If you're really serious about getting into the backcountry, watch for incoming tides, tidal waves, and sudden storms. Even bigger and wilder, **Strathcona Provincial Park** (tel 250/954-4600) is a set of ragged mountain peaks with honest-to-goodness beasts roaming through the woods and drinking from the lakes. From Victoria, head north on Route 1 about 160 miles, then hang a left and continue 50 miles west. Heck, the possibilities don't even end there. You could venture even farther north to places with names like Alert Bay, or west to places like Hot Springs Cove. But we're running out of breath. You're just gonna have to find 'em by yourself.

And even more islands... One of the amazing things about Vancouver Island is that, in addition to all the great stuff packed into that one big island—and it is *big*—are all the tiny islands scattered up and down its coast. These places are each a little different in character, but a hitchhiking-is-the-transit and a golden-arches-only-over-my-dead-body ethos prevails on all of them. Each harbors its own rather curious mixture of personalities, too: On any given island you'll find aging draft-dodging hippies running clothing-optional B&B's, fishermen working hard to make a buck, young granola types puffing happily away on giant spliffs, bona fide painters and musicians (some of them quite famous), and pockets of rich people (they're the ones with the yachts who interact as little as possible with all the others). With its extensive services up and down the coast, **BC Ferries** (tel 888/223-3779) makes it easy to see a smattering of these islands during a Van-couver Island trip; just remember that while the ferry system is generally well-run, schedules and fares change frequently. One of the very hippest of the islands you can hop to is **Salt Spring Island,** reachable from Van-couver *and* Sidney (north of Victoria). We're talking three ferry docks, a huge mountain, and more art gal-leries per capita than you'll probably find anywhere else in the Western world. Salt Spring's been discovered by city types, but nearby **Mayne Island** hasn't—yet. Maybe that's because it's a much more difficult ferry ride to arrange from Victoria. This is a place where cows and lambs graze beside rolling breakers, and the B&B options are truly out of control. Nanaimo locals have been hopping the short shuttle ferries out to **Newcastle** and **Gabriola** islands for years, secure in the knowledge that these relatively undeveloped spots are great for walking (no cars are allowed on Newcastle), wildlife, and maybe a pint of ale afterward.

Work up some pecs appeal... All this activity, all these lean, tanned bods whizzing by—the mood can be catching. While not the best cycling city around, Van-couver does offer eye-opening routes on the waterfront and around the Seawall. You can rent a bike from **Bayshore Bicycles** (tel 604/688-2453, 1601 W. Georgia St.) or **Spokes Bicycle Rentals** (tel 604/688-5141, 1798 W. Georgia St.). Remember to wear your helmet: It's the law! In-line skaters can outfit them-selves at **Bikes 'N Blades Rental** (tel 604/602-9899, 718 Denman St.). All three are close to the Georgia Street entrance to Stanley Park.

Row, row, row your boat... Seeing Vancouver from water level gives you a fresh perspective on the city. Paddle off around Granville Island in a rented canoe or kayak from **Adventure Fitness** (tel 604/687-1528, 1510 Duranleau St.), or along False Creek to English Bay, and Jericho Beach. You can go as far as Siwash Rock in Stanley Park, but *not* under the Lions Gate Bridge. Currents and boats make it dangerous, and besides, it's illegal. Energetic types can paddle right around Point Grey. For real wilderness boating, load the canoe on your vehicle and head for **Deep Cove**, your embarkation point for **Indian Arm** and overnight camping. For an easier ride, **Blue Pacific Yacht Charters** (tel 604/682-2161, 1519 Foreshore Walk, Granville Island) can rent you a 30-foot sailboat or powerboat—or larger. Anything over 40 feet, though, calls for a 7-day minimum cruise. If it's a breezy day, go check out the kite-flyers in Vanier Park just west of the Island.

Peachy beaches... Ski in the morning, sail in the afternoon, and sun your buns every chance you can get. Which stretch of sand you plop your towel down on depends on your age. Honed bodies strut their stuff at **Kitsilano Beach,** just across the Burrard Street Bridge next to Vanier Park on the West Side, perhaps taking time out for a game of volleyball or a lap or two in the waterfront public pool (tel 604/731-0011). Only a few minutes west is a rocky stretch below the expensive homes of Point Grey Road. There you'll encounter fallen logs, perhaps the occasional guitarist—it's a tranquil place, ideal for watching the sun set. At low tide, you can make your way farther west through the pebbles and seaweed to the first of the series of beaches that stretches right to the end of Point Grey. **Jericho Beach** is lively with sailboats and surfboards. Out on the wooden jetty, Portuguese and Vietnamese families drop crab traps or sink lines to try to catch supper. Keep heading west and you come to **Locarno Beach**, followed by **Spanish Banks Beach**. Both draw family crowds. Little kids go bananas when the tide goes out and turns the area into the city's biggest sandbox. This is a popular picnic spot, but be warned: In summer, there's often a roadside check to see that you're not bringing alcohol to the beach. Keep walking west at low tide, and you'll eventually come to the city's most notorious stretch of sand, **Wreck Beach**. Clothing is optional; if acres of flesh is your thing, this is the spot—where else can you buy lunch from a buff-naked hot-dog seller? If you're shopping downtown and get the sudden urge to do a slo-mo barefoot run along the sand, hop a cab, and five minutes later you're at **English Bay Beach** at the south foot of Denman Street, a huge swathe of golden sand that stretches right into Stanley Park. It's always been a popular escape for West Enders—check out the bathhouse, which dates back to 1931, and the fairy-tale bandstand across the street. Pick up some take-out sushi on Denman Street and dine alfresco on one of the big logs at the edge of the sand. Located on its western edge, Stanley Park's **Second Beach** and **Third Beach** are more serene, unlike **Ambleside Beach** across the water in West Vancouver. Summer weekends, it's nose-to-nose rich kids flaunting their new bikinis and boom-box-equipped convertibles. The only escape? The area at the east end of the beach, where dogs and their owners play endless games of throw the stick in the water. Call Vancouver Parks & Recreation (tel 604/257-8400) for info on all these beaches.

One, two, three, fore... Even if you forget to set up reciprocal arrangements with one of the private golf clubs, you can still play a round on a public course. There are three municipal courses within city limits, all toward the southern reaches. The oldest—and the most popular—public course in Canada is the tree-dotted and scenic **Fraserview Golf Course** (tel 604/257-6919, 7800 Vivian Dr.), a 6,700-yard, par-72 course with plenty of elevation changes, wide fairways, a few sand hazards, a single water hazard—and the edge on good looks. Its length alone is a challenge to many golfers. One block east of Cambie Street, just south of 49th Avenue, **Langara Golf Course** (tel 604/257-8357, 6706 Alberta St.) has the biggest, most undulating greens, sand traps, and a bit of water to keep you busy along its 6,085-yard, par-71 course. **McCleery Golf Course** (tel 604/257-8181, 7188 Macdonald St.) is a fairly flat, 6,200-yard, par-71 course, but with plenty of water and sand to make up for it. You can book any of these up to five days in advance through a central reservations line (tel 604/280-1818, open only after 7pm). Expect to pay about $36 for 18 holes on weekends. Out near UBC is another public course, the **University Golf Club** (tel

GETTING OUTSIDE | VANCOUVER

604/224-1818, 5185 University Blvd.). You'll find plenty of sand, a water hole, tree-lined fairways, and few hills on the back nine of this pleasant, 6,584-yard, par-72 course.

Best places to get teed off on the Big Island...

Duffers and Japanese tourists already know it, and now you do, too: Vancouver Island is justly famous for its golfing. Whether you're a truly awful hacker or someone who can actually hit the ball into the middle of the fairway—no comment on which category *we're* in—you'll easily find something to suit your taste, skill level, and price range. There are a half dozen courses within Victoria's city limits; the most proletarian is probably **Cedar Hill Municipal Golf Course** (tel 250/595-3103, 1400 Derby Rd.), a par-67 course with very reasonable fees that dip even lower the later it gets in the day. **Cordova Bay Golf Course** (tel 250/658-4444, 5333 Cordova Bay Rd., Saanich) is a bit farther out of town (and nicer) and ratchets up the price an additional notch. Finally, if money is no object or you're the kind of nuts-about-golfing golfer who heads for dripping St. Andrews, Scotland in the middle of winter, head to the **Olympic View Golf Club** (tel 250/474-3673, 643 Latoria Rd.), just east of downtown Victoria. (This place is so cool that it has its own *waterfalls*, for Pete's sake.) Try not to let the stratospheric greens fees, tam o'shanters, and expensive duds ruin your pure golfing pleasure. In nearby Nanaimo there's another unexpected crop of mid-priced courses, which draws the Japanese business set. (It's actually cheaper for them to fly here and play 18 than to tee off at home.) Of the local six-pack, try the **Nanaimo Golf Club** (tel 250/758-2451, 2800 Highland Blvd.). It's tougher than it looks, but the gorgeous ocean views compensate for all those lost balls.

Merchant-Ivory country...

The click of the ball on a willow bat, the white flannel trousers...throw in some cucumber sandwiches, and you could be in jolly old England. Terms like "silly mid on" and "silly mid off" are typical of a game whose rules are impossibly complex to neophytes. Still, it's a pleasurable way to while away some time for free, but be warned, an entire game can last four or five hours, or longer. The places to hit are Brockton Oval in **Stanley Park**, or **Connaught Park** north of 12th Avenue, between Vine and Balsam streets in Kitsilano. Teams are made up of local amateurs: Vancouver residents who hail from the U.K., India, or anywhere else where there's a strong cricket culture.

Kicking up a racket... Twisting the knife, new Vancouverites love to call home to Toronto or Montreal—anyplace cold—on Christmas Day, and boast how they've just played a game of tennis. The city has 180 public courts, and they're all free. "First come, first to serve" is the rule. Showing up bright and early, or around dinnertime, often cuts the wait. The largest concentrations are in **Stanley Park** (17 courts near the Beach Avenue entrance); **Kitsilano Beach**, just southwest of the Burrard Street Bridge, which has 10 courts; and **Queen Elizabeth Park**, the big chunk of green east of Cambie Street between 29th and 37th avenues, which is home to 17. They're all hard courts, and they're not lit for night play. Tennis fanatics often sneak in for a game at high school courts when school's out.

Going to great lengths... You can leap in the ocean pretty much year-round in Vancouver (witness the thousands who dunk every New Year's Day at the Polar Bay Swim), but if you want a more controlled setting and lockers to leave your clothes in, you've got several options. The award for the pool with the best view—which means mountain peaks and sun-gilded hunks—is **Kitsilano Beach Pool** (tel 604/730-0011). Huge, heated, and filled with sea water, it's open from Victoria Day, May 24, to mid-September. Across town in Stanley Park, **Second Beach Pool** (tel 604/257-8370) is a freshwater pool right next to the Seawall. The enormous brown building on Sunset Beach just west of Burrard Street Bridge is the **Vancouver Aquatic Centre** (tel 604/665-3424). It has a 164-foot pool, whirlpool, sauna, and a pool for kids, as well as a weight room. The downside is that it closes for a month each summer for maintenance. Out near the University? The **UBC Aquatic Centre** (tel 604/822-4522) at 6121 University Boulevard has all the facilities of the downtown one, plus sauna, steam room, and gym. All charge a few bucks for use of the pool and facilities.

Sloping off in ski season... No, they're not UFOs. Those vertical rows of twinkling lights hanging in space signal night skiing, not little green men. By the time they go on, the powder-crazy will already be halfway to the world-class slopes of **Whistler/Blackcomb**. But the rest of us—locals with day jobs—head home after work, gear up, take the bus to North Vancouver, and are on the slopes soon after. **Grouse Mountain** (tel 604/984-0661, 604/986-6262 to check on conditions) has a vertical drop of 1,200 ft., 22 runs, and aerial trams to take you up the ski area; the magnificent city view is a bonus. Even raw beginners can have fun here—but so can experts— during a season that normally runs from late November to mid-March. Snow-making equipment supplements the average annual 140 inches of white stuff. **Mount Seymour** (tel 604/718-7771), in **Mount Seymour Provincial Park** to the east, has almost the same vertical drop as Grouse Mountain; its 25 runs are accessed by chair lifts and a tow. Snowfall averages 120 inches a year. Four out of five trails here are geared to beginner and intermediate skiers, so it's a popular destination with Mom, Pop, and the kids. Drive west and you'll come to **Cypress Bowl** (tel 604/419-7669), which has a vertical drop of 530 meters, about the same snowfall as Grouse, and as many runs (for all skill levels) as Seymour, one of them 2.5 miles long. Chairs, chair lifts, and tows take you aloft. Cross-country skiers head here, too, for the peace and quiet of well-groomed trails, some of which are lit for night skiing. The growing leagues of snow-boarders are happy in any of these places.

Grinding up Grouse... "The Grouse Grind" isn't a local coffee brew. Depending on your viewpoint, it's an ago-nizing, exhilarating, or downright dumb hike up **Grouse Mountain** that's best described as steep—make that straight up. In just 1.8 miles, you climb 900 feet. Know thy body, and act accordingly. The less in-shape, or more sen-sible, take the **Grouse Mountain Skyride** (tel 604/984-0661), which skims above the treetops and deposits you, with energy to spare, 3,700 feet above sea level, almost at the top of the mountain—which you can get to via the **Peak Chairlift**. Mountains behind you, ocean before you, islands way in the distance—do you rule the world, or what? Trails lead from both locations. The one-hour amble around Blue Grouse Lake, near the SkyRide, is good for beginners.

Where to face down a bear, or soar like an eagle... A 40-minute drive from downtown puts you in rugged back country. Even if their usual hike is only as far as the corner store and back, out-of-towners still get a thrill from visiting the **Lynn Headwaters Regional Park** (tel 604/224-5739), if only to take a snapshot of the bear warnings at the entrance. Laden with backpacks, day packs, and trekking sticks, wilderness seekers set off on trails that pass through true mountain country. Towering cedars, thick brush, rushing creeks: This is very rugged terrain. Unless you know what you're doing, leave the longer hikes for the experts. You can instead spend a pleasurable hour or so following the **Lynn Loop Trail** beside a creek. If you do tackle a longer trail—some of them take six hours or more—remember that the weather around here can change in a heartbeat from sunshine to thick fog. Stay on the path, time your adventure carefully, and always let someone know both your route and approximately when you plan to be back. For up-to-date hiking and trail conditions, call 604/985-1690.

Heart of the rain forest... Fallen logs are furred with vivid green moss, rivers rush far below, and sunlight filters through the tree canopy hundreds of feet above. It may be in North Vancouver, but **Capilano River Regional Park** (tel 604/224-5739) definitely has a tropical feel. Winding through its lush grounds are 26 kilometers (15 miles) of well-maintained trails. Some start at the Cleveland Dam, a good photo op for an unobscured view of the mountain peaks known as the Lions. From there, you descend along the Capilano River until you reach sea level, and "civilization"—**Ambleside Park** in West Vancouver. A passionate ecologist, Manfred Scholermann of **Rockwood Adventures** (tel 604/926-7705) leads excellent guided tours of the North Shore, including **Lighthouse Park** and **Bowen Island**, with gourmet food included. Those of you who can't tell the difference between a Douglas fir and a hemlock can sign up for a walk through the **Seymour Demonstration Forest** (tel 604/987-1273) with a professional forester.

VANCOUVER | GETTING OUTSIDE

ping

A tide of
cosmopolitan
transplants from
Asia, Europe, and
other Canadian
cities has turned
once-dowdy

Vancouver into an international shopping bazaar, where big-name designers share floor space with fresh-off-the-boat Asian imports and native artworks. No longer can visiting Londoners and Parisians sneer at the locals' attempts at fashionable dressing ("so...*last season*..."). These days, the city is well-supplied with designing talents, the best of them famed internationally—Zonda Nellis, Martha Sturdy, Christine Morton, Patricia Regehr, Ron Leal. With three separate fashion design schools in town, a new generation is making a name for itself, gravitating like iron filings to the low-rent magnets of Cordova Street and the East Side. In Vancouver, you can easily come away with this season's hottest Chanel suit—or an Australian akubra, textiles from the Punjab, a Northwest Indian ceremonial mask, or a locally produced bottle of fine wine.

Target Zones

Don't let anyone tell you **Robson Street** is Vancouver's hippest shopping area. It ain't, not by a long shot. But it believes its own hype, and because Robson links the West End with downtown and has lots of restaurants and coffee shops, it's continually thronged by tourists and young locals. A handful of individual stores hang on because of the streams of passersby, but in general it feels like Any Mall, Anywhere. Rents have climbed to the point where only the big honchos like **Gap**, **Armani A/X**, and **Club Monaco** can afford to hang out their shingles on the main strip between **Burrard** and **Jervis streets.** It's still fun, though, to browse Robson Street on a sunny afternoon in a go-with-the-flow sort of way—wear black in the winter, shorts in the summer, and you'll blend right in. The hub of downtown shopping is the intersection of **Granville** and **Georgia streets,** where you'll find **The Bay**, and the city's last remaining downtown department stores. Turn south along Granville Street and you'll find street fashion; turn north and you'll find, er, not very much. Most of the downtown shopping action, if not underground, is at least out of sight. The biggie, **Pacific Centre**, stretches two blocks along Granville Street between Georgia and Pender streets, connecting with office towers and a SkyTrain station. The two-story older section, low-ceilinged and claustrophobic, is anchored by The Bay and **Sears,** with the huge **Holt Renfrew** fashion store the major pit stop along the way, just a few steps north; the newer section, linked by a glass walkway across Dunsmuir Street, is a vast improvement, with three levels of stores around a central, day-lit atrium. Along with the usual mall fare—$10 tank tops; mass-market shoe stores; fashions for the slim, little, and large—are several luxury stores on the upper level, conveniently sited for those staying at the attached Four Seasons hotel. Pricey designer import stores predominate at the **Sinclair Centre** at Granville and Hastings streets, a smart conversion of four historic buildings, including an elegant clock-towered structure that was built in 1910 as the city's post office. Another old neighborhood southeast of the downtown shopping core, formerly rows of warehouses, has been reborn as **Yaletown**. If you're looking for Italian pottery, a wowser silver top, or anything else that makes a design statement, you'll likely find it on these narrow streets. Follow Granville Street south from here toward the bridge and you'll pass through inflatable-doll and triple-X-rated-movie land; once across the bridge, however, as the road climbs, the shopping landscape switches into a more genteel gear. **South Granville** is Vancouver's version of Bond Street or Fifth Avenue, known for stores selling butter-soft Scottish cashmeres, sharply tailored suits, fin-de-siècle brass candlesticks, Georgian chairs, 19th-century prints, and Limoges porcelain, along with a mix of affordable clothing stores and even a few trashy dollar stores. Had you gone west from here into **Kitsilano** in the 1960s, you'd have run into the hippie center of Canada, its 4th Avenue a laid-back main drag where you could buy hookahs, love beads, and tie-dyed T-shirts. These days, the scent of patchouli has been replaced by espresso, with throngs of crisp young professionals on Saturday afternoons buying Cuisinart saucepans and hunting for amusing picture frames for their new condos. A ride on the SkyTrain will take you to **Commercial Drive** (get off at the Broadway station), currently the funkiest neighborhood in the city, with subversive art galleries and multicultural grocery stores alongside Italian coffee shops that haven't changed in decades. Do what everyone else does: Shop your way up one side and down the other. Catering more to the well-heeled, several other areas are worth checking out, including **West 10th Avenue** out near the University of British Columbia, **41st Avenue** west of Arbutus Street, and **Marine Drive** in West Vancouver.

Bargain-Hunting

When the Canadian dollar was closer in value to the green-

SHOPPING | INTRODUCTION

back, gaggles of 20-somethings would pile into Tracey or Mary-Lou's Honda and blitz down to the States for a frenzied day of shopping the factory outlets. Not anymore—these days, they have to rely on what's here at home. But bargains are everywhere; with Canada's West Coast economy stagnant for the past few years, stores offer sales, markdowns, and drastically reduced merchandise on a regular basis. January and July are the best months to score big-time. Deal-minded locals also keep their eyes open for factory and sample sales, usually listed in Tuesday's *Vancouver Sun*.

Trading with the Natives

This is Vancouver the Nice, so service is almost always congenial. The city vibe is ultra-casual—as in L.A., savvy store staff are aware that a customer in baggy shorts and a ratty T-shirt may be but a computer chip away from a billion bucks. Leave your checkbook at home. Some stores will accept checks, but many won't. Travelers' checks are okay just about everywhere, with Canadian or U.S. dollars equally welcome. If, for some reason, you do run up against attitude, feel free to gripe, bitch, and moan with gusto, both to the store and to the city's tourism people. You'll get results.

Hours of Business

Most stores open at 9:30 or 10am and close at 6pm. On Thursdays and Fridays they stay open until 9pm, and on Sundays are only open from noon to 5. That's the general rule, but there are exceptions. In parallel with their customers' lifestyles, hipper independent stores open and close later than the norm. Really small stores may shut up shop while the owner pops out for a cappuccino. Check The Index, below, for any anomalies.

Sales Tax

Vancouverites are used to the fact that the price on the hang tag is most definitely not what you pay at the cash register. Canadians are taxed to the hilt: Almost everything, barring groceries, books, magazines, and kids' clothes, gets hit with a 7 percent Provincial Sales Tax (PST). On top of that, you're dinged another 7.5 percent for the national Goods and Services Tax (GST). There is a bright side, though: If you're visiting from outside the province, shipping your goodies home (rather than taking them with you) can exempt you from the PST. If you're from outside the country, a little red tape can also get you back the GST you've forked out for those Roots boots or your hotel room. It doesn't apply to money spent at restaurants, or on gas, or those fat Cuban cigars (yes, they are indeed legal here!), or other tobacco products. Save your receipts: If your bills top $200—which means you've paid $14 in GST—you can claim it back from Revenue Canada. Ask at your hotel for the necessary form.

The Lowdown

Labels to lust after... Sited to catch the rich tourist's eye on Burrard Street is **Chanel**—yes, the real deal: braid-trimmed suits with chain-lined hems and shoes with the double-C logo. Wealthy Asians are the major customers here, so it tends to carry lots of small sizes. A few blocks away on Granville Street, **Holt Renfrew** (note: Call it just "Holt's" if you want to pass for a local) can outfit you with an authentic bit-and-bridle Hermès scarf—there's a whole boutique filled with them. This is where Vancouver jet-setters buy their cashmere—or is it *still* pashmina this year?—shawls, and every major designer is represented. Holt's men's department is famously label-heavy, too. Look to the store's house lines, though, for smart clothes at fair prices. It's a brief walk north to **Leone** in Sinclair Centre, which houses expensive Italian fashion upstairs—Dolce & Gabbana, Armani, and an entire boutique of Versace house-wares—Versace clothing too—and its own affordable and hip A-Wear below. **Plaza Escada** is right next door, and if you have to ask how much its European lunch-at-the-Ritz elegance costs, you can't afford it, baby. Still haven't reached your credit limit? A trip to **Boboli** for more Italian labels should solve that.

Tomorrow's Armanis and Donna Karans... Cordova Street, a block south of Gastown, is the epicenter for Vancouver's up-and-comers. As you'd expect with avant-gardists, these boutiques often don't open until 11am. **The Block**, one of the first names in town to take a chance on Canadian women's fashion, carries local names as well as happening designers from all the way across Canada in Toronto and Montreal—even some L.A. labels, too. Run your manicured nails down the racks of affordable but edgy careerwear and drop-dead cocktail dresses. There's a neat little coffee bar, too, where you can take a breather before plunging on. Down the street, **Dream Apparel & Articles for People** is where new fashion grads often first show their wares. Prices are generally low, finish is not always perfect, but hey, if you want a unique dress at a chain-store price.... Swerve over to Gastown's Water Street and into **Jacqueline Conoir Boutique** if you want a killer suit, sinuously cut to display female curves—they're Paris-trained RozeMerie Cuevas's specialty. Stylish Kitsilano residents make tracks for the 4th Avenue/Macdonald Street crossroads, where coolly elegant **Style Box** looks more expensive than it is. Owner and designer Dinny Lansdowne does separates and dresses in luscious colors and useful neutrals (and, hooray, they're machine washable!). Across at **The House Gallery Boutique**, owner April Peters stitches clothes inspired by a bygone era, cutting velvets and brocades into long dresses with laced bodices: very popular with new romantics. Movie and arts types willingly trek to East Vancouver to find **Point in Time**, a tiny gem of a shop in a former corner store. It has the most vibrant local fashion in town, all of it made by B.C. designers—linen shifts printed with tongue-in-cheek symbols, extravagantly trimmed jackets, bias-cut silks, and other fresh fashion ideas.

Where the stars shop... Vancouver is no more celeb-obsessed than the next town, but who bought what little doodad by which designer does invariably make the gossip columns. Silk and satin lingerie bearing designer Christine Morton's Christine Vancouver label has slithered over the bods of Sharon Stone, Diana Ross, and Gwyneth Paltrow; **Holt Renfrew** downtown carries a good sampling of her teddies, slips, and bias-cut nightgowns. For knockout ballgowns in lustrous silk and rustling taffeta, big names in the Canadian entertainment biz go to **Catherine Regehr**, as do brides with an eye for froth-free elegance. Her swanky by-appointment-only premises are just off South Granville Street. To be honest, Vancouver's social calendar has too few grand occasions to keep Regehr thriving in her hometown—sales are huge in the United States, so in recent seasons she has also turned her hand to pieces that are luxe, but more casual. From there, it's a hop and a skip to the store that shares a name with its designer, **Zonda Nellis**, whose sophisticated atelier is an ideal backdrop for the lustrous wovens that made her name. These days she also creates timeless pieces from intricate velvets made up especially for her in Italy.

Clothes make the man... Women here often bitch about the sloppy looks of most Vancouver men—and with reason. Fashion is not a major concern for the typical B.C. guy. Those who do Make An Effort eventually find their way to the major designer labels at **Mark James**, in Kits. Hugo Boss and Armani are the monikers if you're into that body-conscious European cut. American fashion-followers can groove on Calvin Klein or Donna Karan. For waxing the Ferrari or similar weekend pursuits, the favored names are Boss Sport and Replay. Guys in the financial business favor **Quorum Fashion Emporium** downtown. The draw? Designer styling for less, thanks to a cross-ocean link with factories in France and Italy (the same ones that make...sorry, they don't want to name names). Another attraction here is the offbeat dress shirts and belts. Rich kids get their sartorial thrills downtown at **Boys' Co.** as they flip through the racks of Versaces, Moschinos, and DKNYs. Boys' Co. has even expanded lately into branches in the 'burbs, which is a hopeful sign that the city's male population may be starting to look more seriously at what it wears.

In-your-face fashion... The more outrageous clothing shops cluster together on Granville Street just south of Robson Street, where teens rave over the ultra-cool styles and hip-to-the-minute style of the stores. Goth, grunge, whatever's down. The Canadian chain **Le Chateau** has been around since the '60s, but for contemporary fashion, it still knocks spots off anyone else; the Burrard Street store shows off skintight fits for pencil-slim chicks and dudes. Yaletown's **Atomic Model** brings in hot labels from New York City and L.A., while the Brit pack makes a beeline for **Vasanji** in Yaletown, which imports street-sharp style direct from London.

Squeezing that fashion dollar... In the spirit of how

Kits used to be, **Ethel's Boutique** on 4th Avenue is known for clothes at down-and-dirty prices. Moroccan rayons, Indian cottons, slinky coordinates—sometimes the labels are scissored out, sometimes they're not. Funky-but-chic skirts with wicked back slits, layered chiffon dresses—it's a grab bag. Basic leggings and bike shorts here are always at rock-bottom prices. **Banshee** has two outlets—one on West Broadway just west of Macdonald Street; one on Commercial Drive. Owner Darlene Browman brings in samples, over-cuts, or whatever other trade terms apply, and shoppers are frequently overheard gushing about how they've just seen this ankle-length $35 skirt or that $25 sheer blouse at double or more the price in trendy downtown boutiques. **Danier Leather Factory Outlet** offers such great buys, it's a regular stop for Japanese tour buses. Ask for suede hot pants here, and staff will come back with "What color?"—scarlet, emerald green, they've got it, and everything goes for a song in this huge warehouse on the east side. Since you're already in the area, stop in at **Roots Factory Outlet,** selling discounted items from the popular Canadian chain with its own logo'd brand of outdoorsy wear.

Recycled and retro... No one's shy about wearing secondhand here—real estate agents trawl consignment stores in search of pre-owned Armanis, and spiky-haired nouveau punks scout thrift shops for finds. Gen X-ers with a hankering for the past hang out at **Mecca**, on the Commercial Drive strip, rooting for the perfect tux or a diamanté-trimmed cocktail frock. They also prowl, alongside fashion and film students, through the enclave of retro wear that centers on Cordova Street. **Deluxe Junk** is the granddaddy, where the longer those 1940s twin sets or 1960s mini-shifts hang on the racks, the lower the prices drop. There's a huge range here, from dainty Victorian nightgowns to tons of jeans and leather jackets. Blaze a trail through **Tapestry** if you're heavily into Ginger Rogers bias-cut satin, Fred Astaire jackets, rhinestone necklaces, or hippie flares.

Shoe, shoe, who's got the shoe... Maybe it's the casual lifestyle, but this is not a city serious about footwear in the same way that London or Paris is.

Among mainstream stores, the most avant-garde styles are at downtown's fashion department store **Holt Renfrew**. Other than that, the biggest beacon in the dark—and it's a huge, blazingly international one—is **John Fluevog**, whose store on Granville Street just south of Robson Street is a must for the pierced and magenta-haired. The decor hasn't changed since the 1970s (it's now back in style), but the shoes are light years ahead: Heels inspired by horse hooves, platforms so high they make your ears bleed, "wok 'n' roll" sandals...if your wardrobe has slipped over to the safe side, a pair of Fluevogs will jump-start it.

To top it all off... In a circus atmosphere complete with gaily colored posters and memorabilia, **Big Top Hat Shop** is crammed with everything from simple foldable cottons to swooningly romantic, flower-garnished straws. It's one of the bright spots in otherwise tourist-trap Gastown. A seething mass on weekends, **Edie's Hats** on Granville Island can fit you out with a handmade velvet cap, a $4,000 panama hat, or a fedora. One of the biggest names in local design, **Martha Sturdy**, creates jewelry that routinely appears in the pages of *Vogue* and *Elle*. Bold simple shapes are her specialty. Visit her shop on South Granville Street to splurge on a pair of Martha's dramatic earrings, or plain silver hoops, with individual gewgaws to hang on them.

The big two... Joined, if not at the hip, then by the underground maze of shopping centers, the city's last remaining department stores are clustered around the Georgia and Granville streets crossroads. Strictly speaking, only its size qualifies **Holt Renfrew** to be in the department store group. Its stock in trade is almost exclusively fashion, though there are a few amusing housewares, such as airy but warm mohair blankets. What's there changes with the season, and with store buyers' whims. The red-, yellow-, and green-striped blankets at **The Bay** haven't changed since the Hudson's Bay Company first sold them at its fur trading posts that opened up Canada's west. Having pared down its name to The Bay, this department store (like most) is in the throes of redefining itself. Cruise around the junior wear—its "Real" house brand offers the best buys—but you'll also see a smattering of Vancouver designers represented. The shoe department's worth cruising, and so are the housewares, if you're into Italian pottery painted with pears and plums. Across from The Bay is the white, largely windowless monolith of a building that houses Sears, formerly Eaton's. That Canadian institution—rural seniors grew up with "the Eaton's catalogue"—was always operated with the democratic notion of being all things to all people. Eaton's had tried—but failed—to keep up with the times, and closed at the (most recent) turn of the century; intervention by (gasp!) the American department store chain saved the day. Now, however, Sears has taken over for good.

Swanning around Granville Island... This is one tourist attraction that actually merits all its hype; in addition to the setting, views, and Public Market, Granville Island is ace for shopping. On a weekend, it seems the whole city descends on **Edie's Hats** in the Net Loft (a collection of inviting stores selling clothing, cookware, books, and more, all under one roof) to try on a Borsalino or 1920s-style cloche. Nearby **Maiwa Handprints** is an exotic bazaar of a place whose owner works with village artisans in India to create the bed and table linens, cushion covers, and fabrics she sells. Prices are miraculously low, given the intricacy of the work. Also check out Maiwa's own line of locally made women's skirts; big, floppy shirts; and dresses in soft, heavy linen. Across the way, the French-accented **Nancy Lord** sells flawlessly cut classic clothing in lustrous silks, buttery leathers, and the softest linens. If your heart is set on a cashmere pea jacket, here's where to come.

Food, glorious food... Affluent West Siders pick up takeout crab cakes, chutneys, and drippingly ripe French cheeses at **Lesley Stowe Fine Foods**. Prices are high, but you do get what you pay for—the parmesan "crisps" are addictive, and her lemon dacquoise dessert is to die for. Mixing local supermarket, gourmet store, coffee shop, and take-out counter, **Meinhardt Fine Foods**, on the high-rent South Granville Street strip, can sell you a quart of milk, a loaf of bread, champagne vinegar, or an entire foie gras from France, where owner Linda Meinhardt has a chateau. They pack up some great picnic baskets, too. On 4th Avenue in Kits, chocolatier Greg Hook makes evil little treats at **Chocolate Arts**. The fruits used in his fillings are all organic (everyone knows organic foods contain fewer calories, right?). For a fine souvenir, get one of the chocolate Haida "masks," made from molds by noted First Nations artist Robert Davidson. B.C. wine makes another excellent take-home gift, but skip the government liquor stores—the most interesting vineyards don't make enough wine to supply them. Shop instead at private wine shops; the North Shore's **Edgemont Village Wines** has the biggest selection. To decompress afterward, try one of the exotic black, green, or flower teas—or even just a shot of quality imported ginseng—from the **Ten Ren Tea & Ginseng Co.** in Chinatown.

Home sweet home... Creative types have alchemized the Yaletown district, a clutch of old warehouses south of the downtown hub, into one of the city's most interesting areas. Studios, galleries, restaurants, ateliers, bars—it's a buzzy place, and so are the stores around here, especially **Liberty Design**. (It's not connected with Liberty of London, by the way, all you international travelers.) Darling young couples come here to poke through the cushions, candleholders, and tchotchkes—the place is looking ripe for a double-page spread in some shelter magazine. Flanked by huge stone columns and accessed by a flight of steps, **Chintz & Company** houses furniture, furnishings, fabrics, and a gazillion little tempting thingies to buy for your home. Staff are often cheek-to-cheek with interior designers, so don't expect the usual hand-holding service.

My great-granddad brought it over... Face it. At little more than a century old, Vancouver itself hardly qualifies as an antique. Those of a mind to furnish their pads with early Victorian or Georgian have to rely on what's come from Europe. South Granville Street is one popular source; a few notches down (in price and quality) is Antique Row on Main Street, starting at about 25th Avenue. For that furniture-found-in-my-granny's-cottage look, hit **Folkart Interiors** in Kitsilano—they just may have that antique icebox, pine armoire, or farmhouse table you need for your newly reno'd home in trendy Point Grey. For a pedigreed chair, gilt chandelier, or magnificent silver centerpiece for your Georgian table, pop into

Uno Langmann just south of the Granville Street Bridge. Some of the pieces here date back to the Renaissance. Sharp Vancouverites home in on the monthly auctions at **Love's Auctioneers** and attempt to snatch bargains from under antique dealers' noses—Art Nouveau mirrors, Limoges porcelain pieces, Oriental rugs, diamond rings, strings of amber, and whatever's up for grabs.

Gear up and go... With awesome peaks and rushing rivers right on the doorstep, locals are seriously into sports. Officially you have to be a member to shop at **Mountain Equipment Coop**, but you can join as you go in the door of this vast emporium, then happily root through the camping, hiking, climbing, and biking clothes and equipment. If that doesn't pan out, stride athletically over to **Taiga Works Wilderness Equipment**, which manufactures its own line of jackets, pants, tents, and sleeping bags. Nearby peaks, beaches, and plenty of empty sidewalk means boarding of all kinds is big in Vancouver. Snowboarders, surfboarders, and skateboarders congregate around the 4th Avenue and Burrard Street crossroads, where their favorite stores are located. At **Thriller**, owner Mike Jackson (yes, really) sells his own line of boards, clothing, and "Grubby" backpacks. Several blocks west, at **Hot Shop**, boarders rely on local snowboarding legend Peter "P.D." Ducommun to steer them toward the latest trends.

Kidding around... **Kids Only Market** is an entire building at the entrance to Granville Island, bursting with everything that turns a small person's crank. Moms and Dads favor it too, because this isn't one of your mass-market outlets: Barbie and Ken dolls are notably absent, and so are toys calling for batteries. Instead, you'll find handcrafted, well-made imported dolls and trains; crafts supplies; clothes; and colorful kites to fly at nearby Vanier Park. They also sell food and offer a play area to encourage shoppers to linger—needless to say, it's a zoo on weekends. Young readers love to pore over the shelves at **Kidsbooks** on West Broadway in Kitsilano—they've got both old faves and new titles—you won't find a better selection in the city. If you're stuck for ideas, ask the staff. As you swing back toward town, stop off at **The House**

Gallery Boutique, which purveys the kind of fairytale frocks that make many a 6-year-old girl go into a frenzy.

Naughty secrets... Under Vancouver's sedate exterior beats a black leather heart. The somewhat raunchy **Mack's Leathers**, at the sordid end of Granville Street downtown, sells clothing and sex gadgets; you can get a few extra piercings here while you're at it. **La Tienda Shoe Salon** specializes in heels high enough to give you a nosebleed, and no, they're not for walking, staff will explain patiently. They're mostly for working girls—and not the kind who work in banks and law firms. Even "girls" with boat-sized feet will find something to fit.

Read my aura... Need a shot of wheatgrass? Wind chimes? A meditation tape? All three, and you want *choice*? Are you ever in luck. In Vancouver, several blocks of West Broadway are New Age heaven, with more herbal remedies and alternative-lifestyle accessories than anywhere else in the city. Whimsical window displays make **Gaia Garden** stand out; inside you'll find lavender flowers by the gram, herbal remedies, books, and plenty of help if you're new to the natural way of life. **Banyen Books & Sound** is a gentle place filled with irritatingly gentle people, thousands of books, and tapes of whale songs and other natural sounds meant to mellow you out. A block east, **Escents Aromatherapy** sends out wafts of geranium, rosemary, and lavender to entice you through the door; the sweet-natured staff then wins you over to the serene pleasures of aromatherapy oils or fizzy bath bombs, all made in Vancouver.

Between the covers... Feeling homesick? You can pick up out-of-town newspapers at **Mayfair News** on the West Side, as well as at shoebox-sized **Magpie Magazine Gallery** on Commercial Drive, where you vie for space with graphic designers and social activists checking out the vast amount of eclectic reading material. Kerbam! Splat! Pow! Fans of Superman, Spider Man, and the Green Lantern head for what neighborhood? Kitsilano, to browse through **The Comicshop**'s collection of new and vintage stock. Loyal readers pick up the new Carol Shields or Margaret Atwood a few blocks west at locally owned **Duthie's Books**. Sci-fi fans, cinephiles, and computer nerds are well catered to at the **Granville Book Company** downtown, which stays open until midnight; it also carries more mainstream works, even those of Danielle Steele. Out near UBC, science fiction and fantasy orbit around the shelves at **White Dwarf Books**. In Point Grey, the feminist **Women in Print** bookshop does carry works by men—but they're all about the female gender. Downtown, **Little Sister's Book and Art Emporium** is the literary source for gays and lesbians. (Not known for its broad-mindedness, Canada Customs gives them a hard time periodically when they attempt to bring in books that no other store would have problems importing.) Travelers whet their appetites in Kitsilano with **The Travel Bug**'s guides, maps, equipment—and the noticeboard at the rear of the store where customers offer rides to South America or exchange names of cheap hotels in far-flung places like Phuket. Downtown, a good travel resource is the phenomenally well-stocked **International Travel Maps and Books**. Amateur chefs can find more cookbooks than they ever dreamed possible at **Barbara-Jo's Books to Cooks**; this Yaletown shop also includes a demonstration kitchen where classes are held by local chefs and big names on the book tour circuit. At the **Wanderlust Travel Store** in Kits, footloose and fancy-free types scan the racks of travel books. For out-of-print and secondhand volumes, rummage your way through **MacLeod's Books** downtown, a rabbit warren of bookshelves (clearly marked, thank goodness) that's a bibliophile's dream.

From the city that brought you Bryan Adams... A plethora of audio stores makes for fierce competition—which explains why CD prices in Vancouver are among the lowest in North America (which means the lowest in the world). On Seymour Street downtown, you can zip back and forth between **A&B Sound** and **Sam the Record Man** to compare deals. A&B stocks books and videos too—at the top of the escalator (Top 40 is downstairs, classical upstairs); cop a free view of whatever movie is playing on the home theater set-up. Installed downtown in what was once the main branch of Vancouver's Public Library, the blockbuster **Virgin Megastore** lets you plug into listening stations to sample music before you buy; classical music buffs can bliss out in their own soundproof room, where there's no risk of acid rock wrecking a fugue. As its name suggests, **The Magic Flute** in Kits has a classical bent, especially good for CBC (Canadian Broadcasting Corporation) and local recordings. So does **Sikora's Classical Records** downtown, which also carries sheet music; most customers here look like they've briefly escaped from the symphony. There are two indie-record standouts in Kitsilano: **Black Swan Records** is a popular haunt for jazz, world music, hard-to-find stuff, and imports—new or used, CD or vinyl, this store carries it all. Independent labels, new wave, and pop rule at **Zulu Records**.

No home should be without one... Considering how often it rains in Vancouver, umbrellas are a must. Some locals buy cheap and buy often; sager ones invest in built-to-last bumbershoots from **The Umbrella Shop** downtown, a family business in operation since 1935. Most of its stock is made on the premises; hand-painted umbrellas are a specialty, as are brollies built on sturdy Fox frames imported from England. Right down the street, Vancouver's paranoids slink into **Spy City** for phone recorders or pinhole video cameras ideal for keeping an eye on the nanny. Counter-surveillance devices, books on Internet terrorism and laundering your ill-gotten gains—many items here are bought as gag gifts (take it from me, you don't want to run into the guy who *seriously* wants to bone up on *Contingency Cannibalism*). Down in Gastown, **Button Button**'s name is self-explanatory. Large, small, leather-covered, rhinestone-encrusted, and they've got beads in every color under the sun: African buttons made from a termite nest, vintage buttons, cork buttons—you'll have fun just poking around, and few can walk out the door without sifting through the vast container of "Button Soup." For not only buttons, but also fake fur, sequins, doodads, gewgaws, foot-deep fringe in neon green, and gazillions of other things connected with textiles, **Dressew Supply** is close by. Service is occasionally snarky, a big security guard skulks by the door, and forget getting help by phone, but this is the kind of offbeat place that can be fun to prowl around. A few steps east, **Salmagundi West** hangs out in an 1880s flatiron building. Iron bedsteads, wicker baskets, and Oriental rugs on the sidewalk lure you into the grandmother's attic of your dreams—jewelry, antiques, vintage drapes, oil paintings, glassware, china, beads, greeting cards, books, vases, feathers, Victorian passementerie, lamps.... Once you've had your fill of the upstairs, take the vertiginous steps down to the basement—and you'll come upon more. Don't miss the Chinese apothecary's cabinet, its 100-plus drawers holding party tricks, puzzles, water flowers, and other small treats. For less tasteful stuff—anatomically correct pencil erasers, faux eyeballs, and such—pop into nearby **Oddball**. "If you don't need it," say staffers, "you'll find it here."

Souvenirs you can take home without wincing...

Get this straight: Smoked salmon is a *staple* here, so don't be lured into paying more than it's worth. Skip the downtown souvenir stores and stock up at the **Granville Island Public Market**. Actually, you can pick up a stash in most local supermarkets, but the Granville Island market is a fun experience no visitor should miss. Seekers of authentically native mementos should also beware: Those armies of miniature totem poles you see in the souvenir stores were *not* carved by aboriginal hands in the mists of far northern B.C. For the real thing, spend some time at **Hill's Native Art** in Gastown. The staff knows its way around the carved silver Haida bracelets, button blankets, and bentwood boxes and masks; the same is true at at the **Leona Lattimer Gallery** near Granville Island. Other good bets are the gift shops at the Vancouver Museum and Museum of Anthropology [see Diversions]. Hordes of Asian tourists flock to **Roots Factory Outlet**, at the corner of Burrard and Robson streets, to outfit their kids in authentic Canadian jackets. The brainchild of two Torontonians, Roots has now expanded even beyond Canadian borders. (Its best-known item is a red fleece reversed cap that one of the British royal princes vaulted onto the front pages.) Browsing around Chinatown should net you hand-embroidered linens, authentic cheongsams for that Suzie Wong look, or brocade by the yard; teens go for the over-size brushes meant for Chinese painting but ideal for applying makeup. Over on Commercial Drive, **The Doctor Vigari Gallery** showcases the skills of local artists, crafters, and furniture makers. Glassware, intricately framed mirrors, inventive candle-holders—what's there changes constantly, but is always intriguing. Finally, they're illegal to bring back home to America, of course, but if you've got a hankering for Cuban cigars, **La Casa del Habano** imports 'em directly from that country's biggest exporter and stashes them in a top-flight humidor. Just don't think of trying to sneak those stogies back onto the plane home (unless home happens to be a country other than the U.S.). Smoke 'em or eat 'em.

Shopping the island... Vancouver Island might not be the shopping equal of Vancouver, but it ain't bad, either. Downtown Victoria alone boasts the stalwart Canadian department store **The Bay,** which is about what you'd expect, plus a honkin' assortment of shops that sell everything from kitschy souvenirs to five-figure antiques that came over from England before there even *was* a Canada (or a U.S. of A., for that matter). Government Street is your easiest diving-in point; just begin behind The Fairmont Empress Hotel and walk west. Any of the cross streets is also likely to bear fruit. It's unbelievable how many shops here sell English tea sets, tweed caps, and Scottish kilts, and you'll soon overdose on the tweeness of it all. Try to hold to a few stops, such as **W&J Wilson, British Importers,** or the very Irish-y **Avoca Handweavers,** all specializing in clothing and woolens. You're gonna want to pick up a slab of salmon at some point during your trip to bring back home for the in-laws, so look no further than **Canadian Impressions** in Victoria for your supply. Need a book? **Munro's Books** is your place, with a concentration in island and natural history. Besides Government Street, there are several other areas you might hit; one of the best is the very nice Antique Row area stretching along a few blocks of Fort Street east of the harbor. Among the stars here are the silver experts at **Jefferies & Co.** and the period English offerings at **David Robinson Antiques,** but really any shop is just as likely to yield a find or two. Finally, the island's a great place to find items crafted by the native peoples of Canada's Northwest. Government Street is lined with the bulk of the traders in these goods—some very high-quality, some rather tacky. **Hill's Indian Crafts** is the acknowledged king, and better than it looks at first glance. Other options—and there are many—include the **Indian Craft Shoppe** in Victoria and, up-island about 35 miles in Duncan, the **Quw'utsun Cultural and Conference Centre.**

SHOPPING | THE LOWDOWN

The Index

A&B Sound. Central source for CDs and tapes. Frequent sales.... *Tel 604/687-5837. 556 Seymour St. Granville Station SkyTrain.* **(see p. 146)**

Atomic Model. Women's fashions you won't see anywhere else in town.... *Tel 604/688-9989. 1036 Mainland St. Bus 15.* **(see p. 139)**

Banshee. Fun, funky clothes at budget prices.... *Tel 604/254-7240. 1566 Commercial Dr. Bus 20. Also tel 604/731-7247. 2813 W. Broadway. Bus 9.* **(see p. 140)**

Banyen Books & Sound. Music to meditate by, and books that tell you how to do it.... *Tel 604/732-7912. 2671 W. Broadway. Bus 9.* **(see p. 145)**

Barbara-Jo's Books to Cooks. Culinary speciality shop in Yaletown.... *Tel 604/688-6755. 1128 Mainland St. Bus 15.* **(see p. 146)**

The Bay. Downtown department store is the modern-day descendant of the early fur-trading Hudson's Bay Company.... *Tel 604/681-6211. 674 Granville Street. Granville Station SkyTrain.* **(see pp. 134, 141)**

Big Top Hat Shop. Circus decor, lively staff, and a wide range of hats.... *Tel 604/684-7373. 73 Water St. Buses 3, 4, 6, 7, 8, 50.* **(see p. 141)**

Black Swan Records. Jazz, world, folk, and blues music on a groovy stretch of Broadway.... *Tel 604/734-2828. 3209 W. Broadway. Bus 9.* **(see p. 147)**

The Block. Fave source for fashion from all across Canada.... *Tel 604/685-8885. 350 W. Cordova St. Buses 3, 4, 6, 7, 8, 50.* **(see p. 137)**

Boboli. Eurofashion for him and her on the main shopping drag.... *Tel 604/257-2300. 2776 Granville St. Bus 8.* **(see p. 137)**

Boys' Co. Upmarket imports for rich kids. Branches in Richmond, Burnaby, and South Vancouver.... *Tel 604/684-5656. 1044 Robson St. Bus 5.* **(see p. 139)**

Button Button. Buttons of every size, shape, color, and description.... *Tel 604/687-0067. 422 W. Cordova St. Buses 3, 4, 6, 7, 8, 50. Closed Sun.* **(see p. 147)**

Catherine Regehr. Sumptuous "big evening" wear and bridal gowns.... *Tel 604/734-9339. 1529 W. 6th Ave., Suite 111. Bus 8. By appointment.* **(see p. 138)**

Chanel. Classic suits, shoes, and accessories with the "double C" logo.... *Tel 604/682-0522. 900 W. Hastings St. Bus 22.* **(see p. 137)**

Chintz & Company. Furnishings, furniture, and an admirable selection of fabrics.... *Tel 604/689-2022. 950 Homer St. Bus 15.* **(see p. 143)**

Chocolate Arts. Excellent chocolates made on the premises by master chocolatier Greg Hook.... *Tel 604/739-0475. 2037 W. 4th Ave. Bus 4.* **(see p. 143)**

The Comicshop. Vintage comics, new ones, and scads of memorabilia.... *Tel 604/738-8122. 2089 W. 4th Ave. Bus 4.* **(see p. 145)**

Danier Leather Factory Outlet. Savings on men's and women's leather fashion.... *Tel 604/432-6137. 3003 Grandview Hwy. Bus 27.* **(see p. 140)**

Deluxe Junk. Retro fashion priced low. Lots of jeans and leather.... *Tel 604/685-4871. 310 W. Cordova St. Buses 3, 4, 6, 7, 8, 50.* **(see p. 140)**

The Doctor Vigari Gallery. Intriguing selection of works of local craftspeople.... *Tel 604/255-9513. 1312 Commercial Dr. Bus 20. Call for hours.* **(see p. 148)**

Dream Apparel & Articles for People. Tomorrow's Donna Karans and Calvin Kleins often bring their first efforts here.... *Tel 604/683-7326. 311 W. Cordova St. Buses 3, 4, 6, 7, 8, 50.* **(see p. 138)**

Dressew Supply. Two floors of fabrics, trims, Halloween masks, beads, fake fur.... *Tel 604/682-6196. 337 W. Hastings St. Bus 10. Closed Sun.* **(see p. 147)**

Duthie's Books. Loyal Vancouverites read with this home-grown store, the last of a chain..... *Tel 604/732-5344. 2239 W. 4th Ave. Bus 4.* **(see p. 145)**

Edgemont Village Wines. The widest selection of B.C. labels in the area.... *Tel 604/985-9463. 3050 Edgemont Blvd., North Vancouver. Bus 232. Open until 7pm weekdays, 9 Sat, 6 Sun.* **(see p. 143)**

Edie's Hats. Wild assortment of headgear.... *Tel 604/683-4280. 1666 Johnston St., Granville Island. Bus 51.* **(see pp. 141, 142)**

Escents Aromatherapy. Local aromatherapy store of oils and bath potions.... *Tel 604/682-0041. 1172 Robson St. Bus 5.* **(see p. 145)**

Ethel's Boutique. Great deals on hip clothing—some with famous labels.... *Tel 604/736-0910. 2346 W. 4th Ave. Bus 4.* **(see p. 140)**

Folkart Interiors. Country-style Canadiana of a certain vintage, for the home.... *Tel 604/731-7576. 3651 W. 10th Ave. Bus 10.* **(see p. 143)**

Gaia Garden. Herbal remedies and other natural ways to enhance your life.... *Tel 604/734-4372. 2672 W. Broadway. Bus 9.* **(see p. 145)**

Granville Book Company. Techies, film buffs, and sci-fi enthusiasts buy their reading here.... *Tel 604/687-2213. 850*

Granville St. Granville Station SkyTrain. Open until midnight Sun–Thurs, until 1am Fri–Sat. **(see p. 146)**

Granville Island Public Market. Good hunting ground for food, microbrewed beer and crafts.... *Tel 604/666-6477. 1689 Johnston St. Bus 51. Closed Mon during Jan.*
(see p. 148)

Hill's Native Art. Native bentwood boxes, silver jewelry, blankets, and masks, all authentic.... *Tel 604/685-4249. 165 Water St. Buses 3, 4, 6, 7, 8, 50. Open 9am–9pm, until 10 July–Aug.* **(see p. 148)**

Holt Renfrew. Best fashion store in the city—Jil Sander, Armani, Calvin Klein, plus its own affordable label and some slinky lingerie. Shoes at all price levels.... *Tel 604/681-3121. 633 Granville St. Granville Station SkyTrain.*
(see pp. 137, 138, 141)

Hot Shop. The latest snowboarding gear.... *Tel 604/739-7796. 2868 W. 4th Ave. Bus 4. Open noon–6pm Mon–Sat, closed Sun.* **(see p. 144)**

The House Gallery Boutique. Renaissance-inspired frocks and separates.... *Tel 604/732-8647. 2865 W. 4th Ave. Bus 4.*
(see pp. 138, 144)

International Travel Maps and Books. Serious explorers and armchair travelers can lose themselves here.... *Tel 604/687-3320. 539 W. Pender St. Granville Station SkyTrain. Closed Sat–Sun.* **(see p. 146)**

Jacqueline Conoir Boutique. For designer RozeMerie Cuevas's line of curvy women's suits and separates.... *Tel 604/688-5222. 403–55 Water St. Bus 8.* **(see p. 138)**

John Fluevog Shoes. Way-out shoe styles.... *Tel 604/688-2828. 837 Granville St. Granville Station SkyTrain.*
(see p. 141)

Kidsbooks. The name says it all.... *Tel 604/738-5335. 3083 W. Broadway. Bus 9.* **(see p. 144)**

Kids Only Market. No mass-produced nasties, only handmade

SHOPPING | THE INDEX

and imported toys for the little ones.... *Tel 604/689-8447. 1496 Cartwright St., Granville Island. Bus 51.***(see p. 144)**

La Casa del Habano. Imported Cuban cigars for those who thrill to the feel of contraband.... *Tel 604/609-0511. 980 Robson St. Buses 1, 2, 5, 17.* **(see p. 149)**

La Tienda Shoe Salon. Stratospheric heels and thigh boots for "working" girls and drag queens.... *Tel 604/683-6200. 341 W. Pender St. Buses 17, 22. Closed Sun.* **(see p. 145)**

Le Chateau. Canadian chain famous for edgy duds you squeeze into. Branches in most malls, including nearby Pacific Centre.... *Tel 604/682-3909. 813 Burrard St. Bus 22.* **(see p. 139)**

Leona Lattimer Gallery. Collection of Northwest coast Native art.... *Tel 604/732-4556. 1590 W. 2nd Ave. Buses 4, 50.* **(see p. 148)**

Leone. Dolce & Gabbana little black dresses, Versace bath towels, Armani too, in a restored heritage building.... *Tel 604/683-1133. 757 West Hastings St. Buses 3, 4, 6, 7, 8, 16, 20, 50.* **(see p. 137)**

Lesley Stowe Fine Foods. Gourmet takeout and groceries.... *Tel 604/731-3663. 1780 W. 3rd Ave. Bus 4. Open until 6:30pm daily.* **(see p. 142)**

Liberty Design. Opulent home accessories.... *Tel 604/682-7499. 1295 Seymour St. Bus 8.* **(see p. 143)**

Little Sister's Book and Art Emporium. The city's major gay and lesbian bookstore.... *Tel 604/669-1753. 1238 Davie St. Bus 6. Open until 11pm.* **(see p. 146)**

Love's Auctioneers. Bid for whatever's on the block at antiques auctions held the last week of each month.... *Tel 604/733-1157. 1635 W. Broadway. Bus 9.* **(see p. 144)**

Mack's Leathers. Black leather and fetish accessories.... *Tel 604/688-6225. 1043 Granville St. Bus 8.* **(see p. 145)**

MacLeod's Books. Secondhand bookstore resembling a

rabbit warren.... *Tel 604/681-7654. 455 W. Pender St. Buses 17, 22.* **(see p. 146)**

The Magic Flute. Mostly classical records, including some local recordings.... *Tel 604/736-2727. 2203 W. 4th Ave. Bus 4.* **(see p. 147)**

Magpie Magazine Gallery. Tiny shop with vast choice of reading material.... *Tel 604/253-6666. 1319 Commercial Dr. Bus 20.* **(see p. 145)**

Maiwa Handprints. Unique textiles and clothing from India.... *Tel 604/669-3939. 6–1666 Johnston St., Granville Island. Bus 51.* **(see p. 142)**

Mark James. Designer labels like Hugo Boss and Armani for upwardly aspirational guys.... *Tel 604/734-2381. 2941 W. Broadway. Bus 9. Also tel 604/688-0089. Bus 15.* **(see p. 139)**

Martha Sturdy. Bold jewelry, plus exquisitely designed bowls and vases from exciting local designer.... *Tel 604/737-0037. 3039 Granville St. Bus 8.* **(see p. 141)**

Mayfair News. Scads of magazines, and out-of-town papers.... *Tel 604/738-8951. 1535 W. Broadway. Bus 9. Opens early Mon–Fri and stays open until 10:30pm, until 10 Sat–Sun.* **(see p. 145)**

Mecca. Vintage, pre-owned, and new clothing for Gen X-ers seeking a past.... *Tel 604/251-7390. 1204 Commercial Dr. Bus 20.* **(see p. 140)**

Meinhardt Fine Foods. Exceptional gourmet take-out.... *Tel 604/732-4405. 3002 Granville St. Bus 8. Open until 9pm.* **(see p. 142)**

Mountain Equipment Coop. Giant store with clothes and equipment for camping, hiking, biking, and climbing.... *Tel 604/872-7858. 130 W. Broadway. Bus 9. Open until 7pm.* **(see p. 144)**

Nancy Lord. Classic fashions in luxury suedes, linens, and cashmere.... *Tel 604/689-3972. 1666 Johnston St., Granville Island. Bus 51.* **(see p. 142)**

SHOPPING | THE INDEX

Oddball. Dirty jokes, faux eyeballs, and other equally kitschy stuff.... *Tel 604/632-0090. 439 W. Hastings St. Bus 10 (or other Hastings St. buses).* **(see p. 148)**

Pacific Centre. Downtown's biggest shopping mall.... *Tel 604/688-7236. 701 W. Georgia St. Granville Station Sky-Train.* **(see p. 134)**

Plaza Escada. Classically elegant European fashion for the well-heeled.... *Tel 604/688-8558. 757 W. Hastings St. Waterfront Station SkyTrain.* **(see p. 137)**

Point in Time. Home-grown fashion that'll knock your eyes out.... *Tel 604/255-8407. 1302 Victoria Dr. Bus 20. Closed Mon.* **(see p. 138)**

Quorum Fashion Emporium. Designer labels for Wall Street wannabes.... *Tel 604/684-1223. 525 W. Georgia St. Bus 22.* **(see p. 139)**

Roots Factory Outlet. Sturdy, well-made clothing for couples and kids. Suburban branches.... *Tel 604/683-4305. 1001 Robson St. Bus 5.* **(see pp. 140, 148)**

Salmagundi West. Antiques, textiles, vases, greeting cards, and some highly interesting furniture in a Gastown flatiron building.... *Tel 604/681-4648. 321 W. Cordova St. Buses 3, 4, 6, 7, 8, 50.* **(see p. 147)**

Sam the Record Man. Huge store, featuring excellent prices on everything from heavy metal to Mozart.... *Tel 604/684-3722. 568 Seymour St. Granville Station SkyTrain.* **(see p. 146)**

Sikora's Classical Records. Long-hair CDs and scores right downtown.... *Tel 604/685-0625. 432 W. Hastings St. Bus 10.* **(see p. 147)**

Sinclair Centre. Four heritage buildings converted into an upscale mall.... *757 W. Hastings St. Buses 3, 4, 6, 7, 8, 16, 20, 50.* **(see p. 135)**

Spy City. Stuff every 007 or would-be snoop should own.... *Tel 604/683-3283. 414 W. Pender St. Buses 17, 22. Closed Sun.* **(see p. 147)**

Style Box. Designer Dinny Lansdowne's elegant, affordable coordinates in muted colors that won't break your bank.... *Tel 604/324-1771. 4439 W. 10th Ave. Bus 4. Call for hours.* **(see p. 138)**

Taiga Works Wilderness Equipment. Tackle the mountains in one of this local company's jackets, sleeping bags, or tents.... *Tel 604/875-6644. 390 W. 8th Ave. Bus 9.* **(see p. 144)**

Tapestry. Retro clothing and other vintage finds.... *Tel 604/687-1719. 321 Cambie St. Buses 3, 4, 6, 7, 8.* **(see p. 140)**

Ten Ren Tea & Ginseng Co. Chinatown importer of all sorts of teas and ginseng products.... *Tel 604/6841566. 550 Main St. Buses 1, 3, 4, 7, 8.* **(see p. 143)**

Thriller. Snowboards, boardwear, backpacks, and other accessories.... *Tel 604/736-5651. 1710 W. 4th Ave. Bus 4.* **(see p. 144)**

The Travel Bug. Gadgets, gizmos, books, maps, knowledgeable staff.... *Tel 604/737-1122. 2667 W. Broadway. Bus 9.* **(see p. 146)**

The Umbrella Shop. Umbrellas made on premises by a 4th-generation firm.... *Tel 604/669-9444. 534 W. Pender St. Buses 17, 22.* **(see p. 147)**

Uno Langmann. Fine antiques, silver, *objets*, and paintings in neoclassical surroundings.... *Tel 604/736-8825. 2117 Granville St. Bus 8.* **(see p. 144)**

Vasanji. Cool gear direct from London.... *Tel 604/669-0882. 1012 Mainland St. Bus 15.* **(see p. 139)**

Virgin Megastore. Big, up-to-the-minute music source in the heart of the city.... *Tel 604/669-2289. 788 Burrard St. Bus 5. Open until 11pm Mon–Thur, midnight Fri–Sat, 10pm Sun.* **(see p. 146)**

Wanderlust Travel Store. Yet another good Kitsilano travel bookstore.... *Tel 604/739-2182. 1929 W. 4th Ave. Bus 9.* **(see p. 146)**

White Dwarf Books. Sci-fi and fantasy books. Tolkien fans rejoice.... *Tel 604/228-8223. 4368 W. 10th Ave. Bus 10.*
(see p. 146)

Women in Print. Books by (mostly), for, and about the female gender.... *Tel 604/732-4128. 3566 W. 4th Ave. Bus 4.*
(see p. 146)

Zonda Nellis. Long-established women's-wear designer in South Granville.... *Tel 604/736-5668. 2203 Granville St. Bus 8.* **(see p. 139)**

Zulu Records. New wave and pop music, much from independent labels.... *Tel 604/738-3232. 1972 W. 4th Ave. Bus 4.*
(see p. 147)

VANCOUVER ISLAND SHOPPING

Avoca Handweavers. All Ireland, all the time.... *Tel 250/383-0433. 1009 Government St., Victoria.* **(see p. 149)**

The Bay. Once the proud Hudson's Bay Company, now a department store with a few surprises from the past.... *Tel 250/385-1311. 1150 Douglas St., Victoria.*
(see p. 149)

British Importers. Simply the best men's clothing store on the island.... *Tel 250/386-1496. 1125 Government St., Victoria.* **(see p. 149)**

Canadian Impressions. Canadiana galore, but a cut way above most of the rest in town.... *Tel 250/383-2641. 811 Government St., Victoria.* **(see p. 149)**

David Robinson Antiques. English antiques such as porcelains, period silver, and fine Persian rugs.... *Tel 250/384-6425. 1023 Fort St.* **(see p. 149)**

Hill's Indian Crafts. Good collection of arts and crafts from local native tribes.... *Tel 250/385-3911. 1008 Government St., Victoria.* **(see p. 149)**

Indian Craft Shoppe. Plenty of native-woven clothing, carvings, and other goods.... *Tel 250/382-3643. 905 Government St., Victoria.* **(see p. 149)**

Munro's Books. A top Victoria book nook specializing in local history.... *Tel 250/382-2464. 1108 Government St., Victoria.* **(see p. 149)**

Quw'utsun Cultural and Conference Centre. Amazing sweaters woven by local Cowichan craftspeople, plus totem-pole carving demonstrations.... *Tel 250/746-8119 or 877/746-8119. 200 Cowichan Way, Duncan. From Victoria, drive about 35 miles north on Hwy. 1 and turn off at signs.* **(see p. 149)**

W&J Wilson. Thick, hand-woven sweaters and other men's clothing from the British Isles.... *Tel 250/383-7177. 1221 Government St.* **(see p. 149)**

SHOPPING | THE INDEX

Downtown Vancouver Shopping

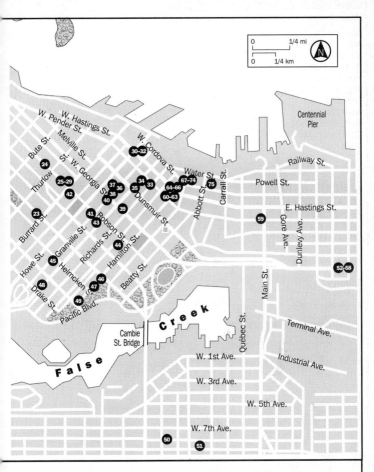

tlife

By and large,
Vancouver rolls
up the sidewalks
at a fairly early
hour. The good
news is, you won't
need to spend

a fortune on cab fares. The city's nightlife is fairly concentrated in one part of town, making club—or brew pub—hopping a simple matter of strolling—or staggering—from place to place. **Yaletown** and **Gastown** are both focal points of action, with Yaletown having the edge in terms of attitude. The **West Side** has a smattering of places whose proximity to home attracts locals and university types. Pumped by the musicians, artists, and writers who live nearby, **Commercial Drive**, on the East Side, is one of the liveliest streets in the city. The *Georgia Straight* (www.straight.com), Vancouver's leading entertainment weekly newspaper, has the most comprehensive listing of what's on in the clubs and pubs. Otherwise, take a gander at downtown lampposts and scaffolding, where emerging bands often staple their posters. Some types of music are notably lacking. Forget its geographic location, Vancouver is not a heavy country 'n' western town. For cowboy music, you'll need to go way, way east of the city limits. And pity the poor club owners of Vancouver, where a fragmented music scene and a multicultural audience mean being all things to all people if you want to make a buck. Soul, blues, Latin, world beat—some places switch identities every night.

Liquor and Smoking Laws

Up until very recently, British Columbian liquor laws were so archaic that they caused visitors from outside the country to snicker in their beers—if they were lucky enough to come across one. Now you may actually be able to ask for a glass of Cabernet in a restaurant without ordering a meal or at least a token plate of nachos just to appease the authorities. That's because, thanks to a recent new law, certain restaurants with a full liquor license—which includes the right to serve hard liquor—can now set aside 10 percent of their seats (but no more than 20) for those who wish to drink without ordering food; previously they couldn't. However, many other restaurants only have a beer/wine/hard cider/wine cooler license—which doesn't include, say, martinis—and in those places you must order at least one food item no matter *where* you sit. You can't buy, or drink, alcohol unless you're 19 years of age or over. Carry photo ID with you in case you're asked for it (as you most likely will be if you are in your 20s, or at least look like you are). Vancouver may have smokin' music, but lighting up is verboten. And that means EVERYWHERE. As of the beginning of the 21st century, restaurants, bars, lounges, diners, cafes—all are totally nonsmoking. Smoking "rooms" are permissible, but go inside and you won't be able to get food or booze served to you. It's also okay to light up outdoors, so expect to see a deluge of patios opening up. A quick word on drinking and driving: Don't. Vancouver police crack down periodically with roadblocks and Breathalyzer vans, and woe betide you if you're over the limit. What people do here is what they do in most other places: They either appoint a designated driver among the group who takes his or her role very seriously while everyone else gets sloshed, drink in the neighborhood so they can totter home on foot, or take a cab.

The Lowdown

The club scene... Completely fluid. Hard to pin down. Will probably have changed by the time you read this. At time of writing, the hottest place around is **Sonar**—a British 'zine included it on a global roundup of great dance clubs. The crowd is twentysomethings eager to dance up a storm to electronic, house, jungle, and drum 'n' bass music. Look the part, and they may pick you out of the lineup. Wednesdays, Fridays, and Saturdays are the tough nights to get in. Even though it's been around forever, **Richard's on Richards**—don't ever call it that, you hick, it's "Dick's on Dicks"—still sizzles, assuming you can handle the attitude. Again, you've got to look right to make the cut. It helps to be on the make once you get inside. Everyone's dressed to the hilt, and everyone's cruisin'. Local bands and some international groups (though not mega names) make up the music, which is enhanced by an ace sound and lighting system. Get set for big lineups on the weekends. Upstairs offers an eagle-eye view of a floor big enough to accommodate movie crews—a scene in Steve Martin's *Roxanne* was shot here. **The Starfish Room**'s live bands are big with the young indie-rock crowd. For more of the same kind of rock from entry-level bands (they play here before they graduate to The Starfish Room), head for **The Brickyard** and join an eclectic audience made up of mega-numbers of bike couriers, musicians with the night off, downtown artists, and other assorted slacker types. **Chameleon Urban Lounge** draws in a similar crowd to Sonar's (both are run by the same people)—a lot of folks go to both. This cave-like space, long on deep colors, velvet, and candles, more than holds it own, as does the music. Latin jazz, house, drum 'n' bass—it's a typical Vancouver buffet played mostly by DJs. **Caprice Nightclub** is a dance club that puts industrial dance first and foremost, but also features old-school, '70s and '80s hits; it replaces Luv-A-Fair, a beloved club that saw some of the most cutting-edge acts of the '80s and '90s. Check to see what's happening which night. Black gothic is the fashion, but the crowd also includes frat boys who think they're cool. Hip-hop and house are the preference of **The Purple Onion Cabaret**, but there's Latin and jazz too. The decent-sized dance room draws the twentysomethings, while cushy sofas in the lounge appeal more to the older crowd. On the wrong side of town, **The Columbia** used to be a seedy dive where old fogies went for cheap beer—a makeover has made it more of a draw. These days, heavy metal fans go for the same reason—but more for the very loud music played by bands you've never heard of. It's a crap shoot: Some nights you may luck into a group that's on its way up. Other nights, the kindest thing you can say is they're on the low end of average. Back downtown, funky **DV8** combines live or DJ music with decent food, but skips any attitude. Mind you, the purple and gray decor's pretty cool. Not far from Dick's on Dicks, **Wett Bar** brings in a crowd from the action on Richards Street: The kind of snowboarder and skater types you might see at Sonar, but younger. It's the kind of place where people come up and talk to you...whether you want them to or not. A honkin' huge space (which can sometimes mess with the sound), **The Rage** hosts shows on Fridays and Saturdays only—Flashback Fridays, and top-40 dance—with a flying saucer special effect that dates back to the place's glory days during Expo '86. Gridlock at the door isn't uncommon, but the place is so big, you'll get in eventually.

Trending upward... You'll no doubt want to make the scene at some point to impress your spouse or traveling companion. **Richard's on Richards** is the ultimate trendoid spot, but there are better choices if you actually want to hear each other. **Cloud 9 Lounge** is the place to begin or end your night on the town on a high—literally. The bar sits 42 stories above the city, affording great views of mountains, islands, and city lights if it's not raining. Don't fancy the view? Just sit tight; the bar revolves gently, doing a full 360. The **Alibi Room** is one of the coolest, attracting a Holly-wood and Hollywood-wannabe crowd. Dine upstairs in the quiet restaurant, or slink downstairs to the equally subdued lounge, where you can browse through a library of scripts that actually got made into films; the crowd here is full of hopefuls, and you might even catch a bona fide star nursing a drink incognito.

All that jazz... The plaintive wail of a sax or a foot-stompin' New Orleans-style jam have enough fans in Vancouver to justify a dedicated Jazz Hotline (tel 604/872-5200) that will tell you what's happening in clubs tonight. The **Hot Jazz Society** on Main Street draws what's called an "older" crowd, but it's still pretty casual, and if you want to hear horns that'll make your hair curl, this place is hard to beat. Bus along Broadway to the **Jazz Cellar Café** and, depending on the night, you can join Kits enthusiasts taking in fusion, funk, or classic jazz. High point of the year is the Vancouver Jazz Festival held in June, which presents all kinds of jazz at various clubs and theaters around town, not to mention free shows at parks and shopping malls, and (non-free) perfor-mances by the likes of Herbie Hancock and the Pat Metheny Trio. Any time of year, if jazz diva Diana Krall (who hails from Vancouver Island) is in town, pull every string you can to score tickets.

On a global note... Followers of flamenco's captivating rhythms or evocative Romany music find both on var-ious nights at the **Kino Café**, an unassuming little spot on Cambie Street. Picture a Greenwich Village coffee bar in the 1950s—that's the kind of ambience it has. On Commercial Drive, **The Latin Quarter** can set you up with a platter of tapas while you take in some cha-cha or other Latin sounds. Romanian, Middle Eastern, and sometimes flamenco musicians also show up. The crowd is real, the atmosphere thankfully unpretentious, and though foot-tapping is encouraged, there's unfortunately no room to dance.

Having a gay old time, wish you were here...

The West End has the most heavily concentrated gay population in the city. Ergo, that's where you'll find the most gay and lesbian nightspots. The city's drag queens are utterly gorgeous. Cruise around long enough, and you're likely to see Barbara, Dolly, or Marlene, wigged to here, eyelashed to there, and zipped into form-fitting dresses to die for. Sizzlin' go-go dancers and a weekly drag show are part of the fun at **The Odyssey** where style is everything. You don't have to dress up, but you may get looks if you don't. DJ Jules provides commercial house tunes. The scene changes fast. Your best bet is a gander at *X-tra West*, the local gay bi-weekly. Copies are free at coffee shops, hipper stores, and public libraries.

Clubs with a peel...

Vavoom...vavoom. Take it all off, baby, and they do in Vancouver, right down to their birthday skins, odd in a city that's in many ways so puritanical. Not all strip clubs are dimly lit stages with some poor chick from the sticks giving her all while middle-aged men drool into their beer. At **Number Five Orange**, you're just as likely to run into a couple in from the 'burbs as a guy down from the far north who's been strip-mining, hasn't seen a woman in months, and now sits thoughtfully chugging down beers. Decor is nothing to write home about, but the audience isn't notable for its Martha Stewart quotient anyway. Long before Yaletown was cool, **The Penthouse Cabaret** was a byword for raciness. Vancouver's shadiest characters have all been here one time or another in the past. These days, its red velvet walls are the backdrop to performers with names like Meryl Stripp.

Mean martinis...

Even if they cut their teeth on beer or wine coolers, Vancouverites have taken effortlessly to the retro drink of the day, the martini. The first to bring 'em back to popularity was **Delilah's** in the West End, and the silver bullets served here will quickly make you legless. The crowd, largely gay and sometimes in drag, certainly has more wit and panache than the vapid types posing at the uptown bars. For drinks with a gruesome touch, settle into **The Crime Lab**, at the west end of Pender Street. Strictly speaking, it's a restaurant, but at the downstairs bar the upbeat staff will happily pour you a "D.O.A." or a "Rigor Mortis" more than capable of doing away with your appetite. In between scanning the luxe-y room for celebs, you can knock back an exceptionally svelte version of a martini, as you settle back in the big comfortable chairs at **Gerard Lounge**, downtown. A block north, the Hotel Vancouver's convivial bar staff in **900 West** also make a mean martini in appropriately elegant surroundings. The bar provides a ringside seat for people-watching from where, depending on how the evening progresses, you can tumble off into the lounge or the restaurant.

Hang with your peers... Ad agency art directors and brokers who've made a killing settle in downtown at **Joe Fortes**, as they elbow each other around the big U-shaped bars, play "my portfolio's bigger than yours," and eyeball the women descending (slowly) the huge staircase from the powder room. Movie-biz wannabes cut straight to the chase at the **Alibi Room** (see above) in Gastown, either settling in with the script of *Star Wars*, *Fargo*, or anything else from the script library—they even have *Ace Ventura: Pet Detective*—or bringing their own script hot from the PC to one of the monthly open mike readings and praying a producer will be in the audience. At **Bukowski's**, a high-energy eatery on Commercial Drive, the literati and other creative types congregate for poetry readings or live bands. The older and more well-heeled crowd has found their newest haunt with the recent opening of the **Gotham Cocktail Bar** downtown. Sit at the bar, light up a stogie, order up a well-aged scotch, and discuss the declining state of the younger generation. Despite its name, you won't run into wall-to-wall Aussies at **The Anza Club** just off Main Street; it's more a social club these days. Most downtown clubs cater to those who wore diapers in the 1970s. If rubbing shoulders with those of barely legal drinking age is your idea of a good time, go ahead. Otherwise you'll feel more at home at **BaBalu Tapas**

Lounge. On Sundays, big band sounds rule, and dance lessons are included. Otherwise it's funk, soul, a bit of everything, plus house band Smokin' Section, which plays funk, soul, jazz, swing, Latin—just about anything except top-40. Musicians in town, even famous ones fresh from nearby concert gigs, are known to find their way to the downtown **Railway Club** to hang out. Sign the guestbook, and you're in the door of this skinny, second-floor, downtown club.

Set 'em up, Joe... Vancouver just doesn't have the kind of bars you find in New York or Chicago, where—assuming you're in the mood—the barman deals out wisecracks as he pours you a shot, and the walls are soaked in a million memories. Fed up with the rain, Vancouverites pretend they're in Spain at downtown **La Bodega**. Lower-echelon movie types, radio producers, those who did the European thing in the '70s and want to recapture the feeling—it's a mixed crowd, but a friendly one, especially after a jug or two of sangria. If you just want a quiet drink and a staggering view of English Bay—especially at sunset—settle into the undersung bar at the **Sylvia Hotel**. Glamorous it's not, nor is the crowd—part tourists, part unattitudinal locals—but you can't beat the vista. The most glamorous bar in town is at the Wedgewood Hotel in its **Bacchus** lounge. Fresh from the law firms hereabouts, groomed-to-the-teeth women and their consorts discuss meaningful problems, such as whether to head down to Maui or Palm Springs this weekend.

Brewed on the premises... Well, honestly! You would think that, given its British heritage, Vancouver would be alive with quaint little pubs full of wizened expats crowded around the piano for a singalong. Sorry, they're all home watching reruns of *Fawlty Towers*. The liveliest spots are the microbreweries that have taken the town by storm (although Vancouver still has nowhere near as many as Portland, the Pacific Northwest mecca for suds-lovers). **Sailor Hagar's** pulled its first homegrown brew in 1986, and it's well worth boarding the SeaBus to North Vancouver to taste its big seller, the honey pilsener. There's a slew of others worth trying too—another reason to rely on public transit. If shouting yourself hoarse at the game has left you with a raging thirst, **Dix Barbecue & Brewery** is right across from BC Place Stadium. Shoot some pool, gnaw on some BBQ ribs, or sip your beer while you sit at the bar or at a counter that actually looks in on the heart of the action. High ceilings, vintage photos of historical Vancouver breweries, and mighty beams make it feel like it's been around forever. In fact, it's one of the newer contenders on the city's microbrewery scene, and it's still reasonably quiet, except on game nights, when it's jock city. The beer's good too. Owned by the same conglomerate, the big, rambling **Yaletown Brewing Company**, five minutes away, has been around long enough to make it the place to hang out for Yaletowners who work, shop, or live in the trendily converted former warehouses. The city's first brewpub, the large **Steamworks**, has a fireplace, comfy leather chairs and sofas, and a great harbor view. All are lures to the downtown office crowd who treat it like their "local." If you're new to the game, sink a Lions Gate Lager or Coal Porter (named after Coal Harbour). Huge windows framing a False Creek view straight off a postcard make up the "decor" at **The Creek Restaurant, Brewery, and Bar.** It's a chic, happening restaurant, brewery, and bar on Granville Island where you can join in the verbal one-upmanship at the long bar or—a far nicer way to spend the time—sip an UpYourHeiny Pils and stare out at the water.

Cheek to cheek... Vancouver old-timers speak fondly of the days when you could go for dinner and dancing at The Roof, the restaurant at the summit of the Hotel Vancouver. That's history. Now, places are few and far between for those who want to go dance the old-fashioned way, holding on to their partner. The Italians never lost their talent for romance, and "That's Amore" often floats across the air at a couple of places on Commercial Drive on the east side. **Al Ritrovo** is in a dicey area down near the tracks, but you'd never know it once you're inside on a weekend night—after stoking up on pasta, well-padded Italian poppas steer well-corseted mommas around the dance floor. Decor is of the moonlight-in-Venice variety, and you'd swear the band has been there since the day they opened the doors, but if you want to fox-trot or samba your way round the room it's a hard place to beat. Even if the only Italian you speak is fluent cappuccino, you'll still be welcome. The younger crowd makes its way to **Federico's Supper Club** on Commercial Drive, where two generations of the Fuoco family play live ballroom, Latin, old standards, and whatever else the diners want.

The black leather crowd... We're not talking about the bikers who hang out with their Harleys at the Starbucks on Robson Street. No, these are places for those who know that "B" and "D" stands for "bondage" and "discipline," and who get thrills from playing Slaves and Masters and wearing leather or rubber from head to toe. Drop by one of the fetish stores [see Shopping] and you can pick up flyers advertising upcoming events. Formerly known as the Betty Page Club (until Betty put her foot down), the **Body Perve Social Club** holds monthly events in Gastown at The Lotus where you can socialize, take in some music, or—once in a while—see somebody get spanked. (As a disclaimer, I'd like to add that I don't have direct knowledge of these activities. Honest.)

Luck o' the Irish (and English)... Vancouver's Anglo heritage means it's blessed with a clutch of British and Irish pubs. Wearers of the green need not fret: Their country is well represented. The **Blarney Stone** and the **Irish Heather Pub,** nearly across the street from each other on Gastown's Carrall Street, both offer a party atmosphere and plenty of shamrockin' music. The Heather is probably the more authentic of the pair, with great pub grub to match; the Stone's a little louder, with better live music on the weekends. Both could have been plucked straight off the Emerald Isle.

Victorian nights... Victoria isn't exactly the most exciting town on the planet; in fact, it's rather buttoned-down. Still, with a little hunting you can find some pretty cool spots. Inside the big Fairmont Empress Hotel [see Dining], the **Bengal Lounge** is a must-see slice of the Empire from back in those days when the sun never set on it. You half expect two white-clad Indian attendants to begin fanning as you drink a stiff one, but the crowd isn't too snooty for comfort. If you're pressed for time, you could do a lot worse than to head for the nearby Strathcona Hotel [see Accommodations]: It's possible to hit a half-dozen different theme bars here, no cab rides or designated drivers required. **Big Bad John's,** one of them, is a much different experience from the Bengal: It's almost a dive, to put it politely. Bar fights aren't unheard of, so don't go shooting off your mouth *too* loudly. Finally, if you care more about the beer than anything else, make tracks for two brew pubs near the Johnson Bridge. **Swans Brew Pub** and **Spinnakers Brewpub** both serve equally delicious microbrewed ales in renovated surroundings. Why fight about which one's better? Hit both; they're within a mile of each other.

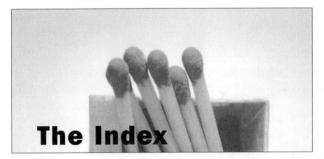

The Index

club these days. Live bands run the gamut.... *Tel 604/876-7128. 3 W. 8th Ave. Buses 3, 8. Closed Sun. $20 membership. Cover $5–10.* **(see p. 169)**

BaBalu Tapas Lounge. A few gray hairs, even a wrinkle or two won't earn you snotty looks at this uptown spot for over-30s. Swing nights Sundays.... *Tel 604/605-4343. 654 Nelson St. (in the Comfort Inn). Buses 4, 5, 6, 7, 8, 10. Cover varies.* **(see p. 169)**

Bacchus. Among the city's most elegant place to have a drink. In the Wedgewood Hotel across from the Law Courts, so clientele includes many already called to the bar.... *Tel 604/608-5319. 845 Hornby St. Bus 5.*
(see p. 170)

Blarney Stone. Irish pub featuring great live music on weekends and a party-hearty crowd.... *Tel 604/687-4322. 216 Carrall St. Buses 1, 4, 7.* **(see p. 172)**

Body Perve Social Club. Formerly the Betty Page Club until Betty put her foot down. The leather-and-handcuffs set gets together on the last Saturday of every month.... *Tel 604/688-4947. 455 Abbott St. Buses 1, 50.*
(see p. 172)

The Brickyard. Gastown hangout for high-decibel rock and alternative, usually by local bands. DJ plays metal Sundays to Tuesdays.... *Tel 604/685-3922. 315 Carrall St. Buses 1, 50. Cover $5–6.* **(see p. 165)**

Bukowski's. High-energy eatery where literati and other Commercial Drive types congregate for poetry readings or live bands.... *Tel 604/253-4770. 1447 Commercial Dr. Bus 20. No cover.* **(see p. 169)**

Caprice Nightclub. Rockin' dance club for Brit pop, indie rock, house, and more.... *Tel 604/685-3288. 1275 Seymour St. Buses 4, 6, 7, 8, 10. Cover varies.*
(see p. 166)

Chameleon Urban Lounge. Trendy uptown hangout for Latin jazz, house, and other genres, played mostly by DJs.... *Tel*

604/669-0806. 801 West Georgia St. Granville Station SkyTrain. Cover varies. **(see p. 165)**

Cloud 9 Lounge. Central high-rise bar takes you high above Robson Street to look down upon the masses; the drink prices match the altitude.... *Tel 604/687-0511. 1400 Robson St. Bus 5.* **(see p. 167)**

The Columbia. For aficionados of heavy metal and cheap beer.... *Tel 604/683-3757. 303 Columbia St. Bus 8. Cover $3–5 Wed–Sat.* **(see p. 166)**

The Creek Restaurant, Brewery, & Bar. Watch slick young 30-somethings complain about their high-paying jobs at this humming Granville Island spot. Better yet, sip an UpYourHeiny Pils and stare at the water.... *Tel 604/685-7070. 1253 Johnston St. Bus 50.*

(see p. 171)

The Crime Lab. Unpretentious little place down near Coal Harbour. Commendable menu, and martinis with suitably gruesome names. Anyone for a "D.O.A."?... *Tel 604/732-7463. 1280 W. Pender St. Take a cab.*

(see p. 169)

Delilah's. "Love your dress, dah-ling!" Campy crowd makes for lotsa fun, especially when "les girls" are around. Prix-fixe dinners, and standard-setting martinis.... *Tel 604/687-3424. 1789 Comox St. Bus 6.* **(see p. 168)**

Dix Barbecue & Brewery. Cavernous brew pub and BBQ joint across from BC Place Stadium. Best when it's crowded.... *Tel 604/682-2739. 871 Beatty St. Stadium Station SkyTrain.* **(see p. 171)**

DV8. Funky, cool, and no-attitude hangout for younger crowd. Eat sushi, quesadillas, and burgers while you listen to live indie bands, or new CDs and upcoming releases.... *Tel 604/682-4388. 515 Davie St. Bus 6.* **(see p. 166)**

Federico's Supper Club. If you're Italian, or you just wanna dance and chow down on some pasta, this new-ish supper

NIGHTLIFE | THE INDEX

club fills the bill.... *Tel 604/251-3473. 1728 Commercial Dr. Bus 20.* **(see p. 172)**

Gerard Lounge. Comfortably wealthy clientele, often seasoned with in-town movie stars. Nice place to sip a martini.... *Tel 604/682-5511. 845 Burrard St. Bus 22.*
(see p. 169)

Gotham Cocktail Bar. Sip some scotch and puff on a stogie at this classy new hang downtown off Granville Street.... *Tel 604/605-8282. 615 Seymour St. Take any downtown bus to Granville St.* **(see p. 169)**

Hot Jazz Society. Traditional Dixieland and mainstream have been its drawing card for years.... *Tel 604/873-4131. 2120 Main St. Cover varies.* **(see p. 167)**

Irish Heather Pub. Extremely authentic pub, right down to the whiskey and stout.... *Tel 604/668-9779. 217 Carrall St. Buses 1, 4, 7.* **(see p. 172)**

Jazz Cellar Café. Jazz selection ranges from fusion and funk to classic jazz at this high-energy West Side spot.... *Tel 604/738-1959. 3611 West Broadway. Bus 9. Cover varies.* **(see p. 167)**

Joe Fortes. The Rolex crowd hangs here, hoping to connect as they sip martinis at the U-shaped bar in this New York–style fish restaurant.... *Tel 604/669-1940. 777 Thurlow St. Bus 5.* **(see p. 169)**

Kino Café. Unpretentious, friendly spot showcases flamenco on Thursdays, Fridays, and Sundays; Romany music on Monday.... *Tel 604/875-1998. 3456 Cambie St. Bus 15. $10 minimum on show nights.* **(see p. 167)**

La Bodega. Friendly bar in a downtown Spanish restaurant is a good place to escape the rain.... *Tel 604/684-8814. 1277 Howe St. Buses 1, 2.* **(see p. 170)**

The Latin Quarter. Live Latin, flamenco, and sometimes Middle European or Middle Eastern music plays while you eat tapas.... *Tel 604/251-1144. 1305 Commercial Dr. Bus 20.* **(see p. 167)**

900 West. Sophisticated bar and lounge sections of The Fairmont Hotel Vancouver's flagship eatery makes great martini escape from downtown.... *Tel 604/669-9378. 900 W. Georgia St. Bus 22.* **(see p. 169)**

Number Five Orange. Guys and girls watch girls take their clothes off. One of the less sleazy strip joints around.... *Tel 604/687-3483. 203 Main St. Buses 4, 7. Cover $3 until midnight.* **(see p. 168)**

The Odyssey. Stylin' gay hangout features go-go dancers and weekly drag shows.... *Tel 604/689-5256. 1251 Howe St. Buses 4, 6, 7, 8, 10. Cover varies.* **(see p. 168)**

The Penthouse Cabaret. If walls could tell tales, you'd run screaming from this ages-old strip joint.... *Tel 604/683-2111. 1019 Seymour St. Buses 4, 6, 7, 8, 10.* **(see p. 168)**

The Purple Onion Cabaret. The lounge has live bands, funk, acid jazz, classic jazz—it varies. The nightclub's DJ spins top-40 and, Saturday nights, hip-hop and R&B.... *Tel 604/602-9442. 15 Water St. Buses 1, 50. Cover $3–7.* **(see p. 166)**

The Rage. Live bands, assorted music, in humongously huge space.... *Tel 604/685-5585. 750 Pacific Blvd. Buses 1, 2. Cover varies.* **(see p. 166)**

Railway Club. Off-duty local (and sometimes national) bands drop in here. A club, but no problem joining.... *Tel 604/681-1625. 579 Dunsmuir St. Granville Station SkyTrain.* **(see p. 170)**

Richard's on Richards. Mega-night club is still one of the hottest in town. Have style, be beautiful, and the doorman may wave you in past that lengthy line.... *Tel 604/687-6794. 1036 Richards St. Buses 4, 6, 7, 8, 10. Cover varies.* **(see pp. 165, 166)**

Sailor Hagar's. Way before brewpubs became the in thing (like the mid-1980s) this North Vancouver fave was packing them in. Call for a honey pilsener, and you'll fit right in.... *Tel 604/984-2567. 221 W. 1st St., North Vancouver. SeaBus.* **(see p. 170)**

Sonar. Currently the hottest spot in town, this dance club plays hip-hop, house, soul, drum 'n' bass music.... *Tel 604/683-6695. 66 Water St. Buses 1, 50. Days open vary. Cover varies.* **(see p. 165)**

The Starfish Room. Live rock place is a favorite with bike couriers and downtown artist types.... *Tel 604/682-4171. 1055 Homer St. Bus 15. Closed Sun–Tues. Cover varies.* **(see p. 165)**

Steamworks. Gastown brew pub was the city's first. Downtown after-work crowd considers it their "local." Seasonal beers. In summer, you can sink a framboise made from local raspberries.... *Tel 604/689-2739. 375 Water St. Buses 1, 50.* **(see p. 171)**

Sylvia Hotel. Old-fashioned hotel bar is nothing to write home about, but it does offer sublime views, especially over a gin at sunset.... *Tel 604/681-9321. 1154 Gilford St. Bus 6.* **(see p. 170)**

Wett Bar. Assorted music, reggae, hip-hop, underground jazz, major dancing.... *Tel 604/662-7707. 1320 Richards St. Buses 1, 2. Cover varies.* **(see p. 166)**

Yaletown Brewing Company. Happening brewpub in groovy Yaletown. Jeans or designer duds—it's your call.... *Tel 604/688-0064. 1111 Mainland St. Bus 15.* **(see p. 171)**

VANCOUVER ISLAND NIGHTLIFE

Bengal Lounge. One of several eating and drinking rooms inside the grand Fairmont Empress Hotel, an enclave of Jolly Old England.... *Tel 250/384-8111. 721 Government St.* **(see p. 172)**

Big Bad John's. Completely unpretentious place where the music cranks and there are no airs. Not the place to go spouting leftish philosophy.... *Tel 250/383-7137. 919 Douglas St.* **(see p. 173)**

Spinnakers Brewpub. Canada's original brewpub, and still

NIGHTLIFE | THE INDEX

one of its best.... *Tel 250/386-2739. 308 Catherine St.*
(see p. 173)

Swans Brew Pub. Terrific pub serving products of the Butterfield Brewery in the basement. The adjacent jazz club keeps things hopping.... *Tel 250/361-3310. 560 Pandora St.* **(see p. 173)**

enterta

7

inment

Nobody in Vancouver sits at home anymore, wistfully moping over *The New York Times* and complaining that there's nothing to do around here. Not in a city that has its own symphony, opera, and international fame for contemporary dance. The three major cultural areas are all within the city limits: Two are downtown, close to most of the major hotels; the other's on the East Side, a 10-minute cab ride away. Four blocks south of the downtown shopping hub, side by side on Hamilton Street are the glass-fronted **Queen Elizabeth Theatre** and the **Vancouver Playhouse**, a quarter of the size; both are part of the same complex built in the 1950s. That behemoth building across Georgia Street on Homer Street is the Ford Centre for the Performing Arts, forced to close its doors due to its owner's financial problems—but one can always hope it will reopen.

For drama of the less cerebral variety, two of Vancouver's major sports facilities are just to the southeast. **General Motors Place** (everyone calls it GM Place) is where the local professional hockey team hangs its jock straps. Topped with what looks like meringue, **B.C. Place Stadium** is a massive arena that echoes, at various times, with football games, high-decibel concerts, and exhibitions. Be sure you know which gate you need (it's printed on your ticket)—on a rainy night, the walk around the stadium gates can be long and chilly.

Back in the days of vaudeville, Granville Street south of Georgia Street was riotous, neon-lit, and rife with live theater. Now, amid its panhandlers, runaways, porn shops, and creeping gentrification, all that remains are the intimate **The Vogue** and the opulent, 2,800-seat **Orpheum Theatre** which, in its heyday, hosted Bob Hope, Charlie Chaplin, and the Canadian premiere of *Gone With the Wind*.

Events on the East Side mirror the tastes of the hip young artists, musicians, and writers whose day-to-day epicenter is Commercial Drive. Don't expect to see anything "safe" on the stage of the **Vancouver East Cultural Centre** (known in these parts as "The Cultch") or at the small theater in the **Havana** restaurant.

Never a city to do things by halves, Vancouver has more festivals than you can shake a stick at, giving locals a chance to binge on comedy, movies, books, and folk music. What this city doesn't do, oddly enough, is fall hard for the charms of touring blockbuster musicals. More than one impresario has had to close a run early because folks in this 'burg just aren't keen on recycled Broadway.

Box-office stars like The Rolling Stones, Bob Dylan, and

Eric Clapton usually include Vancouver in the L.A.–San Francisco–Seattle loop of a North American tour, and the venue is invariably B.C. Place Stadium. It seats thousands, so chances of getting a ticket are usually promising, but you may end up squinting down at a matchstick-size figure. But don't despair—even being in the audience here may be your ticket to stardom. One of the legends oft told around here is how boda-cious *Baywatch* babe Pamela Anderson Lee was first spotted when a bigger-than-life shot of her in the bleachers appeared on the giant screen.

The Lowdown

What's on where... Concerts, events, plays, and other ways to have fun are covered in the city's two daily papers. Devoted exclusively to entertainment, the *Vancouver Sun*'s "Cue" section is well worth a look. Arguably containing the most comprehensive listings, the *Georgia Straight*, an opinionated news and entertainment weekly, is available free at movie theaters, coffee shops, and street stands. *Vancouver* magazine includes a calendar in each issue. The **Talking Super Pages** (tel 604/299-9000) link you with recorded announcements from certain major cultural and sports organizations, although the commercials you're forced to listen to first are a major pain. Press menu option 6 to get listings. Of course, not all events make the mainstream media. More offbeat concerts and emerging bands often rely on a guy with a backpack full of posters, a staple gun, and sticky tape to publicize their next gig on empty store windows and lampposts.

Getting your mitts on tickets... The one-call-does-it-all is usually to **TicketMaster** (tel 604/280-4444), which adds a $3 to $6 service charge to your ticket price. The front section of the local Yellow Pages displays floorplans of local theaters and sports arenas. Seat numbers are so microscopic as to be fairly useless, but they do give you a rough idea of where you'll be sitting. Subscribers to the Vancouver Opera or Symphony are quick to snap up their usual seats at the front of the balcony. Otherwise Vancou-verites are an odd lot, usually waiting until the last minute to buy their tickets. If that major rock show is all sold out, hang in there—promoters sometimes release blocks of tickets at the last moment. Scalpers? Sure. They run classified ads in the dailies and lurk around concert venues. Whether you pay their price, and run the risk of getting a lousy seat for your money, is up to you.

The grand old lady of Granville Street... Walk into the ornately decorated **Orpheum Theatre** and you really feel you're out on the town. If walls could talk.... Built in 1927 as a "picture palace," this was the place that drew lineups to see Sophie Tucker, Fanny Brice, and Jack Benny, or to take in the new Astaire and Rogers flick. Spanish Renaissance is the official term for the architecture used here, which combines influences from Seville, Granada, Morocco, and Spain. Grand staircases, scores of arches, everything gilded and plastered to within an inch of its life—the Orpheum even boasts an original Wurlitzer organ. It's still raised up once in a while as an accompaniment to a classic silent movie. Mostly, the chandeliers shine down on the **Vancouver Symphony Orchestra**. Even if you can't make one of its concerts, you can still get an inside glimpse of the **Orpheum Theatre** in its glory days on one of the guided group tours led by theatrical old-timers.

Music, maestro please... Under the leadership of Music Director Bramwell Tovey (who took over the baton in September 2000), the **Vancouver Symphony Orchestra** has evolved into a tour de force. This venerable orchestra is remarkably young at heart. All the better to lure in new generations of music lovers, right? Snooty it ain't. While concerts often put internationally known performers such as Yo-Yo Ma, Pinchas Zukerman, and Nana Mouskouri in the spotlight, programming ranges from the works of the great composers to pops concerts that get the audience rockin' with a tribute to Duke Ellington, or carnival music from Rio and "N'Awluns." And let's not forget the "Tea and Trumpets" series that precedes pleasantly schmaltzy Viennese waltzes or rousing marches with a cuppa, and cookies—if your ears don't tune into something you like, you're not trying. During the summer, the orchestra often puts on free outdoor shows in Deer Lake Park in Burnaby, or on Grouse Mountain. **Vancouver Recital Society** founder and director Leila Getz's claim to fame was bringing dishy Italian singer

Cecelia Bartolli to Vancouver long before she rocketed to fame. "Whatever Leila wants, Leila Getz" is the buzz in musical circles, and the Society shines among those of its kind across the country, says one local music critic. Its usual venues are the **Vancouver Playhouse, The Chan Shun Concert Hall at the Chan Centre for the Performing Arts,** and, once in a while, the **Orpheum Theatre.**

If it's curtains for you... Maybe it's Vancouver's British heritage, or its distance from other major centers, but either way, the city's live theater scene is jumping. The roomy, contemporary waterfront **Arts Club Theatre** presents mostly middlebrow modern productions, some Canadian and original works, and what one critic calls "dandy date shows" like *The Odd Couple.* While the theater's Granville Island location is pretty (and its lounge bar is a great place to hang out), the space can't hold a candle to the **Stanley Theatre** on South Granville Street. Once home to vaudeville, then a movie theater for a 60-year stint, it swerved dangerously close to a retail future before concerned locals intervened in 1992. A major makeover in 1930s art deco style has produced a gem of a home for lively musicals, Shakespeare, and other crowd-pleasers. You're more likely to walk out into the night feeling challenged if you attend a **Vancouver Playhouse** production where the broader (and some would say, more intelligent) repertory often reins in edgy plays hot from the hands of young local playwrights. Downtown on Granville Street, in what used to be "theater row," **The Vogue** is the venue of choice for individual performers and cabaret-style performances. Big-ticket road shows along the lines of *Showboat* and *Sunset Boulevard* used to touch down at the magnificent **Ford Centre for the Performing Arts**. Designated as the "star" of Vancouver's entertainment area, but sidelined by its producer's financial problems, its future is now up in the air. And those big splashy shows? We mostly don't get 'em.

Culture at the Cultch, and other offbeat places... The most risk-taking theater in town shows up at "the Cultch," the local term for the **Vancouver East Cultural Centre**. Mingle with a hip, arty crowd in a restored 1914 church close to Commercial Drive before trooping in to see gut-wrenching raw dramas, lesbian comedians, and provocative dance, not to mention music which ranges from local groups and touring world beat artists to big-name performers like Canadian folkie Ian Tyson. Likewise, you never know what to expect at the **Vancouver Fringe Festival** in September. Productions are unjuried so hopefuls can strut their stuff. While successes can lift you to your feet in a standing ovation, failures can make you cringe with sympathy for the poor wannabe up on stage. Festival events center around the Commercial Drive and Gastown areas. An unfamiliar name on the marquee doesn't necessarily mean you're wasting your money—some of the most dynamic productions around are the work of beginners. Achingly honest monologues, mind-blowing performance art, and unforgettable one-acts are just some of the hundreds of productions spaced over 10 dramatic days. Artistically fearless and fast making a name for itself, **The Electric Company** is a brand-new company of actors who have gone through Langara College's theater program. Productions are few, so check local listings. If the electricity is flowing, grab a ticket, and fasten your seatbelt. Among the best theatrical buys around is Langara College's **Studio 58** where professional directors and a large pool of talented young actors combine to create productions with a big-budget look. Over on Commercial Drive, **Havana** is a fave hangout for locals, and not just for its Cuban cuisine. As well as an art gallery, there's also a small theater behind the scenes. Typical shows include *The Thousand Year Itch*, an ongoing "soap"—"episodic variety theater" is the technical term—satire, music, movies, and *Chicks on Top* (a look at losing virginity, selling condoms, and the female take on *Godot*). Saying it's a varied program is like saying that Cuba makes decent cigars.

Aria ready for some opera?... Socialites in Armani, rumpled artists, and Mr. and Mrs. Jones in from the 'burbs all schmooze comfortably together at the **Vancouver Opera,** which presents a mainstage season of grand opera each year at the **Queen Elizabeth Theatre**. At its best, the company can raise the rafters—regulars still talk about hearing now-famed B.C. tenor Ben Heppner do *Peter Grimes*. Then again, there was that lusterless performance of *Carmen* one year.... Formed in the 1950s, the company has had its share of glory over the years. When Richard Bonynge helmed it as Artistic Director in the 1970s, several productions featured his missus, soprano Joan Sutherland. These days they don't have the cash to bring in the big names but manage to keep up the quality nevertheless—it's only the rare production that falls flat on its face. More recently, the company commissioned a full-length opera, *The Architect*, and introduced the works of Janáček to Vancouver audiences. Newbies who don't know their bass from their *Don Giovanni* arrive early at performances to bone up on music and story at free info sessions in the lobby. Held the Sunday before each opening night in the downtown branch of the local Chapters bookstore, an informal get-together known as Opera Café combines cappuccinos and comments from cast and production crew. Mention "The Three Tenors" in Vancouver and you'll get scowls. At a much hyped "see the New Year in" concert some years back, the trio sang lustily for awhile but then scampered offstage well before "Auld Lang Syne." The memory still rankles.

Dance pointers... Tutus and pliés are passé for Vancouver balletomanes. *Swan Lake* and the rest of the classics drift into town via touring companies, but aficionados consider the work of homegrown groups far more sizzling. **Ballet British Columbia** has had its ups and downs but current artistic director John Alleyne is putting the group on the map again. Breaking new ground, the group is famous for cutting edge movement, complex choreography, and fast but refined footwork. It's about as far from *The Nutcracker* as you can get—and **Kokoro Dance Theatre Society** is even farther. Bodies painted white, heads usually shaved, dancers wearing only loincloths, and sometimes appearing mother-naked—it ain't your typical troupe of droopy swans by a long shot. Usually seen at the **Firehall Arts Centre**, and led by cofounders Barbara Bourget and Jay Hirabayashi, this is Canada's only *butoh* (a Japanese dance form) company. Screams, erotic grunts, sobbing, laughter...audiences have come to expect anything and everything, from frenetic steps, to almost exruciatingly slow movement. For primal, earthy works, ballet fans keep their eyes on the **Karen Jamieson Dance Company,** which often taps the ancient legends of B.C.'s native peoples for inspiration.

Shakespeare in the sand... The raising of the big, striped, open-ended tent at Vanier Park is one of Vancouver's official signals of the start of summer. Under the canvas, you'll see Hamlet, Romeo, and Lady Macbeth strutting their hour upon the stage, led by actor and director Christopher Gaze. On a serene midsummer's eve, **Bard on the Beach** is a tough act to follow. Productions have tended to be the better-known plays. Added in 1999, a smaller studio stage is destined for lesser-known plays such as *Measure for Measure.* (Whether Gaze will expose gentle Vancouver audiences to the gory *Titus Andronicus* remains to be seen.) There's far less demanding fodder, intellectually speaking, at **Theatre Under the Stars** in Malkin Bowl at Stanley Park. Folks who complain they want to leave a show humming a tune are big fans. How could they not be when the cast (a mix of pros and amateurs) never stretches beyond *West Side Story, Kismet,* and other Broadway warhorses?

Music U'll appreciate... Envy the UBC music students who perform their first concerto or partita at **The Chan Shun Concert Hall at the Chan Centre for the Performing Arts.** The acoustics here are terrific, so great in fact that audiences compare the experience to being inside a musical instrument. The hall actually adjusts to the performers: A counterweighted acoustic canopy can be raised or lowered, and motorized velour banners drop from the ceiling to mask the walls. Mind you, the venue can be a mixed blessing. Every nuance will ring out with crystal clarity for the next Gould or Rubenstein—and so will every wrong note. In its first couple of years, the space has already snared a number of international names like tenor Ben Heppner, Pinchas Zukerman, and the Duke Ellington Orchestra. Right now, public performances take place only on weekends during the school year. The rest of the time, this marvelous space belongs to UBC students.

On the REALLY big screen... Awesome landscapes, large, often ferocious animals, wide skies, mighty oceans, and outer space. Well, given their screen size, you'd hardly expect either the **Omnimax** or **CN IMAX** theaters to show the sort of movies set at chess clubs or research labs. Oh sure, maybe your hometown has one or the other of these big-screen behemoths, but we'll bet Vancouver beats it for location. **Omnimax Theatre** is housed in the "golf ball" of Science World British Columbia at the end of False Creek, so you knock both off your "must-do" list on the same trip. Out where the cruiseboats tie up in Vancouver harbor sits the **CN IMAX** theater. It's ironic to watch tourists line up to eyeball faux wall-to-wall scenery when it's going on live, right behind them—but that's life in the movies.

Movie premieres, repertory, and the red-eye special... Despite the onward march of the dreaded multiplex, Vancouver still boasts a clutch of independent cinemas. A staple on fridge doors across the city is the schedule for the **Ridge Theatre,** whose program and prices more than justify the 15-minute bus-ride from downtown over to Kits. Most nights, the Ridge screens $5 double features such as a brace of Altman movies or an all-Canadian double bill. Other times, you can catch the local premiere of that Oscar-winning documentary or an obscure foreign flick. Renovated some years back, the 1950 theater nixed its antique sound system but kept the Crying Room, a small separate room with a glass wall overlooking the screen and piped-in sound, where parents can take little ones along without raising hackles. Oh yes, and that's real butter on the popcorn. Also in Kitsilano is the **Hollywood Theatre**. Founded in the 1930s and still in the hands of the same family, it has a pleasant time-warpy feel, right down to the art deco details and the balcony. Double features—$3.50 on Mondays, $5 the rest of the time—plus recent releases bring in students in droves, who stock up on date bars and coffee before hunkering down to catch Jean-Claude Van Damme taking out the bad guys for the umpteenth time. More sophisticated types can take their pick of the latest foreign and art flicks at **Fifth Avenue Cinemas** on Burrard Street. Technically only **Pacific Cinematheque** members can attend the showings of Hitchcock classics, obscure Iranian documentaries, and other offbeat screenings, but membership is just an on-the-spot $3 formality (which gives you 50 percent off your first admission: $7.50 for one flick, $8.50 for a double feature). Over at **The Blinding Light!!**, on the fringe of Gastown, you'll come upon programming that's way beyond the mainstream. Cycling movies, punk documentaries, an international horror festival all show up to the cheers, and jeers, of the hip, usually youthful, audience. Ardent movie buffs should time their vacation to coincide with late September's **Vancouver International Film Festival**. It may lack the cleavage and glitz of Cannes, but it's a super bet if you want to be the first on your block to see that obscure Transylvanian love story or the latest yuk-fest from the U.K. Tickets are reasonably priced, but be prepared to wait in line for the more popular screenings.

Did you hear the one about?... What's this about Canadians not being known for their sense of humor? Can you spell M-i-k-e M-y-e-r-s? J-o-h-n C-a-n-d-y? The high point of the stand-up year is the **Vancouver International Comedy Festival**, held every August on Granville Island. Some events call for tickets (which are reaonsably priced and easy to get) but many are free— although the free ones tend to appeal to a more juvenile idea of what's funny. For razor-sharp analyses of contemporary trends, get your yuks at a comedy club. Grin or groan through your beer at **Yuk-Yuk's Comedy Club** as the touring comedians of the week take their turns at the mike. Tuesday pits hard-core professionals against guys and gals who've always been told they should make a career of it. College types and those on the lower rungs of the corporate ladder make up most of the audience, but older folks won't feel out of place, and the jokes, while occasionally raw, rarely draw complaints. At press time, Yuk-Yuk's was shopping for a new venue; now that's not funny. Anyhow, call 'em for the latest details. Down at Granville Island, the award-winning **Vancouver TheatreSports League** goes mano-a-mano in classic improv at the Arts Club's new Revue Stage. When they're on form, you'll die laughing. If neither of these tickles your ribs, take a look through the local papers. Reading about B.C.'s wacko political scene should definitely crack you up.

Words, words, (and) blowin' in the wind... Given its name, it's hardly surprising that **Bukowski's** reels in writers and poets eager to test their words on a captive audience. **The Alibi Room** is another spot you can catch new talent, this time in the film-scripting department, as wannabes read aloud from their yet-to-be-filmed works.

Bookstores and the main branch of the Vancouver Public Library also periodically nab visiting authors for an hour or so of reading and book signing. A fixture on every bibliophile's calendar is the **Vancouver International Writers Festival**, held in October, which imports Canadian literary luminaries like Margaret Atwood and international names such as Isabel Allende, as well as more mainstream writers like P.D. James and Maeve Binchy, to read aloud from their works. Do they sell books too? You betcha—and sign them as well. From meaningful written words, it's a short hop to songs with a message. Held on a July weekend each year, the **Vancouver Folk Music Festival** is a night and two days of global music and singing. Long-haired hippie types in from the Gulf Islands, families with toddlers, old and young of all nationalities—it's a colorful slice of humanity like you wouldn't believe. Detractors call the event a throwback to the 1960s, but for the thousands who joyfully gather in Jericho Beach Park to bliss out, it's one of the highlights of the Vancouver summer. Traditionally, when the gates open, festival-goers race to be first to spread out their Mexican blankets or patchwork quilts up close at the main stage.

Farm animals, stomach churners, and galloping hooves... It's on again, off again, but right now the **Pacific National Exhibition** still has a home in the east of the city. Known (and loved) as the "P.N.E.," it's part agricultural show, part fairground that runs from late August through Labor Day—and it's been around forever. Don't make judgments about the lowbrowness of it all: Arm yourself with a dozen miniature donuts and go with the flow. Knives guaranteed to pare a tomato in slices you can read through, pennies bearing the Lord's Prayer, and "miracle" cleaners are all awaiting you—shop first, then take in the entertainment. The Demolition Derby is a perennial thrill for those who think cars destroying one another is cool. The dog show is appealing, as are the prize-winning chickens and newborn calves—and where else can you see award-winning pickled green beans, or *The Last Supper* in crochet? Take the bus on Hastings Street, heading east from downtown; parking is tight, and though locals stand their kids at street corners to offer a private arrangement, it's not worth the effort. Shrieks and carousel music will guide you into **Playland** (which merges seamlessly with the P.N.E.). The view from the top of the Ferris wheel is worth the fear, and the old-time roller coaster is notorious. Only the strong of stomach should ride on another contraption from hell called "the Mighty Mouse." Fans of the track come to this blocks-long area mid-April to mid-November for the action at the **Hastings Park RaceCourse** with its grandstand view of the mountain peaks. What the heck? Even if your nag limps in last, you can still take in the scenery. Bets as low as $2 mean you can have a fine time for a $20 bill. Play your cards right—in other words, go with the favorites—and you may even walk away with a profit. Major races from the United States and Hong Kong are also beamed in via the tube for long-distance wagering.

Let's play ball... One theory is that the balmy climate melts down their reflexes. Be that the reason or not, the city's pro sports teams sure haven't been making much of an impact in recent years. Even so, ever-optimistic Vancouverites keep on coming. The **Vancouver Canadians** baseball team was sold, but a new franchise with the same name took over right where the old one left off. Only difference is, this team plays at the AA level, a notch below the former AAA Canadians—but, hey, baseball is baseball, so check it out. The Canadians batter up at Nat Bailey Stadium, adjacent to Queen Elizabeth Park [see Diversions]. Lackluster performance also annually plagues the **Vancouver Canucks** NHL team—and this in a country famed for its hockey. Meanwhile, the **B.C. Lions** football games hardly raise a roar in B.C. Place Stadium, though aficionados still remember that Grey Cup championship in 1994.

It's curtains for Victoria... As with most of the action on Vancouver Island, the bulk of its concerts and plays take place in Victoria. Except for some tiny, hard-to-find pockets of life, the rest of the island is basically a cultural void. As you might expect, Victoria's a town that goes heavy on the Shakespeare-in-the-park and other classical genres. One of the best is the **Theatre Inconnu** (tel 250/360-0234), which keeps a low profile during most of the year, then explodes onto the scene with two big annual festivals celebrating Fringe (a mélange of comedy, music, and more) and (we warned ya) Shakespeare. **Intrepid Theatre Company** puts on a more regular series of performances throughout the calendar year. Either one's worth a look if something's playing. Classical music hounds will want to check out the program of the **Victoria Symphony,** which performs a full season of standards at a renovated downtown theater. (The season opener is normally a freebie on the harbor, so catch it if you can.) And, yeah, this town's got opera, too—not one company, but two! The biggie's the professional-caliber **Pacific Opera Victoria,** which can afford to try something daring once in a while. The more modest **Victoria Operatic Society** tends to fill its bill with many of the usual crowd-pleasers you've come to know and love—but they're a comparative bargain if you're on a budget. Not into all that stuffier stuff? This city's also nuts about jazz. The biggest event of the summer might be the boppin' **TerrifVic Jazz Party** each April—which is followed up by **JazzFest International.** Call Victoria's local Jazz Society (tel 250/388-4423) for the latest on other performances and goings-on. Folkies aren't forgotten, either; there's a smattering of folk performances in various bars and clubs around town, particularly of the Celtic music variety. In June, the **Folkfest** brings acts of wider acclaim to town. You can buy tickets for most of the events and performances listed above at individual box offices—or get them in one fell swoop at Victoria's waterfront visitor center (tel 250/953-2033 or 800/663-3883, 812 Wharf St.).

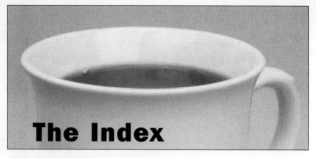

The Index

The Alibi Room. A-a-and action! While diners down tapas, hopefuls expose their movie scripts at monthly readings. Cut!.... *Tel 604/623-3383. 157 Alexander St. Buses 4, 7.* **(see p. 190)**

Arts Club Theatre. The main stage provides the theatrical equivalent of easy listening: Popular comedies, classics, and the occasional new play are the mainstays here. The Revue Stage features edgy live improv. Great bar.... *Tel 604/687-1644. 1585 Johnston St., Granville Island. Bus 8, then 51.* **(see p. 185)**

Ballet British Columbia. Artistic director John Alleyne has taken this Vancouver-based (but frequently touring) dance company to new heights after some low moments. Complex choreography, and refined footwork, is their forte. Few performances in their home town—catch them when you can (most likely at the Queen Elizabeth Theatre).... *Tel 604/732-5003.* **(see p. 187)**

Bard on the Beach. "But soft, what light through yonder window breaks?..." It's just your typical West Coast sunset, which, combined with live Shakespeare and real live mountains just beyond the stage, makes a beguiling combination on summer nights in Vanier Park. Look to the Mainstage tent for the bard's more crowd-pleasing works; the smaller Studio Stage presents lesser-known plays.... *Tel 604/739-0559 or 737-0625. 1101 W. Broadway. Bus 22. Mid-June–Sept.* **(see p. 188)**

The Blinding Light!! Alternative cinema from established and emerging video artists from around the globe. Art, cross-cultural, context-expanding, and none of it to be found at the multiplex.... *Tel 604/684-8288. 36 Powell St. Buses 4, 7. Closed Mon.* **(see p. 189)**

ENTERTAINMENT | THE INDEX

B.C. Lions. It last took the Grey Cup in 1994 but these days Vancouver's CFL football team has lost its edge. Do the fans care? Nah. Maybe it's the weird rules. Games in B.C. Place Stadium.... *Tel 604/930-5466 or 604/583-7747. June–Nov.* **(see p. 192)**

B.C. Place Stadium. The big marshmallow-in-bondage is home to the B.C. Lions, major rock concerts, the B.C. Sports Hall of Fame and Museum, and a plethora of exhibitions.... *Tel 669-2300. 777 Pacific Blvd. Stadium Station SkyTrain.* **(see p. 182)**

Bukowski's. Not nearly as grungy as it should be, given its inspiration. Cerebral decor, sensual global food, and spoken word on the East Side.... *Tel 604/253-4770. 1447 Commercial Dr. Bus 20.* **(see p. 190)**

The Chan Shun Concert Hall at the Chan Centre for the Performing Arts. Superb acoustics attract major names on the concert circuit to this recently opened UBC facility.... *Tel 604/822-9197. 6265 Crescent Rd. Buses 4, 10, or any to UBC bus loop. Performances mostly weekends-only during the academic year, also during the week throughout the summer.* **(see pp. 185, 188)**

CN IMAX. Five-story screen plus wraparound sound put you right in the desert, outer space, or wherever else is the "star".... *Tel 604/682-4629. Canada Place. Waterfront Station SkyTrain.* **(see pp. 188, 189)**

The Electric Company. Mind-expanding theater by an envelope-stretching troupe of young actors that performs all too rarely. A company to watch, say those in the know. Check entertainment publications such as the *Georgia Straight* for listings.... *Tel 604/253-4222. 1885 Venables St.* **(see p. 186)**

Fifth Avenue Cinemas. Five screens of foreign, art, and "talkie" flicks.... *Tel 604/734-7469. 2110 Burrard St. Bus 4.* **(see p. 189)**

Firehall Arts Centre. Broad assortment of rule-bending productions in a converted church on the East Side. Kokoro Dance usually performs here.... *Tel 604/689-0926. 280 E. Cordova St. Buses 3, 4, 7, 8.* **(see p. 187)**

Ford Centre for the Performing Arts. Nothing has played at this spectacular new facility since the owner's money problems forced its closure. Got a bar mitzvah coming up? Call them—they'll probably think about renting it to you.... *Tel 604/602-0616. 777 Homer St. Bus 5.*
(see p. 185)

General Motors Place. The Vancouver Canucks NHL hockey team plays here. So do Neil Diamond, Cher, rock concerts, and Disney ice shows.... *Tel 604/899-7889. 800 Griffiths Way. Stadium Station SkyTrain.*
(see p. 182)

Hastings Park RaceCourse. Here's where to drop money on the horses. If your horse is losing, at least you can still gaze at the mountain view.... *Tel 604/254-1631. McGill St. at Renfrew. Buses 4, 10, 16. Open mid-Apr–mid-Nov.* **(see p. 192)**

Havana. A neat little theater is holed up backstage at this Cuban restaurant. Independent groups present highly original productions. "Soaps," music, movies, whatever: It's the art focus of Commercial Drive. Check local media for events info, or swing by the restaurant yourself and pick up a fresh schedule.... *Tel 604/253-9119. 1212 Commercial Drive. Bus 20.*
(see pp. 182, 186)

Hollywood Theatre. You'll feel like you're caught in a time warp in this 1930s original. Recent releases mostly. What the big theaters charge for popcorn will get you a double feature here.... *Tel 604/738-3211. 3123 W. Broadway. Bus 9.* **(see p. 189)**

Karen Jamieson Dance Company. Ancient myths and traditions of B.C.'s native peoples are the inspiration behind many of their primal works.... *Tel 604/685-5699.*
(see p. 187)

Kokoro Dance Theatre Society. Crackling with originality, body paint, and states of undress, Canada's only *butoh* dance troupe usually appears at the Firehall Arts Centre.... *Tel 604/662-7441.* **(see p. 187)**

Omnimax Theatre. Totally awesome movies on the giant screen inside the golf ball known as Science World British Columbia.... *Tel 604/443-7443. Science World British Columbia. 1455 Quebec St. Main Street Station SkyTrain.*
(see pp. 188, 189)

Orpheum Theatre. A Vancouver landmark on what was once "theater row," the Orpheum was built in 1927 and is worth a tour even when the Vancouver Symphony Orchestra isn't playing.... *Tel 604/665-3050. Smithe at Seymour St. Buses 4, 6, 7, 8, 10.*
(see pp. 182, 184, 185)

Pacific Cinematheque. Specializes in themed movies, major Hitchcock, and French classics, interspersed with foreign movies you're unlikely to see anywhere else. Membership required, but you can join on the spot for $3.... *Tel 604/688-3456. 1131 Howe St. Buses 4, 6, 7, 8, 10.*
(see p. 189)

Pacific National Exhibition (P.N.E.). See Heather the prize cow and the Demolition Derby, put some money on a win-place-show, and eat cotton candy 'til your teeth ache. Tacky but fun, and kids love it.... *Tel 604/253-2311. Hastings and Renfrew Sts. Buses 4, 10, 16. Open mid-August–Labor Day.* **(see p. 191)**

Playland. Next to the P.N.E. in the city's east end. The elderly roller coaster will still turn your knees to water, and the Mighty Mouse ride is only for the stout-hearted. The alternative? Trying to burst enough balloons to win an over-sized stuffed giraffe. A day-pass here is a kid's idea of heaven.... *Tel 604/253-2311. Hastings and Renfrew Sts. Buses 4, 10, 16. Open weekends, Apr on; daily mid-June–Labor Day.* **(see p. 192)**

Queen Elizabeth Theatre. The Vancouver Opera, Ballet B.C., touring Broadway musicals, concerts, and more all show up here.... *Tel 604/665-3050. Hamilton at Georgia St. Buses 5, 17.* **(see pp. 182, 186)**

Ridge Theatre. Real butter on the popcorn and a glassed-in Crying Room for parents saddled with rugrats are bonuses.

ENTERTAINMENT | THE INDEX

But it's the intelligently paired double features at bargain prices that make this 1950s picture palace a Kitsilano icon.... *Tel 604/738-6311. 3131 Arbutus St. Bus 16.*
(see p. 189)

Stanley Theatre. From Shakespeare to swing musicals, this recently renovated former vaudeville and movie theater in tony South Granville shines its light on them all.... *Tel 604/687-5315, or 604/687-1644 (Box office). 2780 Granville St. Bus 8.* **(see p. 185)**

Studio 58. Student talent on stage in often impressive productions at Langara College. Shows take place during school year only.... *Tel 604/323-5652. 100 W. 49th Ave. Bus 49.* **(see p. 186)**

Theatre Under the Stars. Crowd-pleasing musicals in Malkin Bowl at Stanley Park. Wrap up—the air cools off once the sun goes down.... *Tel 604/687-0174. Take a cab. Mid-July–mid-Aug.* **(see p. 188)**

TicketMaster. Central source for tickets for major events. Charge by phone, or drop by outlets around town [see Hotlines].... *Tel 604/280-4444.* **(see p. 183)**

Vancouver Canadians. Vancouver's AA-level baseball team plays in Nat Bailey Stadium, adjacent to Queen Elizabeth Park.... *Tel 604/872-5232. 4601 Ontario St. May–Sept.*
(see p. 192)

Vancouver Canucks. Some seasons are better than others for Vancouver's NHL team, but the locals keep coming out to cheer on the Canucks at General Motors Place.... *Tel 604/899-4625. Sept–Apr.* **(see p. 192)**

Vancouver East Cultural Centre. A converted 1914 church, "the Cultch" lists offbeat, often provocative, drama and musical events and productions on its multi-facted programs.... *Tel 604/254-9578. 1895 Venables St. Bus 20.* **(see pp. 182, 185)**

Vancouver Folk Music Festival. Bare feet and a tie-dyed shirt are de rigueur at this good-humored mid-July weekend celebration of global music held in Jericho

Beach Park.... *Tel 604/602-9798. Jericho Beach Park. Bus 4.* **(see p. 191)**

Vancouver Fringe Festival. Even the rawest newcomers can have their moment in the spotlight here. The talent is unjuried, so you never know what you'll get at this annual September happening centered on Commercial Drive and in Gastown. Expect pleasant surprises.... *Tel 604/257-0350.* **(see p. 186)**

Vancouver International Comedy Festival. Annual July laugh riot on Granville Island. Many events free.... *Tel 604/683-0883.* **(see p. 190)**

Vancouver International Film Festival. A half-dozen movie theaters around the city screen more than 300 flicks from 50 countries.... *Tel 604/685-0260. Late Sept—early Oct.* **(see p. 190)**

Vancouver International Writers Festival. Celebration of the written word brings international literary figures and local luminaries to Granville Island.... *Tel 604/681-6330. October.* **(see p. 191)**

Vancouver Opera. From *Carmen* and *Traviata* to lesser-known operas. The company stages four works each season at the Queen Elizabeth Theatre.... *Tel 604/683-0222. Oct–May/June.* **(see p. 186)**

Vancouver Playhouse. Hot young playwrights and strong production values are this company's hallmarks.... *Tel 604/665-3050. Hamilton at Dunsmuir St. Buses 5, 17.* **(see pp. 182, 185)**

Vancouver Recital Society. Impresario Leila Getz is famed for discovering top talent on its way up. Summer Chamber Music Festival, plus regular season, at various venues.... *Tel 604/602-0363. Sept–Apr.* **(see p. 184)**

Vancouver Symphony Orchestra. Great composers, pops concerts, the popular "Tea and Trumpets" series—if your ears don't tune into something you like, you're not trying. Performances are usually at the Orpheum.... *Tel 604/876-3434.* **(see p. 184)**

ENTERTAINMENT | THE INDEX

Vancouver TheatreSports League. Award-winning teams go head to head in classic improv at the Arts Club's Revue Stage on Granville Island.... *Tel 604/738-7013. Bus 50. Wed–Sat.* **(see p. 190)**

The Vogue. Former art deco movie house on city's former theater row is venue for cabaret-style shows and concerts.... *Tel 604/331-7900. 918 Granville St. Buses 4, 6, 7, 8, 10.* **(see pp. 182, 185)**

Yuk-Yuk's Comedy Club. Downing beers while they do it, a younger crowd hurrahs or heckles the stand-up comedians who show up—sometimes with big names. Wednesday is amateur night.... *Tel 604/687-5233. Call for current location.* **(see p. 190)**

VANCOUVER ISLAND ENTERTAINMENT

Folkfest. Annual late-June gathering of mellow, guitar-strumming types in Victoria's Inner Harbour.... *Tel 250/388-4728. Some performances free, others $2 and up.* **(see p. 193)**

JazzFest International. Annual late-June music festival of jazz, folk, blues, and more.... *Tel 250/388-4423. $38–45 per show.* **(see p. 193)**

Pacific Opera Victoria. Variety of opera performances by the city's biggest and best company.... *Tel 250/385-0222 (schedule) or 250/386-6121 (tickets). Performances at McPherson Theatre, 3 Centennial Sq. $20–80.* **(see p. 193)**

TerrifVic Jazz Party. Victoria's biggest musical party kicks off in late April, showcasing Dixieland and other forms.... *Tel 250/953-2011. $28–40 per day, $90 for all 5 days.* **(see p. 193)**

Victoria Operatic Society. Lower-profile opera company; sticks mostly to the popular favorites.... *Tel 250/381-1021. McPherson Theatre, 3 Centennial Sq. $12–20.* **(see p. 193)**

Victoria Symphony. Orchestral performances in the heart of downtown. Kicks off the season with a freebie on the harbor.... *Tel 250/385-9771 (general), 250/381-0820 (schedule), or 250/386-6121 (tickets). Royal Theatre, 805 Broughton St. $15–30.* **(see p. 193)**

hotlines & other basics

Airports... **Vancouver International Airport (YVR)** occupies Sea Island in the Fraser River 13 km (8 miles) from the downtown core. The information line (tel 604/207-7077) has recorded information on checking in, parking, customs, and immigration. It won't tell you flight arrival and departure times, but it does list the phone numbers of individual airlines so you can call them. Considerably expanded in the last couple of years, YVR is light, airy, logically laid out, and with seriously good shopping, restaurants, and public sculpture. None of this comes free. Be prepared to pay an Airport Improvement Fee when you leave (unless you're under two years old, or flying in and out on the same calendar day). Otherwise, the charge is $5 for flights within B.C. or to the Yukon, $10 for destinations in North America including Hawaii and Mexico, and $15 outside North America. You can pay by cash (Canadian or U.S. dollars) or credit card. **Victoria International Airport (CYYJ)** (tel 250/953-7500), about 20 miles north of Victoria proper, is much smaller. It's best for connecting flights from Vancouver or Seattle, which a number of carriers offer. Get information about flights, parking, and anything else from the airport hotline.

Airport transport to downtown... You'll need to take two regular buses to get downtown from the airport (Bus 100, then Bus 8), a major drag when you're laden with luggage. A better idea is to catch one of the pastel green **Vancouver Airporter** buses, which run every half hour. One-way tickets cost $12 round-trip. Airporters stop at major downtown hotels, the Main Street bus depot, Granville St. and Broadway, and Granville and 41 sts. Call for times (tel 800/668-3141 or 604/946-8866). A **cab** is about $25. A limo is only a few bucks more. Try **Limojet** (tel 604/273-1331 or 800/278-8472) or **Star Limousine Service** (tel 604/685-5600 or 800/803-9222). Worth it to have people peer through those dark glass windows and think you're a rock star. Getting from Victoria's airport is a little tougher; there's no public transit, just cars for rent and a handy private shuttle service called the **Airporter** (tel 250/386-2525, 250/386-2526, or 877/386-2525); tickets on the shuttle cost $13 one-way. Cabs from this airport are fairly expensive ($45), though quite a bit faster than the shuttle bus.

All-night pharmacies... You're clubbed out, and a killer headache is pending? You got lucky, and you need condoms? For 24-hour service, stagger into **Shopper's Drug Mart** (tel 604/685-6445, 1125 Davie St.; 604/738-3138, 2302 West 4th Ave.). Victoria has no all-night pharmacies.

Baby-sitters... Larger hotels can arrange for someone to take care of your offspring. Give them plenty of notice. Other possibilities are **Drake Medox Doula Services** (tel 604/682-2801, 856 Homer St., Suite 203) or **Moppet Minders Child & Home Care Services Ltd.** (tel 604/942-8167, 1075 Dolphin St., Coquitlam). In Victoria, there's **Wee Watch Daycare** (tel 250/382-5437), among others.

Buses and public transit... Trains, boats, and buses are all part of **BC Transit**'s citywide system. For instructions on how to get where you're going, call Customer Information (tel 604/521-0400, 6:30am–11:30pm). The deal is cash-only on the buses (drivers don't carry change), and for the SkyTrain and SeaBus, ticket machines. A fare buys you 90 minutes of traveling time in any direction. Be sure to obtain a transfer when you pay your fare. Ticket prices are based on when and where you travel. A dollar-fifty will take you most places in the city—and anywhere in the system on weekends or after 6:30pm. Weekdays, you'll pay $2, $3, or $4 depending on how many zones you cross. A Day-Pass is $8. Kids and seniors pay less. If you're a student from out of town, tough. You're stuck with paying full fare. You can buy tickets on buses, at SkyTrain and SeaBus stations, and from FareDealers identified by a red-and-blue sticker—7-Eleven and Safeway stores are a couple of sources. Part of the system, **SkyTrain** and **SeaBus** are worth taking just for the fun of it—except during rush hour. Tickets to ride are included in your regular transit fare (see details above). Computer-operated, the SkyTrain is a fabulous ride that winds and dips along elevated tracks through the suburbs, providing a great view of the coastal mountains. The SeaBus, especially at sunset, provides a panoramic vista of the harbor. Night-owl alert: Apart from a few buses that run until 3am, most services shut down by 1am. Timetables are free at public libraries, city and municipal halls, community centers, Travel InfoCentres, chambers of commerce, and the B.C. Transit Lost Property Office. "Discover Vancouver on Transit" is an invaluable pocket-sized book on how to get to major attractions. Add a "Transit Route Map & Guide" for $1.50. If you're bound for West Vancouver, catch a blue bus—while a separate system, it does accept transfers from the BC Transit system, and vice versa. You'll also find maps and route information in the **Yellow Pages**. On Vancouver Island, public transit is almost nonexistent outside of Victoria; **VIA Rail** (tel 888/842-7245) does run a once-daily train from Victoria north, but it only goes partway up the island, as far as Courtenay. Within Victoria, you can take the bus (tel 250/382-6161 for transit info) or the little **Harbour Ferries** (tel 250/708-0201) that cruise both the downtown area and a wider, more scenic swath too. More expensive options include horse-drawn carriages and limos. For the coolest local option, though, hop on one of the local pedal-powered rickshaws operated by **Kabuki Kabs** (tel 250/385-4243). Warning: They're not cheap.

Car rental... If you want to make a splash, **Exotic Car & Motorcycle Rentals** (tel 604/644-9128, 1820 Burrard

St.) can rent you a Ferrari, Porsche, Corvette—or an ass-kickin' Harley Davidson. **Rent-a-Wreck** (tel 604/688-0001, 1083 Hornby St.) can put you behind the wheel of a Chevy Cavalier or Corsica. For your regular Neon or Taurus (plus all the usual names) the following have locations downtown and at the airport: **Avis** (tel 604/606-2869 or 800/879-2847, 757 Hornby St.); **Budget** (tel 604/668-7000 or 800/299-3199, 1705 Burrard St.); **Hertz** (tel 604/647-4598 or 800/847-4389, 1128 Seymour St.); **Thrifty** (tel 604/606-1666 or 800/327-0116, 1015 Burrard St., Century Plaza Hotel). Bear in mind that taxes can increase the price severely. Pick up a $49.99 daily special from the airport, and your credit card slip may show almost double that once you've factored in various government taxes, optional insurance, an environmental tax, and a little sting in the tail called an "airport concession recovery fee." All the usual names—**Avis** (tel 800/879-2847 or 250/656-6033), **Budget** (tel 800/268-8900 or 250/953-5300), **Enterprise** (tel 800/325-8007 or 250/475-6900), **Hertz** (tel 800/263-0600 or 250/656-2312), and **National** (tel 800/227-7368 or 250/386-1213)—can be found at Victoria's airport, and most also maintain offices in or near downtown Victoria as well.

Currency exchange... Most places welcome U.S. dollars; some accept Japanese yen too. Rates aren't always in your favor, so just use your ATM card wherever possible. Better bets are **American Express** (tel 604/669-2813, 666 Burrard St.) or **Thomas Cook** (tel 604/687-6111, 701 Granville St.; tel 604/641-1229, 999 Canada Place. You can change your cash at the airport too, or at major banks downtown. In Victoria, banks, ATMs, and change offices line Government, Douglas, and Yates streets.

Dentists... Ouch! Cracking down on that crab claw cracked a crown? Call the **Association of Dental Surgeons of B.C.** (tel 604/736-7202, weekdays only, 8am–4pm) for telephone numbers of dentists in your area. No dental insurance? They'll send you to a low-cost dental clinic. If you're in real agony, take yourself and your throbbing tooth to the nearest hospital emergency department. Victoria's got a more local service called **Dentists Emergency Referral Service** (tel 250/595-3377), plus a dental clinic—**Cresta Dental**

Care (tel 250/384-7711, 3170 Tillicum Rd.)—that's actually open all week *and* weekend until 5pm.

Doctors... Your first efforts at roller blading have left you with what might be a sprained ankle. An upset stomach has had you in misery for the past 24 hours. Whatever the reason, you want some professional advice. Major hotels usually have a doctor on call. Otherwise, head for a walk-in medical clinic, such as the downtown **Medicentre** (tel 604/683-8138, 1055 Dunsmuir St.) or **Care Point Medical Centres** in the West End (tel 604/681-5338, 1175 Denman St.). Consultation fees are around $40. In downtown Victoria, try **James Bay Medical Treatment Centre** (tel 250/388-9934, 230 Menzies St.), which is open weekdays and Saturdays—though not at night.

Emergencies... Call 911 for fire, police, or ambulance in the Greater Vancouver area. The nearest downtown hospital is **St. Paul's Hospital** (tel 604/682-2344, 1081 Burrard St.). On the West Side, you'll find **Vancouver General Hospital** (tel 604/875-4111, 899 W. 12th Ave.) and, on the UBC campus, **UBC Hospital** (tel 604/822-7121, 2211 Westbrook Mall)—its official name is the Vancouver Hospital & Health Science Centre. **The Children's & Women's Health Centre of British Columbia** (tel 604/453-8300, 3644 Slocan) specializes in obstetrics, gynecology, and children's medicine. The **Vancouver Crisis Centre** can help those in emotional distress (tel 604/872-3311). Victoria's two most central hospitals aren't all *that* central. Getting to **Victoria General Hospital** (tel 250/727-4212, 1 Hospital Way) requires a drive west on the Highway 1 expressway some three miles out of the city. **Royal Jubilee Hospital** (tel 250/370-8000, 1900 Fort St.) is a little closer to the center but still somewhat east of downtown, near the suburb of Oak Bay.

Events hotlines... B.C. Tel's **Talking Super Pages** (tel 604/299-9000) can tell you about the cool new band coming in from the U.K., what's playing at the theater, who's the featured artist at the symphony, movie showtimes, and more. The service is free but you're a prisoner to draggy commercials before they'll give you the info. In Victoria, call the **Community Arts Council's** hotline (tel 250/381-2787). But the best place, by far, to find listings in Victoria is in **Monday Magazine** (see below).

Festivals and special events...

JANUARY: The year kicks off with the **Polar Bear Swim** (tel 604/665-3418) when thousands of sturdy Vancouverites leap into the water. Car buffs stare lasciviously at the newest models at the **Pacific International Auto & Light Truck Show** (tel 604/214-9964). The date of **Chinese New Year** varies from year to year; it's sometimes February before the dragon parade winds through Chinatown (tel 604/687-6021).

FEBRUARY: Budding Martha Stewarts make tracks for the **BC Home and Garden Show**, B.C. Place Stadium (tel 604/433-5121) (BC Home Show in October).

MARCH: A dead loss in terms of events.

APRIL: Heralded as the best in Canada, the **Vancouver Playhouse International Wine Festival** (tel 604/873-3311) brings in hundreds of wines and dozens of winemakers, growers, and experts from around the world. Neophytes will find the tasting sessions an eye-opener.

MAY: Would-be cowpokes drive an hour out of town for the **Cloverdale Rodeo**, the second biggest in Canada (tel 604/576-9461). Meanwhile, talent converges at **New Music West** (tel 604/684-9338). A don't miss event for parents is the **Vancouver Children's Festival** in Vanier Park (tel 604/708-5655). For runners, it's the **Vancouver International Marathon** (tel 604/872-2928).

JUNE: Summer activities kick off with the **Alcan Dragon Boat Festival** (tel 604/688-2382), and the **International Jazz Festival Vancouver** (tel 604/872-5200).

JULY: Calendars are jammed this month, kicking off with flags and fireworks at Canada Place, July 1, in honor of **Canada Day** (tel 604/666-8477). Arrive well before dark if you want a harborfront view. Soon after, you can go **Dancing on the Edge** (tel 604/689-0691) at the Firehall Arts Centre, which highlights dynamic contemporary dance. Don your tie-dyed pants, light an incense stick, and go barefoot to the **Vancouver Folk Music Festival** at Jericho Beach Park (tel 604/602-9798). Far more sedate are the **Early Music Festival**, UBC Recital Hall (tel 604/732-1610), and the **Vancouver Chamber Music Festival**, at Crofton House School (tel 604/602-0363). You need to make time this month too for the laff-riot **Vancouver International Comedy Festival**, Granville Island (tel

604/683-0883) and **Caribbean Days Festival** (tel 604/515-2400) when Lonsdale Quay erupts with steel drums, parades, and limbo dancers. As July wanes, the **Celebration of Light** (tel 604/738-4304) international fireworks competition brings out the crowds. The center of the action is English Bay. Check media for info.

AUGUST: Catch the **Powell Street Festival** for Japanese culture and cuisine in Oppenheimer Park (tel 604/739-9388). Part agricultural show, part fairground, the **Pacific National Exhibition (P.N.E.)** is a city tradition (tel 604/253-2311).

SEPTEMBER: Love it or hate it (as many locals do, especially those who live near the "circuit"), you can't ignore **Molson Indy Vancouver** at Concord Pacific Place (tel 604/684-4639). Less ear-shattering is the **Vancouver International Fringe Festival**. Expect alternative—often outrageous—theater. (tel 604/257-0350). Offbeat, and art movies are the focus of the huge **Vancouver International Film Festival** (tel 604/685-0260).

OCTOBER: ...The literati descend in droves on the **Vancouver International Writers Festival**, Granville Island (tel 604/681-6330), while nest-builders make tracks for the **BC Fall Home Show** (tel 604/433-5121).

NOVEMBER: The **Vancouver Storytelling Festival** (tel 604/876-2272) is a multi-ethnic event held at various venues around town. There's also the **Snow Goose Festival**. Watch 'em head south from the **George C. Reifel Migratory Bird Sanctuary** (tel 604/946-6980) in Delta.

DECEMBER: Vancouverites bundle up warmly to watch the parade of **carol ships** (tel 604/878-8999) and the dazzling **Festival of Lights** at **VanDusen Botanical Garden** (tel 604/878-9274). For the skinny on a few of Victoria's best music festivals, see Entertainment; for more on some of Vancouver Island's wackier annual events, see You Probably Didn't Know.

Gays and lesbians... The latest copy of the free newspaper, *Xtra West* (tel 604/684-9696), will swiftly clue you in to local events, issues, and who's on where. Look for it at movie theaters, public libraries, clubs, community centers, and coffee shops. For the lowdown on gay-friendly hotels, pubs, beaches, and businesses, pick up a free map of Gay Vancouver at **Little Sister's Book and Art**

Emporium (tel 604/669-1753, 1238 Davie St.)—and incidentally the city's top source of gay lit. For more information, or just some emotional support, call the **Pride Line** (tel 604/684-6869). Around in the summer? Don't miss the **Gay and Lesbian Pride Parade** the first Sunday in August in the West End.

Money... The Canadian one-dollar coin is bronze-colored and is called a "loonie"—because it has a loon on one side; the $2 coin is a bronze disc ringed with silver, and bigger, and is known as a "two-nie" (because it's a two-dollar coin—get it?). Five-dollar bills are dark blue; $10s are purple; $20s are green; $50s are orange; $100 bills are a chocolate brown. Bank machines are common, and many stores let you pay by direct transaction. Almost all stores and restaurants accept U.S. dollars.

Newspapers and magazines... Vancouver's two daily morning newspapers are both published by The Southam Group. The difference? The *Vancouver Sun* appears weekdays and Saturdays; *The Province*, a tabloid in size and content, publishes weekdays and Sundays. If you're looking for more in-depth coverage, pick up Canada's nationals, the *Globe and Mail*, and *The National Post*. Community papers are free. The *West Ender* focuses on downtown. *Xtra West* is geared to the gay and lesbian community. The biggest news and entertainment weekly is the free *Georgia Straight* (www.straight.com). You can pick these up at movie theaters, coffee shops, public libraries, community centers, or at marked boxes on the street. Victoria's local daily paper is the *Times Colonist,* though you'll probably find the free weekly *Monday Magazine* (www.mondaymag.com) much more useful for entertainment listings.

Parking... The handiest parking lot if you're downtown in Vancouver for any length of time is the underground one at **Pacific Centre.** Another huge one is at **Library Square.** After 6pm, it's a buyer's market, and most lots charge about $3 for the whole evening (although you'll pay considerably more near **B.C. Place Stadium**). Be aware that street parking meters are active until 8pm seven days of the week, and rush-hour parking is banned on many downtown streets. Be aware, too, that guys fairly low on the food chain are waiting to hitch their tow truck to your nice shiny Miata the moment the clock strikes three. Outside the downtown core, street parking can be a problem. Lobbying by locals has led to most West End street parking (and some areas in Kitsilano) being designated "residents only." Don't risk it. Grab the first legal spot you see, and walk where you're going. Parking in Stanley Park is a huge challenge in high season. Take public transit if you can—and the same applies in compact Victoria.

Passports and visas... You'll need a passport to get into Canada. If you're a U.S. citizen, and you don't have a passport, bring your birth certificate, or Certificate of Naturalization plus photo I.D. If you're from some countries, you'll also need a visa. Contact your nearest Canadian consulate, or ask your travel agent.

Postal services... Mailing your postcards costs 46 cents within Canada, 55 cents to the United States, and 95 cents internationally; standard-size letters run the same. You can buy stamps at many convenience stores. **Canada Post**'s main downtown post office in Vancouver is at 349 W. Georgia St. Victoria's main post office is at 714 Yates St. (tel 250/953-1352), and many local drugstores also sell postage.

Smoking... Light up in most places, and you'll incur wrath, irate looks, and a reminder that you mustn't. "Thou shalt not..." is the rule almost everywhere, which explains the knots of people standing outside office buildings sadly puffing away even in cruel weather. Right now, it's okay to smoke in a pub or a bar, and some restaurants circumvent the rule with designated smoking lounges.

Taxes... Provincial Sales Tax is 7.5 percent, Goods and Services Tax is another 7 percent. What you see on the label isn't what you end up forking out by a long shot. Depending on where you're from, rebate schemes may help you get some of your money back. See Shopping for more information. Note too that the tax on liquor and accommodation is 10 percent.

Taxis... Don't think you can just go out on the street and hail one. Vancouver is a city that plans things. Major hotels are the most fruitful places to find a ride. The drop charge is $2.50, and you pay $1.35 per kilometer (a little over a half-mile) after that. There's no surcharge for luggage or extra passengers. Normally cabs arrive within five or ten minutes of calling them. The worst times are wet evenings. **Black Top & Checker Cabs** (tel 604/731-1111 or 604/683-4567); **MacLure's** (tel 604/731-9211 or 604/683-6666); **Vancouver Taxi** has regular cabs and wheelchair-accessible vehicles (tel 604/871-1111); **Yellow Cab** (604/681-1111 or 800/898-8294 toll-free from a pay phone). Fares are similar (just a little bit less, actually) in Victoria. Try **Blue Bird** (tel 250/382-1111, 250/382-4235 or 800/665-7055), **Empress** (tel 250/381-2222), or **Victoria** (tel 250/383-7111).

Telephones... British Columbia uses two different area codes: 604 for Greater Vancouver, the Fraser Valley, and Whistler; 250 for the rest of B.C., including Victoria. Canada's country code is 1. You'll find plenty of call-boxes on Vancouver streets, and in major stores and malls. If you're making a local call, just plug in 25 cents and wait for the steady hum of the dial tone. You can reach the AT&T operator at 800/575-2222, Sprint at 800/877-8000, and MCI at 800/950-1022.

TicketMaster... This is the major conduit for tickets to big sports events, concerts, and plays. You can charge by phone (tel 604/280-4444) and pick up your tickets at the door. You can also purchase tickets at **TicketMaster** locations around town. Handy ones in the city are in the **Pacific Centre** (701 W. Georgia St.), **GM Place,** the **Arts Alliance** at **Tourism Vancouver's** main location (200 Burrard St.). If you're on the north shore, Capilano Mall (935 Marine Dr., North Vancouver). A $3 to $6 booking fee is added on to the ticket cost. If you want to know where you'll be sitting, the **Yellow Pages** includes plans of major theaters and sports venues.

Trains... If you've choo-choo-ed your way across the Rockies on a **VIA Rail** train (tel 888/842-7245) or journeyed along the Pacific Coast on **Amtrak** (tel 800/872-7245) you'll arrive at Pacific Central station on Main Street. The station is normally about a 20-minute drive from downtown. Worrywarts allow longer, knowing it may be slow negotiating Stanley Park and the Lions Gate Bridge. Vancouver Island's limited **VIA Rail** service (one route) starts at Victoria's train station on Pandora Avenue near the Johnson Street Bridge, walking distance from downtown.

Travelers with disabilities... Vancouver is exceptionally user-friendly due in large part to local hero Rick Hansen who proved some years back that a wheelchair is no barrier to circling the world. Sidewalks are sloped at corners; elevators in new buildings have buttons at wheelchair height; the majority of restaurants are wheelchair-accessible. Special **BC Transit buses** equipped with wheelchair lifts or ramps run on more than 100 routes. Look for the international wheelchair symbol at the bus stop, and the letter "L" on the timetable. You can also wheel onto **SkyTrain** and **SeaBus**.

Tipping... The standard is 15 percent in restaurants. Adding the P.S.T. and G.S.T. together, and throwing in a bit more is how most people figure it here, more if someone has made a special effort. Fifteen percent across the board, including cab drivers and hair stylists. Also plan on a couple of bucks for hotel bellstaff. Coffee shops where staff hand you a croissant and cappuccino across the counter frequently leave a mug beside the cash with a few coins in it as a hint. It's your call.

Visitor information... Locals, for the most part, are highly in favor of tourists. Your big whack of dollars helps the economy. Besides which, many Vancouverites are just plain nice. Stand on a street corner perusing a map for only a minute, and chances are someone will offer to show you the right route. **Tourism Vancouver**'s website (www.tourism-vancouver.org) can help you with pre-trip planning. Once you're here, head straight for its excellent **TouristInfo** office at the north end of Burrard Street and load yourself up with brochures (tel 604/683-2000, 200 Burrard St.); open daily 8–6 in summer, 8:30–5 and Sat 9–5 the rest of the year. In Victoria, head for the easily spotted **Travel InfoCentre** (tel 250/953-2033 or 800/663-3883, 812 Wharf St.), right by the big waterfront Fairmont Empress hotel. It distributes tons of info with a smile, sells tickets to lots of events, books accommodations if you need 'em, and points you wherever you need to go; it's open weekdays, 9 to 5. Or, to do some pre-trip planning, log on to Tourism Victoria's website (www.tourismvictoria.com).

Weather... Cloudy skies can swiftly change to sunny conditions. Dial for the latest weather (tel 604/664-9010 or 604/664-9032). In Victoria, the same service is available (tel 250/363-6717, then 3502).

Frommer's Complete Guides

The only guide independent travelers need to make smart choices, avoid rip-offs, get the most for their money, and travel like a pro.

Frommer's   WILEY

Available at bookstores everywhere.

NOTES